Relocating
Consciousness

D1559008

Consciousness Literature & the Arts (07)

General Editor:
Daniel Meyer-Dinkgräfe

Editorial Board:
Anna Bonshek, Per Brask, John Danvers,
William S. Haney II, Amy Ione,
Michael Mangan, Arthur Versluis,
Christopher Webster, Ralph Yarrow

Relocating Consciousness

Diasporic Writers and the Dynamics of Literary Experience

DAPHNE GRACE

Amsterdam - New York, NY 2007

Cover Design: Aart Jan Bergshoeff

The paper on which this book is printed meets the requirements of "ISO 9706:1994, Information and documentation - Paper for documents - Requirements for permanence".

ISBN-13: 978-90-420-2252-2
ISSN: 1573-2193
©Editions Rodopi B.V., Amsterdam - New York, NY 2007
Printed in the Netherlands

Contents

Chapter One
Readdressing Consciousness, Locating Diasporas

"You know, Brain, what blows me is that you know yourself and don't know yourself at the same time, and you know yourself knowing yourself and you know yourself not knowing yourself – oh this is getting ridiculous!"

"It's the old paradox," says the Brain, smiling with its many cracks and fissures.

"But what is the paradoxical force that lets you do that? [. . .] What is it that permits you to think about thinking and feel about feeling?"

"Consciousness."

(Tom Robbins—*Even Cowgirls Get the Blues*, 362-3.)

1. Conceptualizing consciousness

"Consciousness" can be understood from within the parameters of its original definition, taken from the Latin *sciare*, 'to know'; thus consciousness is a state of being 'with knowledge'. Literature is part of the self-referral quest of the human being to express consciousness, part of the dynamics of intelligence functioning within itself, an activity of the cogniser cognising itself. The result of this creative output of the human brain is a tangible artefact of intelligence, a text or a work of art, which is sharable with other consciousnesses. If we consider consciousness is the seat of human creativity and knowledge, it must be locatable through its expressions, the arts and literature. Literature should itself be able to tell us something about human consciousness, and indeed it has been argued that:

Literature is an interim report from the consciousness of the artist. [...] Literature is made at the frontier between the self and the world, and in the act of creation that frontier softens, becomes permeable, allows the world to flow into the artist and the artist to flow into the world. (Rushdie 1991: 427)

This lofty description notwithstanding, a quotation from a "cult" novel from the 1970's (*Even Cowgirls Get the Blues*) may seem a strange place to start a text that aims to be a 21st century discussion on world literature and consciousness. It may also seem to confirm all of our suspicions that consciousness is a topic of consideration only relevant to those people living in California and/or those interested in the New Age and its illogical blend of ancient philosophies and contemporary life styles. It serves however to highlight the fact that consciousness as a study has been placed within the category of the weird and the wonderful, the exotic and the esoteric; frequently disrespected and feared in equal measure. For most of the past century, consciousness in its most profound meaning has been at worst negated and at best avoided within western academia. Consciousness is a concept and an *experience* that has been refuted by the very discipline that should and could be promoting its value to education and literary thought most convincingly.

In contrast to the previously existing principle that consciousness should be excluded from the field of academic inquiry, this book is based on the premise that the inclusion of consciousness studies is particularly relevant to a discussion of postcolonial literatures, those that involve "the imaginative legacies" of colonialism (McLeod 2000: 4) and diasporic literature, the literature of people(s) relocated around the globe. This book will argue how experience in today's world is informed by a much-neglected area in academics—that of conscious awareness of alternative modes of experience, as expressed through language, or through fictional explorations of character and plot. This book will explore and develop contemporary notions of consciousness in the light of post-modern and postcolonial theory, related to some dynamic writers and ground-breaking novels. Within parameters of postcolonial studies, it aims to challenge some of the assumptions made by the genre itself, predicated as it is on the revelation of "newness" through the study of power through violence. While in the past, postcolonial theory has been based upon a premise of revolution through violence, these chapters will aim to expand contemporary postcolonial theory beyond the limited dimension of the dialectic of power-based-on-violence, to a more visionary exploration of experience based on consciousness as unity-in-diversity.

Postcolonial literature has, according to John McLeod, been forged from the "dynamic relationship between a writer and the culture(s) about which he or she writes" especially in terms of the unequal power relations inherent in the historical experience of imperialism and the decolonising of both "the mind" and the people (ibid). The suitability of postcolonial literature to exploring notions of consciousness lies in its very nature of implicating the ambivalence and contradictory nature of human experience. The postcolonial has for decades been concerned with rethinking identity, and posing questions about formulations of space, of identity and of power. It has created a genre that thrives on uncertainty, irony, and on exploration of possibility and agency for new ideas. That there are no longer gaps between cultures that have to be overcome, because "they" have become "us", paves the way for a more dynamic and profound understanding of the nature of consciousness itself. Recent debates in culture emphasise the dislocation of national and racial identities, the deterritorialisation of being and belonging in which margins and centre collapse. Traditional bodies of self-identity adjust. Skin colour, re-cognised, becomes a discursive political rather than ethnic signifier.

Colonialism and its long aftermath form for some academics a theoretical framework through which to study literature and societies; it is obviously also a lived reality. Whether from the perspective of the coloniser or the colonised, post-colonisation is about *people* and their personal experience. The sense of disempowerment and dislocation, the "cultural obliteration [. . .] made possible by the negation of national reality" (Fanon 1959: 1), along with accompanying emotions of anger, confusion, humiliation and fear, can occur as much in one's country of birth as in a new location reached either through migration or exile. While the Nigerian Buchi Emecheta writes of her trials in adapting to life in the cold and inhospitable London of the 1960's—a relocation that involved losing wealth and class status whilst becoming the face of the unwelcome black "second class citizen" (1974)—the Nobel Prize winning writer Nadine Gordimer expresses her own experience of growing up in the colonial world of South Africa: "for the child I was, the premise is: Colonial: that's the story of who I am. The one who belongs nowhere" (1999: 120).

This experience and its consequent feelings of confusion have been related by writers such as Hanif Kureishi, Salman Rushdie, and V.S. Naipaul amongst others. Naipaul (1987 and 1994) in fact stresses how migrants (and their descendents) can experience this sense of alienated identity both within their "home" and host countries, both of which are experienced as "illusions". Any journey back home turns out to be a "mythical" quest back to somewhere that only exists in the imagination. Nadine Gordimer provides a further expansion in her comment on the real definition of "home": it is "the final destination of the human spirit beyond national boundaries, natal traditions" (1995: 45). It is great writers, "alternative" writers, she elaborates, who are those on the quest "for the Home that is truth, undefined by walls, by borders, by regimes" (ibid: 69). Caryl Phillips also sees the potential energy generated by the tensions and oppositions within the migratory condition; he sees this and "the subsequent sense of displacement [as a] gift to a creative mind" (2001: 131). The loss of the sense of identity and the search for a sense of "belongingness" is ultimately a journey through consciousness.

2. Ways of gaining knowledge

Knowledge and experience are the two steps of evolution. Knowledge reinforces the experience and provides the ground for more expanded skill in action, which in turn is the platform for deeper understanding on the intellectual level. Whether intellectual or emotional, the knowledge we rely upon to live our lives is determined by the way we categorise it, the way our prejudices, biases, educational and social systems allow us to perceive reality and tolerate "truth". Thus, much wisdom is rejected or misinterpreted through our preconceptions and intellectual mindsets. As Kwame Anthony Appiah expresses it, we can identify

> three kinds of disagreement about values: we can fail to share a vocabulary of evaluation; we can give the same vocabulary different interpretations; and we can give the same values different weights. (2006: 66)

To understand more about the nature of "human-ness" must serve a cross-cultural purpose, one that transcends these types of disagreement. Yet what are the ways of gaining and evaluating knowledge available to us? Perhaps, like Casaubon in *Middlemarch*, we can devote our whole lives to teasing out the key to all knowledge, or like Ganesh, Naipaul's "mystic masseur", we may attempt to purchase all the books published in order personally to "own" wisdom and measure our growing knowledge in terms of inches of paper. Whether within literary genres of the modernist, postmodernist, or post-postmodernist text, revelations through the growth of knowledge coincide with deepening experience of both self and language.

"Consciousness contains all human experience" argue Malekin and Yarrow; human consciousness "exists or operates in different forms, on different levels" (2001: 55). Far from being a "mystery" and "the least understood part of human life" (Sommerhoff 2000: 1), the nature and qualities of human consciousness have been known in their entirety for centuries if not millennia—but this knowledge has either not been available or has been placed within the dogmas of religion: distorted, corrupted and lost. Being relegated to the realms of either religious or subjective experience (and therefore unreliable as unscientific) it has also been devalued in the west. This most profound knowledge of consciousness is in fact a victim of colonial rule, as crucial as any other of the debilitating and disadvantaging results of colonialism and the imperial agenda of suppressing indigenous cultures, traditions and texts, including medical and literary knowledge.[i] This mentality has to a large extent persisted, now under the post-modern rhetoric of suspicion of grand narratives of all types, whether religious, socio-political, or humanitarian. The infamous Macauley Minute is seemingly still at work.[ii]

Yet within academic disciplines we are beset with the problem of what consciousness is; a clear definition of this experience in all its aspects of human-ness has kept writers and philosophers upon an ineffectual search over the centuries. What is consciousness—is it that intelligence behind or before, matter; is it a function of the human mind or does human experiencing project consciousness? Why is the "paradoxical force" that Robbins locates as consciousness so important? The answer to these questions is: because consciousness is the intelligence within all of us, it is experience-able and yet it is apparently unlocatable by the intellect.

This book aims to "relocate" consciousness through the inclusion of theories of consciousness into a discussion of postcolonial novels and through a discussion of the relevance of the conceptualisation of alternative or higher states of consciousness within human experience. The text asserts the relevance of this mode of analysing human experience within the realm of diasporic literature. The global diasporic experience of displacement and disorientation, exile and alienation is one in which a re-evaluation of self is not only appealing but also necessary.

New types of experience require a new type of knowledge. As Salman Rushdie describes in *Imaginary Homelands*:

> The effect of mass migrations has been the creation of radically new types of human being: people who root themselves in ideas rather than places, in memories as much as in material things; people who have been obliged to define themselves—because they have been so defined by others—by their otherness; people in whose deepest selves strange fusions occur, unprecedented unions between what they were and where they find themselves. [. . .] Migrants must, of necessity, make a new imaginative relationship with the world. (1991: 124)

This state of cosmopolitan movement, the "hybridity, impurity, intermingling, the transformation that comes of new and unexpected combinations of human beings" celebrated by Rushdie (1991: 394), is a state of "mass migration" in which we are all living, unless luckily enough to inhabit some remote and inaccessible region of the globe. Moreover, it is within this world that we all, as characters, play out our "quest for wholeness" (ibid: 397).

Stuart Hall claims that "Migration has turned out to be *the* world historical event of later modernity" (1995). While he argues for a "loss" of identity within the migrant situation, one that must be healed though texts that restore "the broken rubric of the past" (1995: 394), he also proposes an analysis of the experience of "one-ness" and for the appreciation of "being" as well as "becoming". He appreciates that in a symbolic sense a return to Africa is the source of identity for many migrant people; this symbolic journey to the source, the sacred homeland that has been lost, is however impossible. Access to deeper and more profound levels of consciousness—which in turn allow access to more refined levels of language—is necessary for the "migrant" author to discover the nature of home in the only place possible—that is to say, within his-or her-self.

3. The impact of globalisation

One of the central concerns of this new millennium must be the affect of globalisation on geographic disturbance of culture and people: both in terms of increased connectivity and (paradoxically) increased isolation. With huge numbers of people on the move, whether as a result of war, famine, nationalist movements, or economic migration in the global trade of qualified workers, traditional concepts of home/abroad, global/local, and national/international are being made obsolete. Mass migration of people, capital, and ideas creates a new global proximity, which also threatens the world with a global culture endorsed through cultural imperialism—a new global capitalist monoculture.

Recent discussions on the impact of globalisation on human cultures and social structures have highlighted transformations in both time and space. Social interactions across huge tracts of space/time are now a daily occurrence for many on the planet. Internet communication with other people, cultures, languages and economies daily homogenise diversity into bland chunks of "information" accessible to anyone in their front rooms or offices. While this is nothing new for most in the west—the situation was for example brilliantly parodied in DeLillo's *White Noise* (1986)—in some cultures this also destabilises spaces formerly dichotomised as home versus market place—traditionally gendered spaces, home being the designated female sphere. Moreover, at the extreme, nationalities are seemingly erased and any sense of cultural diversity nullified. The concept of the world becoming one place is one in which it is tempting to believe, as the relationship between local, international and global fractures, and concepts of identity based on cultural difference rapidly become meaningless.

Yet, as human life appears to interact now more than ever before, for many people, global modernity means an experience of "dis-placement" in both time and space (Tomlinson 2001: 9). The sense of our national belonging is destabilised, and any sense of being "at home" is undermined. Globalisation disturbs our definition of "culture", whether meant in the sense of our social interactions or in terms of academic categorization. While culture has long been defined as the force that defines and delimits societies in terms of fixed spaces, the recent intensification of globalisation means that it is no longer possible to imagine the world as a collection of disparate, autonomous regions. Understanding the relationship of culture to space is one of the challenges set before contemporary "world citizens". In his study on globalisation, Zygmunt Bauman expands the notion of diasporic identity, suggesting that in the postmodern world:

> All of us are, willy nilly, by design or default, on the move. We are on the move, even if physically we stay put: immobility is not a realistic option in a world of permanent change. (1998: 4)

His argument is particularly pertinent here as is his emphasis that the effects of this new condition of change are, moreover, radically unequal. Taking a different stance to the traditional problematic one associated with enforced travel and migrancy of the diasporic identity, he argues that: "Being local in a globalised world is a sign of social deprivation and degradation" (ibid). Giving new spin to the problems of life in the postmodern world of the non-place (as defined by Marc Augé) he distinguishes between the new "us" and "them" (self and other) of the globalised world:

> Some of us are fully and truly "global"; some are fixed in their "locality"—a predicament neither pleasurable nor endurable in a world where the "globals" set the tone and compose the rules of the life game (ibid).

Thus, "being on the move" has different consequences depending on whether you are "on the top or the bottom of the hierarchy" (1998: 4). This usefully extends the emotive associations of diaspora experience(s) to include class as well as national positioning. Space, however, retains for Bauman its binary polarisation of local/global, public/private, within the parameters of confinement, progressive spatial separation, exclusion, and the panopticon control familiar to postcolonial theory. What is new, perhaps, to the late 20th century is the establishment of "extraterrestrial elites" (ibid: 3), not to mention the new controversial category of enforced homeless person—those forcibly seized under "extraordinary renditions", a new state of terror that, as reported in the article "Terror suspect flights defended", Tony Blair recently admitted "has been US policy for years" (BBC: 2005). If localities are losing their meaning, so too is the language of humanity. Moreover, even if identity within global relocation is "lost in translation", individual identity is always part of a larger narrative. Marc Augé's concept of non-place has further been exacerbated by the additional concept of the "non-citizen", one that incorporates moral and cultural dynamics and questions (see for example, the recent [2004] discussions by Bruce Robbins). Concepts of community and nation are fast being overridden with those of larger political or religious identifications and the burgeoning idea of cosmopolitanism—a vision that can seem both liberating and threatening. At the heart of the rapidly propagating fear in the world is found the constantly shifting classification and compartmentalisation of knowledge. "Information" rather than intelligence is at the basis of the world's currently remaining superpower's campaign to define right from wrong, good from bad, "democratic" (i.e. good) from "non-democratic" (bad) countries, religions, and peoples. In this new world of the so-called axis of evil, the epitome of xenophobic othering, the Other has become, through its lack of clear definition, both omnipresent and unlocatable. In this, it resembles Foucault's delineation, more relevant now than ever, of the dangers inherent in the western use of space as a locus of domination and the spread of fear (for example, through the invisible eye of the panopticon, which bestows totalitarian mastery over the environment). He discusses "the diabolical aspect" of the idea of a centralised machine of surveillance in which everyone is caught. "Power", he claims, "is no longer substantially identified with an individual who possesses it or exercises it by right of birth; it becomes a machinery that no one owns" (Foucault 1972: 156).

4. Postcolonial positions on power and knowledge

Postcolonial studies is itself in danger of becoming post- theory unless it keeps up with the rapid changes in the world situation. It must be sufficiently far-reaching and forward-thinking to be able to incorporate new ways of articulation in order to deal with the new world order; it must take a "vertical" as well as "horizontal" approach to knowledge—a quantum mechanical approach as it were. It can no longer be looking exclusively to the faults and fears of the past and concerned—as it was initially formulated to be—with everything that occurred as a result of colonisation, which could now appear too limited even if still applicable.[iii] Yet, of course, despite the apparent demise of imperialism, Western powers have in no way relinquished their control. As Williams and Chrisman explain: "This continuing Western influence, located in flexible combinations of the economic, the political, the military, and the ideological is called neo-colonialism" (1993: 3). In *Culture and Imperialism* (1994), Edward Said elaborates how the mentality of neo-colonialism continues to endorse the imperialist attitudes of superiority of white/western over Black/native colonised, and the supposed right of one to oppress the other. Moreover, the imperial scramble for control now extends beyond the confines of mere planet Earth into the future empire of space. As part of the requirement for new knowledge it is vital that consciousness is no longer excluded from western critical theory as a major consideration. In a discipline that concerns itself most centrally with concepts of self and other, it is paradoxical that neither is fully defined nor understood: this book proposes that the theoretical bases of postcolonial studies must include an understanding of consciousness. Once consciousness is understood as the dynamic substrate to all human experience, it can be argued that such an understanding is fundamental to resolutions of otherness and the problems inherent within the power dynamics of oppression that continue, now decades past the colonial era into the neo-colonial and beyond.

5. New paths for postcolonial literature

While some writers and critics have engaged with explorations of consciousness in the fields of theatre, literature (particularly in the genres of science-fiction and the post-human), the topic has not yet been explored within postcolonial literature sufficiently to produce a new direction in that field of theory and production of literary texts. Within the academy, the teaching of postcolonial studies focuses on a diverse range of literature (and film) representing nineteenth and twentieth centuries to the present. Originally post-colonial theory was formulated to deal with the reading and writing of literature written in previously or currently colonized countries,[iv] together with the ways in which the literature of the colonial powers silence or at best misrepresent the experience of the colonised people, describing the native population typically as childlike, inferior, or inadequate. Secondly, postcolonial studies involve an examination of how individuals or groups negotiate and overcome situations of domination and subordination—often a struggle expressed in terms of ways of being and becoming, of finding fulfilment, freedom and agency. It also analysed ways in which colonized peoples rewrote and reclaimed their own individual and national identity, and their strategies for writing in the face of their categorisation of otherness. This rewriting of the history and past—as championed initially by Frantz Fanon—involves inter-connecting issues of psychology and language, politics and tradition.

Since the turn of the new millennium much debate has focussed on the future relevance of postcolonial studies, yet it would seem that the aim of postcolonial literature and theory in renegotiating identity will continue since postcolonial writers "are fabricating the new subjects of history and are seeking to install these new subjects within the folds of contemporary imagination" (McCarthy 2005: 4). These new "patched together" subjects are both exciting and challenging, and continue to include more multidimensional issues of cultural modernisation ranging from issues of gender and empowerment to ethics and the environment. This is fertile and exciting ground for analysing both stability and change, since, as McCarthy continues:

> Emergent postcolonial literatures register a new structure of feeling, of overlapping and cascading epochs of time, of drifting space, of free associations, of the ample desires and insatiable appetites of the centre and the periphery rolled into one. (ibid)

Yet no matter how far these reassessments have forged some limited knowledge on race, gender and culture, what has been left is a void in the real understanding of a way forward— a future application of this discourse to the rapidly changing world of the twenty-first century. While postcolonial theorists have long urged for a rewriting of a people's past to reformulate both national and individual identity, the source of literary expression is overlooked, if not actively refuted as invalid. While concepts such as subjective experience, history, art, ethics, race, gender, and ecology have all been problematised within postcolonial studies, and while this has forged some limited knowledge about "culture", the way forward is still unclear for a future application of this discourse to *life* in a world crying out for alternatives and peace. The failure of "history" and the credibility of other grand narratives forced postcolonial studies to question and deconstruct concepts of ethnicity, desire, self/other, local/global in terms of power, gender, access to resources and agency, and so on. Meanwhile, the problems inherent within the limited definitions of "the postcolonial", together with the political paradigms it engages, reveal the urgent need for a work that addresses the problems of such limited discourse. The goal of "unproblematising" otherness, for example, can be achieved through the realisation that "other" is an extremely inadequate if not fraudulent notion when seen within the larger perspective of an understanding of consciousness.

The area of the postcolonial together with its continuing relevance is itself currently a topic of controversy and criticism, and is in urgent need of being expanded towards a more holistic framework. The reason for placing my argument within the context of postcolonial literature is intentionally with the purpose to expand and redefine the borders of this genre. It is in many ways the field most suited, and most in need, of an introduction of the understandings of consciousness. The inclusion of a clear understanding of consciousness, accessible through quantum theory in physics, is crucial to this reformulation. In order to avoid following a western liberal line of thinking, which searches exclusively for social or psychological explanations, a more in-depth approach must be employed. The very notion of "consciousness" is still one that is unacceptable to many in this field, which prizes itself on representing and discussing the local and the specific, while shying away from any notions of "universal" truths that smack of totalising, and "imperialist", narratives.

As long ago as 1989, in their groundbreaking formulation of postcolonial studies, Ashcroft, Griffiths and Tiffin argued for the inclusion of indigenous literary theory, especially the theories of Sanskrit poetics into mainstream academia. While admittedly this book has since has been subject to much criticism, this does not explain the fact that little has been done in academia to follow up on this suggestion. They cite the lacunae of academic work on the indigenous literary theory of India, including the interplay between literature, language, and aesthetic experience. Indian literary theory, they explain, embraces "not only an evaluation and interpretation of the text but also a theory of production and consumption" (1998: 120). Furthermore, deeper exploration and utilisation of these theories is in itself "a political act of rebellion against the incorporating tendencies [. . .] of neo-universalism" (ibid: 121).

Indian literary theory is based on the philosophical texts and originally oral histories mostly dating back over two to three millennia. The Vedas, the oldest of which (Rig Veda) is thought to be about five thousand years old, contain in seed form the essence of what was to become an extensive system of linguistics, which was in later centuries also applied in treatises on grammar, literature, performance (theatre) and dance. The implications of Indian theory to performativity and the concept of the sacred space of the theatre have already been explored and elucidated in the texts by Daniel Meyer-Dinkgräfe, Peter Malekin and Ralph Yarrow, in the context of Indian aesthetics and the nature of conscious experience through various stages of higher awareness and receptivity.[v] Although not yet widely studied within these terms, much postcolonial and diasporic literature accesses meaning through experience of the sacred encounter with the source of "being"—as expressed through language, or through fictional explorations of experience and art.

Bill Ashcroft has reiterated (2003) that the sacred has followed the path of being another denied discourse, neglected in academia in terms of theoretical agenda. Yet, he argues, it is the most rapidly expanding means of local empowerment. Here, I shall expand upon the usage of Indian literary theory (in particular the description of possible higher states of consciousness) in its relevance to postcolonial literature. Within this overall framework, I will examine some important aspects of literature, first, how literature must concern itself with this debate if it is to remain of relevance in the twenty-first century. Consciousness and literature must both be understood in their individual as well as social contexts—as expressions of the development of the human mind as well as the community. I will also argue that literature is based on language, and language is based on consciousness: a self-referral state that cannot be defined externally. (In other words, the expressions of language in literature are manifestations of a more subtle level of intelligence *beyond* language. This is analogous to the situation in quantum mechanics, when it was discovered that classical physics could not account for quantum mechanical phenomena. One cannot justify or explain something that is more fundamental from a level that is more superficial.)

In these chapters, I will examine how writers have themselves explored the theme of the diversity of conscious experience within their work: specifically located within literature designated as "postcolonial" and "diasporic"—realms of literature that are particularly exploratory by nature, seeking as they do to redefine and renegotiate notions of self-hood and otherness, identity and belongingness, locating and breaking boundaries of time (in terms of history) and space (in terms of geo-political certainty). A critical analysis of contemporary creative writing contextualises an understanding of consciousness within literature taken from a variety of cultures and languages. This book addresses issues of consciousness within the academy; I also analyse this topic in order to re-formulate a "writing of consciousness" with reference to the works of postcolonial and diasporic African writers, such as Ben Okri, J.M. Coetzee, Abdulrazak Gurnah, Chinua Achebe, Ahdaf Souief and Naguib Mahfouz; and Caribbean writers such as Wilson Harris, V.S. Naipaul and Edwidge Dandicat. The way consciousness is involved in the creative process will also be examined in other contemporary writers who migrate between continents, writers such as Isabel Allende (Chile and California) and Mario Vargas Llosa (Peru and London). As I discuss in the next chapters, the world is a reflection of our own inner consciousness or reality; the world is as we are, a projection of our own desires. It is this metaphysical journey that is explored in much diasporic literature, with examples ranging from Wole Soyinka, through Wilson Harris to Chitra Banerjee Divakaruni. As Divakaruni herself expresses it in her novel *Mistress of Spices*:

> Sometimes I wonder if there is such a thing as reality, an objective and untouched nature of being. Or if all that we encounter has already been changed by what we had imagined it to be. If we had dreamed it into being. (Divakaruni 1997: 16)

6. Locating Literature of the Diasporas

A diaspora, as Robin Cohen analyses in *Global Diasporas: An Introduction* (1997), is a community of people that lives together in one country, that "acknowledge that the 'old country'—a notion often buried deep in language, religion, custom or folklore"—always has some claim on their loyalty and emotions (ix). A member of a diaspora community, moreover, is "demonstrated by an acceptance of an inescapable link with their past migration history and a sense of co-ethnicity with others of a similar background" (ix). With the constant influx of new community members who bring with them "new" values of language, culture and class, diaspora spaces are "dynamic and shifting, open to repeated construction and reconstruction" (McLeod 2000: 207). The diaspora breaks down concepts of local and global. Similarly, this sense of transience or fluidity means that these communities are open to change. The new possibilities that these dynamic communities suggest have also given rise to an exciting and creative wave of literature from writers of the diasporas in Britain and North America.

The diasporic predicament is, for example, tellingly explored in Nadeem Aslam's *Maps for Lost Lovers*, a novel involving Pakistani and Indian families, and the conflicts and resonances of the various communities forging a meaningful space to live in an unnamed English town. Meaning is bestowed on life by close observation of aesthetic minutiae of daily existence, listening to jazz music, breeding butterflies, noting the seasonal changes in nature—events that are independent of politics, religion or the fearful and fragile pocket of their existence in British society. The character Kaukab, a Pakistani mother who had come over to England to marry in her early teens, feels the solitude of life away from the norm of an extended family:

> It was as though, when the doors of Pakistan closed on her, her hands had forgotten the art of knocking; she had made some friends with some women in the area but she barely knew what lay beyond the neighbourhood and didn't know how to deal with strangers: full of apprehension concerning the white race and uncomfortable with people of another Subcontinental religion or grouping. (32)

One morning as she lies in bed worrying about her son's involvement in the recent violence, and the disappearance of her nephew, next door, "her neighbour wonders why her children refer to Bangladesh as 'abroad' because Bangladesh isn't abroad, *England* is abroad; Bangladesh is *home*" (2004: 46). Not all who live in a diaspora may have undergone the experience of migration, however, since a diaspora community or member may be two or three generations removed from the original families who relocated. The sense of belonging to a geographically distant "home-land" may be a more "spiritual" or emotional link to past traditions of the culture, and may be created out of "the confluence of narratives" of a shared history rather than an actual memory of a previous place of residence (Brah 1996: 183). Sometimes this can result in a sense of dislocation, rather than relocation, a jarring sense of being at home in neither world; sometimes the "homeland" is "no more than a mythic place of desire in the diasporic imagination" (Brah ibid: 92). [vi] Any sense of nostalgia may indeed be for a place never known, a place merely located in dream. Avtah Brah argues that diaspora communities are forged out of multiple imaginative journeys between the old country and the new (1996: 183). These diaspora spaces are both physical and emotional spaces, shifting and dynamic. Yet at the heart of the diasporic experience is always "the image of the journey", a movement away, a dispersal *from,* a *dis*-location (ibid: 181-182).

Homi Bhabha regards people in cultures today as living in a "Third Space", an "in-between state", a state of suspension of time, space and identity. The postcolonial emphasis on the search for identity is expanded through his concept of culture being "less about a pre-given identity [. . .] and more about the activity of negotiating [. . .] often conflicting demands for collective self-expression" (1999: 38-43). What becomes apparent within these discussions on the diaspora (led by Hall's notions of dynamic change where the margins become the centre, and Homi Bhabha's formulation of the transformative properties of Third Space) is that despite change, something remains constant.[vii] The relocation of culture or of individual, which is transformational in theory, does not, in practice, change the individual in essence. (One does not usually arrive at a new or unknown destination having no idea of who one is!) If, as Hall has argues, diaspora identities are constantly "producing and reproducing themselves anew" to create hybrid communities that are evolving new dynamic cultures, it is timely to take this projection one logical step further to discuss the "common ground" of human life in consciousness. Relocation of dwelling does cause change in self-appraisal of identity, and yet within that change "original" identity is not lost: something remains the same. Thus, the diasporic experience is a diverse and self-contradictory one involving movement, travel and a re-establishment of "home"; fragmentation and a desire for wholeness; elitism and shifting categorisation of class; a release from but simultaneously a jealous guarding of tradition.

Robert Young recently outlined the new forms of migration that are criss-crossing the planet—they are what he calls the "shadow lines" (after Amitav Ghosh's novel), the abstract and yet real lines of migration north from south, west from east, Africa to Mediterranean, the new flow of human cargo of the migrant routes that operate without borders.[viii] Nationalism is no longer so pertinent to all of this movement as the class wars between Global North and South, between the rich and poor states; the new apartheid is the state of not-sharing of the world's resources (Young: 2005). Literature of the diaspora is thus concerned with the continuing trends of movement of peoples that have been ongoing for centuries. One only has to cite the millions of people who were shifted across the globe during the era of slavery to realise the complexity and longevity of world routes. (The 550 years of displacement and dislocation of African people to the Caribbean, for example, created one of the "worst" experiences of colonial venture. In all more than five million slaves were imported. In the Atlantic slave trade over twelve million were relocated in total to the Americas.) While writers such as Toni Morrison and Caryl Phillips have dealt graphically with issues of slavery and its aftermath, few have dealt with the extermination of the indigenous peoples who lived in these places and who were replaced by slaves. Today these types of radical conquest and displacement are driven by new economic demands—that of access to the last remaining oil reserves for example—and they are also driven though disparity in wealth.

7. Formulating new connections: consciousness studies and literature

Cameron McCarthy locates the direction of postcolonial "fictive worlds" as mapping out new terrains of communication and power that act horizontally, rhizomatically, to challenge both Eurocentrism and "reductive forms of multiculturalism" (1998: 1). He argues that many postcolonial authors (such as Wilson Harris, Michael Ondaatje and others) have already transformed the canon to include "multicultural worlds from which there are not longer exits to retreat" (ibid: 4). This new dynamic of literature with its multicultural and multilingual points of reference *must* include the previously excluded realms of literature that have been previously othered due to their so-called "mystical", "esoteric" or "sacred" connotations.

Definitions give a clue as to the problem here. "Mystical" is defined as "having a spiritual meaning or reality that is neither apparent to the senses nor obvious to the intelligence" (all definitions here are taken from *Merriam Webster Collegiate Dictionary* 11th edition), a definition that will be challenged as this work proceeds. It has been said that the spiritual in life is anything that makes us look within rather than without ourselves, anything that directs the mind within. (The word "esoteric" is originally derived from the ancient Greek meaning "from within".) If we then trace the meaning of 'spiritual' (since it is the defining word within mysticism), we find that it means 'not corporeal, related to religious or sacred matters' and comes from the Latin *spiritualis,* 'of breathing, of wind'. The further one proceeds in tracking back this etymology the more significant it becomes. To go further, we trace the word *religion,* since again this is a central word in the definition of spiritual. *Religion,* meaning 'service or worship of God or the supernatural', comes from the Latin *religare,* which means 'to tie back', 'to restrain, 'to sanction'. (It shares the same stem as the English words 'rely' and 'ligature': something that is used to bind.) In some ways this can be compared to the word *yoga,* which means 'to yoke', to bind to the source, the Self, but *religare* also carries other connotations of forcing or restraint rather than liberation.

While religious sanctions were previously deployed to consolidate notions of white racial superiority, religion is now being used as motivation and justification for the growing opposition to neo-colonialist exploitation. To see how far the meaning of "religion" has come in today's world, one only has to read a recent comment by Hanif Kureishi:

> We know longer know what it is to be religious and we haven't for a while.[. . .] The truly religious, following the logic of submission to political and moral ideals, and to the arbitrary will of God, are terrifying to us and almost incomprehensible. To us "belief" is dangerous and we don't like to think we have much of it. (2005)

In a fictional context, the ambiguous status of religion in the world is wryly depicted in Salman Rushdie's short story "The Prophet's Hair", which plays with the contradictions, the wonders and dangers, inherent within faith and religious enigma, when the mysteries of a religious relic are experienced as simultaneously miraculous and deadly (Rushdie 1995: 35). By extension, it is significant to read in Levy-Strauss's classic structuralist work on human belief systems, his claim of the importance to analyse

> not how men think in myths, but how myths operate in men's minds without their being aware of the fact [...] It would perhaps be better to go still further and, disregarding the thinking subject

completely, proceed as if the thinking process were taking place
in the myths, in their reflection upon themselves and their
interrelation. (1969: 6-10)

The experience of consciousness in its most pure state—one that
can be called transcendental consciousness, since it is "beyond"
thought —is neither mystical nor spiritual nor religious, according to
their definitions. The only possible definition is the Upanishadic *neti
neti*, 'not this not that'. The experience of pure consciousness simply
is pure experiencing, without connotations or associations. (The word
"pure" here denotes sole, entire, or complete, not a state of purity or
piety that would by association imply a converse state of impurity.)
Consciousness is related to knowledge, and the state of pure
consciousness is the state of pure knowledge: a state of complete
knowledge. In this state, knowledge is complete because there is a
unity between the knower, the process of gaining knowledge, and the
known; and knowledge is able to create from within itself. The
location of consciousness as the seat or home of all knowledge can be
applied to the areas of life considered by postcolonial studies: namely
the realms of power, how language is employed in order to control
power, and how the peoples of the world—especially those of the
colonised or developing world—are demeaned or exploited by these
hegemonies. This is not resorting to utopian fantasy, ignoring the
problems as they exist; transcendence cannot and should not imply an
escape from "reality". The aim of developing understanding of
consciousness must be viewed together with its implications in an
ethic of responsibility and compassion. The injustices and inequalities
in the world will never, in fact, be resolved *without* the world
embracing a more profound understanding of human consciousness.

In the decade since Homi Bhabha argued for the fluid, relocatable,
renegotiable nature of migrant identity in the gaps—the Third Space
between national cultures and borders— it is money, the transnational
movement of funds and investment, that has become "extraterrestrial", flexible, and renegotiable. So too have definitions of
illegal/legal, criminality, government, and terrorism—all of which are
used for and determined by political and economic reasons. Tribalism
and globalism, paradoxically interdependent forces, are apparently
reshaping the world. Ten years ago Benjamin R. Barber was able to
write that "McWorld pursues a bloodless economics of profit"; but it
is clearly debatable now just how "bloodless" that pursuit has

remained. He continues, "Responding to McWorld, parochial forces defend and deny, reject and repel modernity wherever they find it" (1996: 12). Now it all seems so much more complex than that.

While the force of globalisation is seen by many to ride on the back of neo-colonisation, issues of globalisation have to be reassessed, not merely in terms of colonisation, economics, trade and so on, but addressing the way a concept of a global country becomes a legitimate "alternative" to one world superpower. In a hopeful vision, the journalist John Pilger (2005) argues that imperialism is being replaced by new values, and he proposes the growth of concern amongst the people is fast creating the alternative super-power, a force of world consciousness against inequality, poverty, and war.

In conclusion, it seems that any physical location on the planet, no matter where it is conceived to be, is a shallow imitation of a real sense of "home". Stuart Hall argues that the "return to the beginning" can never be fulfilled (2004: 402), but remains a symbolic representation of the "infinitely renewable source of desire, memory, myth, search, discovery" (ibid). This search will remain impossible so long as individuals look *outside* themselves to find this long-lost sense of fulfilment. This theme of the search for fulfilment and a sense of wholeness or completion is of course an ancient genre in literature, harking back (in the West) as far as the medieval stories of Piers Ploughman, Gawain and the Green Knight, and the Nordic sagas of heroism and conquest, or poems such as fourteenth century *The Conference of the Birds* in Persia.[ix] The twentieth century *Bildungsroman*, which did not meet its doom with postmodernism, continues in postcolonial contexts in novels such as *The Famished Road*, or *Palace of the Peacock* (both discussed in later chapters). The narrative voice of the displaced, dispersed, and disenfranchised men and women of Africa, India or the Arab world are not far removed from the questing hero narratives of previous centuries. "Birth is a moment of transcendence that we spend our lives trying to understand", writes Rushdie (1991: 421). The search is ultimately for the self, and the self ultimately is consciousness. Consciousness is, to borrow a phrase from Stephanie Newell, one's "potentially irreducible specificity" (2006: 213), if not one's potential limitless specificities.

In order to detail how this claim can be both valid and relevant to twenty-first century literature and the future of postcolonial studies, the next chapter will elaborate the nature of consciousness and the structure of pure knowledge inherent within the human mind. The fact that the experience of heightened modes of consciousness is one that is described across many cultures also endorses a cross-cultural analysis and use of consciousness studies in world literatures. [x]

Discussing the role of the writer in society, Salman Rushdie argues that the role of art is to mediate between the material and spiritual worlds, to offer a "secular" alternative, a "transcendence" that is "that flight of the human spirit outside the confines of material, physical existence" (1991: 421). It is this flight—the "soaring quality of transcendence, the sense of being more than oneself, of being in some way joined to the whole of life" (ibid)—that this work explores. Significantly in the context of the diasporic journeys undertaken by the migrant and the exile, it is worth considering that the journey itself may have value: Rushdie elaborates his theme on writing as adventure, that "in the case of travel adventures, the best of all are those in which some inner journey, some adventure *in the self*, is the real point. [...] Enlightenment is certainly to be had at home, but it's still worth making the long, arduous trip [...]" (ibid: 225, emphasis added).

[i] This exclusion can be argued to be an extension of (British) colonial rule in India where all the sacred texts of the Veda, including Rig Veda, Ayur Veda (the texts dealing with health and medicine) the stories of the Puranas, for example, were banned and relegated to the realms of myth. Doctors of Ayurveda were banned and punished by the British: if found practising the traditional pulse diagnosis, for example, their hands would be cut off. The hymns of the four Vedas, the Puranas etc, were declassified from being stories from history and detail of sacred rites to fantasy and myth.

[ii] Macaulay's Minute on Indian Education (2nd February 1835) was written to explain the rationale behind the funding of education; to argue how a sum of money set aside for the promotion of knowledge of literature and science in the Indian Empire should be spent, for "reviving literature in India". It expounds upon the benefits of the colonial peoples in India receiving an English education in English, rather than promoting any Indian language, since, it was argued, any indigenous learning, including philosophy, astronomy, and medicine, was baseless and lacking in any purpose. Similarly indigenous scriptures and languages (Sanskrit and Arabic) were deemed to be "poor and rude" and indigenous literatures including history and poetry relegated to the realms of childish nonsense. The minute's main message is to reinforce the "intrinsic superiority" of all European traditions and knowledge; and that education of colonial peoples in their mother tongue would be impossible—prejudices that came to form the backbone of the Empire and that lasted well into the twentieth century. We still see the aftermath in surprising places today. The misconception of Vedanta as mysticism can be seen as part of the western undermining of Indian culture.

[iii] Bill Ashcroft, one of the first theorists in formulating "postcolonial theory" as an approach within literary studies, explains that the term "postcolonial" was intended to indicate "post-colonization" (Plenary address "Postcolonial futures" at USACLALS Conference at Santa Clara University, USA, 2002.)

[iv] It is also important to note that the term "postcolonial" (or "post-colonial") is itself a problematic term; most writers in the field today acknowledge that it also involves a certain amount of controversy just to define what it does address in the intellectual, aesthetic and political components involved in its usages.

[v] See for example *Studies in the Literary Imagination* Volume 34, no 2 (Fall 2001), which is devoted to the theme of "Drama and consciousness".

[vi] This often debilitating sense of being "in-between worlds" is obviously not only true of Diaspora communities, but is an experience that may equally apply to an individual who feels out of place in the social structure of their own homeland. To give Thomas Mann's 1903 novel *Tonio Kröger* as an example, the eponymous protagonist is an artist who feels total alienation from the *class* identities (Bohemian vs. Burgher) available to him in Germany, as summed up in his agonised statement, "Ich stehe zwischen zwei Welten und bin in keine daheim." [I stand between two worlds and am at home in none (my translation).]

[vii] Diasporic communities, while absorbing some aspects of "new" life in America or in Great Britain, can be seen to become more traditional and rooted in the traditions of their motherland than those who stay at home. Location may determine the ways in which group identity changes, or does not change: Wembley may be a locus of more traditional values that have long-since been transformed and abandoned with the fast-pace of change in Gujrat/North India. A specific diasporic group such as Cypriot Turks and Greeks, all British Citizens since independence in 1963, live in a state of harmony in London that is as yet unimaginable in the divided city of Lefkosia.

[viii] Robert Young, Plenary address "One Way Street—Walter Benjamin at the Border", European Association for Commonwealth Literature and Language Studies conference, *Sharing Places*, Malta, 21 March 2005.

[ix] Salman Rushdie compares the *Conference of the Birds* with *Pilgrim's Progress* and sees both as "adventure[s]" of purification of winning through to the divine" but that "this allegorical, transcendent adventuring is, these days, more or less completely defunct", since, for one thing "For every Christopher Columbus there is also a Captain Hook, for every lamp-genie there is a fiend". ("On Adventure" in *Imaginary Homelands*, 223). This argument will be challenged later in this book, when I locate several postcolonial novels that deal with such outer and inner journeys, and discover that indeed, "few topographical boundaries can rival the frontiers of the mind" and where "adventure has its dark side as well as a light" (ibid).

[x] The state of pure consciousness, where the self is in a state of being self-referral, a quiet "internal observer", is described as an experience of expansion and utter peacefulness, and is variously defined by different contemplative traditions. It is the absolute one in Plotinus, Atman/Brahman in Advaita Vedanta, and nondual consciousness in Buddhist Vijnanas. It is referred to as "Turiya Chetana" or transcendental consciousness in Vedic Science, according to which, it is "the field of unbounded, unmanifest, pure intelligence, in which reside all the frequencies of Creative Intelligence responsible for the whole manifest universe" (Maharishi 1993: 190-191).

Chapter Two
Exploring Self and Other: Theories of Consciousness

"If only the other parts of the body realised that they are manifestations of absolute consciousness then . . ."
"Maybe we can wake them up," suggests the Brain.
(Tom Robbins—*Even Cowgirls get the Blues*, 363)

1. Exploring concepts of consciousness

Consciousness remains multiply ambiguous from various perspectives ranging from semantic to phenomenological (Antony (2001). As one of the most widely misunderstood and misinterpreted words of our modern world, "consciousness" clearly is in need of redefinition or reformulation. Dictionary definitions have it as being "the quality or state of being aware especially of something within oneself", and as "the state of being aware of some object, state or fact" (Merriam Webster), and this encompasses the sense of being aware of social or political issues. Consciousness "of" remains a concept that misleads in assuming that the mind must have content, must have a state of being that is both fluctuating and temporal. In the wide-ranging debates surrounding the nature of consciousness, it has generally been assumed that an objective study of consciousness is impossible.[i] Gerd Sommerhoff, for example, proposes that the problem is because, "Our own experience gives us merely a subjective, 'first person' view of consciousness, whereas science needs to occupy a detached and objective 'third person' standpoint" (2000: 4). This, however, is faulty reasoning; the observer and the observation can never be independent. From twentieth century physics experiments (as immortalised by Schroedinger's famous cat) we know that the act of observation influences the system being observed, and even enlivens the potentialities within it (Hagelin 2006b). The act of observation also can increase order in that system (a fact upon which chaos theory is based).

The renowned AI scientist and writer Marvin Minsky concludes that although consciousness is a "hot topic" in neuroscience, the word itself is one that confuses at least sixteen different processes (2006: 16). Some theorists believe only humans have consciousness: Daniel Dennett, for example, "sees consciousness as just a cultural product" (3) and "denies subjective states of awareness altogether" (1991: 65). At the opposite extreme, the psychologist Susan Blackmore attributes consciousness to any system that interacts with the environment (Blackmore 1992). Other writers highlight the *qualitative* dimension of consciousness, known as *qualia* or "what it is like to have this or that conscious experience" (Sommerhof ibid: 7). Sommerhof also resorts to his dictionary for definitions and locates consciousness mainly relating to one of three senses: awareness of the surrounding world; awareness of the self as an entity; and awareness of one's thoughts and feelings. He also locates the obsolete use of "consciousness" as meaning a shared knowledge, or shared attitudes—such as in the term "collective consciousness". He proposes that any theory of consciousness must relate to all these aspects as well as providing a unity between them (ibid: 9). All of these meanings are based on the "horizontal" play of semantics, without the "vertical" conceptualisation of the possibility of consciousness existing as a "pure" entity devoid of association. In her more recent work, Susan Blackmore (2005) problematises both physiological and psychological parameters of consciousness, locating as a key question the moment when an individual can locate the "now" of "being conscious". She further extrapolates different modes of experiencing consciousness itself, whether through changes in neurological functioning derived through drugs or meditation techniques such as TM or Zen.

1.2. The bare bones of consciousness

Sommerhof argues for the importance of setting any understanding of consciousness within its biological context; "Modern evolutionary theory leaves little room for doubt that Homo sapiens is a product of the continuous biological development and the faculty of consciousness is part of that product" (2000: 6). His model of consciousness argues that the roots and rationale of consciousness arise "out of an organism's interaction with the external world" (ibid). While this is a limited viewpoint according to the approach taken throughout this book, it is true that, fundamentally, the functioning of consciousness is dependent on the health of the human body and nervous system. Just as knowledge is structured in consciousness, so consciousness is structured in the physiology. If the human body functions from total efficiency all the time, then it is said to be healthy, an effortless circulation of matter converted into pure energy, functioning from a state of wholeness. One theory of consciousness argues that in terms of the human physiology, consciousness can be regarded as the extra "power" that is surplus to the living organism's basic requirements of survival, scavenging for food, and surveillance for safety. Once these have been met, the larger brained mammal, man, is able to direct the energy into channels of higher metal activity. In evolutionary terms, the bipedal body is aiming for maximising its potential—both physical and mental. The upward energy flows through the spinal column of the newly upright Homo sapiens to the frontal cortex where consciousness becomes developed and mental potential becomes expanded. Consciousness then, in terms of evolution, requires the development of the uniquely human ability to expand mental functioning to the optimum, based on the functioning of the body in a state of "wellness", where the physical organism is functioning to its full total potential all the time. This is called health: where the five senses regulate and execute the frictionless flow of the body's perceptive and interactive abilities: physical, mental, environmental, social, and spiritual.

The knowledge that humans use only a fraction of this mental potential available within their brains is now commonplace (psychologists estimate only about five to ten per cent). If the physical system is functioning with maximum efficiency, it is a system where the on/off binary building blocks switches are optimised: creating the frictionless flow of information and energy throughout the body and the channels of communication. When the needs of the human body are met, the excess energy allows the human nervous system and thought processes to cognate, develop, and expand. Consciousness according to this theory is not essence but effervescence: the sparkling bubbling over of human energy, a vivacity not experienced by all.[ii]

Regardless of how human bodies change over time, from childhood to adult to old age, or regardless of our location in space, we still think of ourselves as the same person, there is no difference to our sense of self. By adulthood, our physical bodies contain not one of the original cells we were born with; our bodies have rebuilt themselves many times over—yet we still consider ourselves to be the same "person". While we may talk academically of redefining our identity, few of us, if any, would challenge that we identify with a "core self" that does not change. Yet we cannot analyse this sense of self through the intellect: it is beyond conceptualisation. As in the laws of physics, we cannot analyse something bigger from something smaller. (We can experience the intellect through the self, but not the other way around.) If an individual's mode of activity remains on the level of interaction with the environment, on the surface levels of the mind with intellectual analysis and so on, the experience is always changing and mutable: The ability to access knowledge of self is not possible. If the intellect is not grounded in the self, its discriminating quality will be fluctuating, on a horizontal level of different decisions, not like the true intellect acting in (a vertical) connection to the self. The difference here can be seen in a simple analogy with a television screen. It looks like a moving image but in fact the picture is a direction of a beam of electrons from a non-moving source at the far end of the tube. Or as in the cinema, the narrative of the movie can be enjoyed (or not); when in reality it is just a projection of images on a blank and silent screen.

1.3 Self-referral consciousness

Answering the question "what is consciousness?" Maharishi Mahesh Yogi apparently simplifies the obtuse concept: "Consciousness is that which is conscious of itself" he explains, and continues:

> Being consciousness of itself, consciousness is the knower of itself. Being the knower of itself, consciousness is both knower and known. Being knower and known, consciousness is also the process of knowing. Thus consciousness has three qualities—the qualities of knower, knowing and known—the three qualities of 'subject' (knower), 'object' (known) and the relationship between the subject and object (process of knowing). (1994: 53)[iii]

When these three exist together, consciousness exists. It is appreciated in its qualities of wakefulness, pure intelligence, pure knowledge. Consciousness is a *self*-referral state, which is why it is difficult to define it externally. To be self-referral is the "witness" value of knowing-ness, which can be broken down into this tri-dimensional paradigm of the knower, the object of knowledge and the process by which knowledge is gained. Self-referral is the state of the knower being also the known, and in which the knower is also the process, the flow of gaining knowledge. Consciousness is that state of the mind, awareness, knowing itself, and in this state it can create from within itself. From modern physics we learn that the whole of evolution in nature is self-interacting, dynamic and non-linear—in other words it can create from within itself—and it is due to this quality of "knowing itself" that consciousness is the seat of human creativity and the source of all knowledge (see for example, Hagelin 2006). It is the dynamic and self-referral basis of all manifest creation, the experience of consciousness that lies at the basis of understanding the expressions of consciousness. Here, therefore, the word "consciousness" refers to the intelligence or awareness underlying thought, speech and creativity, where consciousness is not the product of thought but the origin.

Consciousness is the state of being conscious, as distinct from being conscious *of* something. Moreover, it seems the human is the only animal to have the ability, through abstract reasoning, to be conscious of herself, to be able to be knowledgeable of her own existence. This quality of self-referral, or self-reflexivity, is the key to higher consciousness. Where the Upanishads advise, "Know that by which all else is known", they are referring to the Self, the state of pure consciousness in which resides of all knowledge outside the knower. Maharishi Mahesh Yogi explains that "By acting from this level of self-referral [the level of cosmic consciousness, or enlightenment] the self remains free from the limitations and boundaries of space and time and one lives and enjoys the total potential of life in daily living" (2005). Often scientists who have experienced some form of awakening link their experiences of higher consciousness with the profound discoveries of the 20th century of quantum mechanics, quantum field theory, Unified Field Theories and quantum gravity, in which the material phenomenon of the physical world are found to have their origin and explanation in an underlying abstract and non-physical field of intelligence.[iv]

1.4 Axiomatic knowledge

The principle that a self-consistent theory or body of knowledge needs a set of axioms, or fundamental definitions, is absent from many modern theories, of literature, for example, or sociology. This is why "absolutes" are hard to find, and disagreement prevails. To give a parallel: before it was realised that there could be many sets of axioms for different theories of geometry, it was difficult to reconcile the geometry of curved surfaces with the geometry of a flat plane. This is also why the development of quantum mechanics was so problematic. The physicists of that era attempted to understand quantum mechanical phenomena in terms of the principles of classical physics. They failed miserably, for two main reasons. Firstly, the axioms of the theories necessary to understand quantum mechanics are different from those of classical physics, and secondly, quantum mechanics is at a deeper, more profound level of nature. Thus, in the opposite direction, it *is* possible to understand classical phenomena in terms of the principles of quantum mechanics – they are expressions of the quantum mechanical. The quantum mechanical is *not* an expression of the classical.

The comparison between the physical world and the understanding of consciousness is not a trivial one. Many commentators have noted the similarities, parallels, and equivalents between the quantum mechanical/classical relationship in physics, and the expressions found in the literature of many cultures and epochs of human history, that speak of a fundamental level of intelligence or consciousness, which underlies the phenomenal world. The way in which the axiomatic principles are uncovered is often by deduction, in that the discovery is made that they cannot be derived, they must be assumed. This path led to the origin of quantum mechanics, as it was discovered that classical physics could not account for quantum mechanical phenomena. The relationship between the axiomatic and the proven or derived is evident in the expressions of language found in literature. In geometry, we find archetypal forms, which form the basis of all other forms. In literature, there are archetypal relationships between concepts and words, which form the basis of all literary expression. (This is analogous to the way in which complex geometric forms are expressions of certain primordial forms–through which they can be understood—or the way in which complex physical or chemical interactions are expressions of basic, primordial interactions –through which the complex interactions can be understood).

Thus, consciousness is aware of itself; it is both subject and object. Language sprouts from this subject/object relationship in consciousness. This is how our conscious awareness comprehends language. Because our awareness contains the subject/object relationship in its most fundamental form, where subject *is* object, then it can comprehend the subject/object relationships found in language and literature. When the creative writer uses this relationship to form an artistic expression, the reader or listener resonates with this expression, because it evokes the subject/object relationship that already exists in his or her own awareness. We find ourselves stimulated by language and by literature, as dormant expressions of the subject/object relationship are awakened in our own inner experience.

2. The historical place of consciousness in literary studies

Literature is based on language, and language is based on consciousness: a self-referral state that cannot be defined externally. In other words, the expressions of language in literature are manifestations of a more subtle level of intelligence *beyond* language. This is analogous to the situation in quantum mechanics, when it was discovered that classical physics could not account for quantum mechanical phenomena: something more fundamental cannot be justified or explained from a level that is more superficial. As Albert Einstein quipped: "The world we have made as a result of the level of thinking we have done thus far creates problems we cannot solve at the same level of thinking at which we created them" (1972). The understanding at the basis of nature in classical physics and in the first generations of quantum physics was of an inert field underlying creation. The modern field theories of physics, however, show that this underlying field can actually create from within itself. This is crucial in the understanding of how manifestation can spring from the unmanifest, how lively creativity can spring from the field of silence. In terms of language and literature, it is a crucial starting point for the understanding that silent consciousness is the source of all creativity. (That silence is the basis or seed form of manifest verbal expression has been an intuitive experience for many writers, amongst others the poets T.S. Eliot and Ursula Le Guin). Human creativity, the creative process itself, lies in the silent field of awareness, where awareness is aware of itself. It experiences itself as infinite, and in this infinity anything finite can be found. Creativity is then simply the process of discovering these finite values in infinity and bringing them to the surface of life. Just as a diver can pick pearl oysters from the depths of the silent ocean and then bring them to the surface, so the expressed values of consciousness can be seen and appreciated. Thus for an author to locate the dynamism within silence, she must settle in silence through a means of accessing the silent depth of the mind, and then the unboundedness of awareness can create the forms of creative thought.[v]

For the past century or more, what has been thought of as consciousness originates from the days of William James and the psychoanalysts Freud and Jung, both of whom concerned themselves more with the *un*conscious mind, even to the extent of formulating a collective unconscious. In terms of nineteenth century literature, it was George Eliot (who is largely regarded as a writer within the genre of social realism) who produced one of the few explorations of consciousness and the unknown dimensions of the mind, such as a more expanded awareness, which she refers to as "exceptional mental character". Eliot herself, with her lively interest in science as it was rapidly expanding in the mid-nineteenth century, expresses her interest in areas of "the unknown" that may be uncovered through these new developments.[vi]   George Eliot wrote *The Lifted Veil* in 1859, shortly after her first great literary success with *Adam Bede*. Her publishers were too embarrassed to publish it and it was seen—and is still seen by many critics—as an aberration not worthy of serious attention.[vii] The plot centres on the male narrator Latimer and his experience of clairvoyance, a so-called "double consciousness" that allows him to perceive, albeit sometimes unwillingly, the thoughts of others. Just as the narrator perceives a "hidden discourse" within the minds of others that would normally remain inaccessible to a normal mind, so the novel itself contains a hidden narrative of Eliot's own commentary upon the limited discourse of Victorian England. Her theme attacks both the limited perceptions of the intellectual/scientific world, as well as the distortedly restricted patriarchal mind.

Henry James, an author whose novels explore themes of consciousness and morality, discusses in his 1884 essay "The Art of Fiction" the creative moment arising from an intuitive mind that guesses "the unseen from the seen". A heightened state of perception transforms a fragment of idea and the "myriad forms" (194) of reality into a work of literature. In the new twentieth century, other writers such as Virginia Woolf tried to locate the nature of consciousness by analysing the minutiae of each moment in time and every moment and fluctuation in thought, in her technique that became known as the "stream of consciousness". She intuitively felt that the new century had produced a change in human nature, and argued that any moment of any day could be important for the human mind to locate its reality. All these attempts at locating the reality of consciousness were on the *level* of thought, however, and were therefore unable to fathom or access awareness of the source of thought that goes beyond language. By the 1970's, writers such as the Canadian Margaret Atwood were also exploring notions of consciousness as "alternative" narrative structures to patriarchal western society. Her work creates a link between the feminist and the postcolonial, centring the concern of the author on issues of otherness and twentieth century social responsibility. In other postmodern novels the female protagonists overcome the seemingly insurmountable problems inherent within patriarchy—forging new realities and redefinitions of the self.

3. Constructions of the self

In much postmodern and postcolonial thought, the self is constructed through multiple discourses and the effects of power. Theories of subjectivity are anti-essentialist: any totalising narratives, such as Marxism, Christianity, Humanism, and so on, are rejected in favour of *local, shifting* and *contingent* positioning. This fading away of the subjectivity of the author and unreliable nature of the objectively verifiable subject—the knower—leads to a situation where the very nature of consciousness itself must be readdressed. Where is the subject then located, and what is the purpose of creative expression? How does an understanding of the nature of consciousness expand our understanding of the nature of literary expression, the dynamics of literary experience in the flow of meaning between two subjectivities, for both the author and audience? These questions are dealt with in the pioneering work of William Haney II (1993, 2002) for example, which has dealt with deconstruction and a critique of Jameson's notion of the so-called "death of the subject". His argument that the subject as a knower can go beyond conceptual indeterminacy and experience transcendental consciousness (the experience of "going-beyond" thought), proposes a philosophical and linguistic basis to consciousness studies. He puts forward that Sanskrit Poetics, the Indian literary theory based on Vedantic philosophy, provides comparisons to the mechanics of deconstruction in its suggestion of a field of pure possibility at the basis of language, indicating parallel principles of unity in language and consciousness (1993: 1-5). Haney also deals with the apparent contradiction between the notion of consciousness as a "universal" that may be in conflict with the valid postcolonial concern of homogenising experience and eradicating individual difference. He refers to decontextualist philosophers such as Forman and Shear, who, in their discussions on consciousness "argue not for a unity of intentional constructs, but for a unity or identity of nonordinary, nonintentional experiences across cultural and historical boundaries" (Haney 2002: 61). This is a unity of the substrate of conscious experience, of *potentiality*, not the experiences or the individual consciousnesses themselves.

Ralph Yarrow and Peter Malekin similarly have discussed aspects of theatre and the dramatic arts within the framework of sacred space of wholeness and the performativity of consciousness as a mode of self-knowing (Yarrow and Malekin 2001: 54-57). The above writers, all concerned with the dearth of academic examples engaging consciousness as a primary focus of literary analysis, have also examined and differentiated between consciousness as defined by neurobiologists and hard-core reductionists such as F. Crick (1994) who repudiates the idea of awareness pre-existing, or existing independently of, neuro-chemical activity in the brain—and others who view consciousness as a transcendental reality underlying the totality of human life (see for example, Haney 2002: 27-45).

The so-called "hard problem of consciousness" has also led to theories being elaborated in behavioural science, physics, and philosophy; and Haney (citing Francisco Varela) discuses four ongoing basic approaches to consciousness studies: reductionism, functionalism, mysterianism and phenomenology. Here, this text will assume these arguments have been sufficiently dealt with by Haney (in his ground-breaking book *Culture and Consciousness* and elsewhere) and will focus its attention on the paradigm of consciousness as fundamental to, not arising from, the mind or human awareness. As Haney concludes:

> Consciousness studies can help us both to reassess our approach to the fundamental assumptions of contemporary theory and criticism and clarify how aesthetic experience can open awareness to deeper structures. (2002: 176)

Within the arts, as we have seen in comments by Salman Rushdie and others, the techniques of creativity and communication allow for an expression of the diverse modes of consciousness as well as a celebration of what it is to be human. Aspects of aesthetics and ethics come into play within dimensions of both fictional and theoretical terminology. The intellectual and the emotional are integrated in a process in which both are expounded and purified; intuition and revelation are companions on life's journey, which is thereby made less incomprehensible. In an article analysing a personal approach to artistic creativity, Gerda van de Windt details how:

> it is the function of the artist to give unique personal expression to inner truth that is informed by the body. [...] It is the revelation of a mystery and the truth of Being and being human that gives a work of art its authenticity. (2005: 2)

4. Problems and projections: a paradigm of consciousness

In order to refute possible criticisms of such a formulation of consciousness being either utopian or essentialist and oppressive, it is important to provide a clear definition of the functioning of consciousness, and differentiate the use of the word here to other works—whether "new-age", behaviourist, or phenomenological. I am aware of the problematisation within academic literary thought of what constitutes "consciousness" and that it is an overused and abused term, either because, as I have mentioned, it is associated with something mystical or otherworldly, or because it is used in specific terminology such as "political consciousness", "feminist consciousness" and so on, or often contrasted and confused with antonyms such as "unconsciousness", or Jung's collective unconscious—all of which are not the sense in which I use the word here. The notion of higher consciousness, particularly, has been dismissed as either related to mysticism, religion, or some eastern spiritual practices. This has largely been the fate of consciousness within literary studies, until recently.

Post-modern theorist Linda Hutcheon has argued that, "knowing the past becomes a question of representing, that is, of constructing and interpreting, not of objective recording" (2002: 70). This inability to objectively record the past since it does not exist as a unified and accessible entity is compatible with the quantum mechanical view of the universe, existing now for almost a century and yet still widely ignored in the general imagination of the western world. From this viewpoint, the recording of events varies according to the perceiver, collapsing the concept of the observer being separate from his/her observation. So long as recent history in the form of media narratives ignores the subjectivity of documentation, the general public still desperately tries to form a coherent narrative for our present-day world. However, within theoretical standpoints, literature itself has been rethought, casting doubt on the independence of one writer's creativity, and endorsing the notion that a text cannot exist independent of the reader's own interpretation and response. The concept of a unified self of the author has been "decomposed", to produce the autobiographical author as a fragmentary subject that oscillates between presence and absense. Thus, as Hutcheon explains, "Both history and fiction are discourses [. . .] both constitute systems of signification by which we make sense of the past" (1988: 89). With its reference to postcolonial and diasporic literature, this book embarks upon an examination of where postcolonial studies stand in the wake of the post-modern and the post-historic.

Yet it is important to note that one of the main "problems" argued in postcolonial positioning is the importance of referring to local rather than "universal" subjectivity—allowing for the individual differences of ethnicity, nationality, gender, colour, and class, to be emphasised; any theorising that smacks of totalising narratives or of eradicating difference, or homogenising third-world experience, that marginalize one individual or one group's voice in favour of another –

or merges them—indeed any theorising of a "postcolonial perspective" or textual moves that are accused of these "totalising representations" are , as John McLeod warns, "perilous" (2000: 222).

In the light of a more fundamental understanding of consciousness, however, such a problem is alleviated, since this paradigm allows for consciousness being equally expressed in its point value (local) and its expanded (universal) values simultaneously. The point and infinity co-exist, and while seeming to contradict each other's status, they are complementary and co-existing in time and space: one does not exist at the expense of the other; one cannot exist *without* the other. It is from the dynamic relationship of point and infinity that the whole variety of expressions of consciousness becomes possible. Consciousness is "the lively field of all possibilities":

> Consciousness is unity and diversity, both at the same time [. . .] the eternal, self-referral mechanics of transformation exists in the coexistence of the two contradictory qualities of consciousness—singularity and diversity. (Maharishi 1994: 61)

This dynamism, a liquid movement of the imagination in time and space, maintains the relevance of discussing the dynamics of consciousness and literary experience within the framework of the postcolonial. The postcolonial experience and especially the diasporic experience is often characterised by a co-existence of opposites— which is a feature of consciousness, which exists along with other coexistences of silence and dynamism, singularity and multiplicity, manifest and unmanifest. This experience of co-existence is one of consciousness lively in itself—the awakening of creativity—the basis of literary expression.

In terms of human subjective experience, this is clarified in the scientific research on the practice of meditation that leads to the state of pure consciousness. Pure consciousness, or "sheer" consciousness as Forman (1998) terms it, is the state that underlies all conscious experience, and is "the common denominator of being", a state reached through the use of meditation. The experience of this state of consciousness can vary from one individual to another, since clarity of experience depends upon the state of the individual's physiology. "Pure" consciousness, however, is a state usually recognised as associated with feelings of bliss, peacefulness and an upsurge of liveliness and dynamism: a feeling of growth of strength, integrity, and true knowledge. Pure Consciousness is a fourth major state of consciousness, quite distinct from waking, dreaming or sleep. Some traditions refer to this as a state of void or content-less thought; but in actuality the "void" is not empty but full—a lively totality of all possible experiences and expressions in their full potentiality, in seed form. A story from the Katha Upanishad illustrates this concept, when Najiketas shows his son that the hollow banyan seed contains all the potential forms of the adult tree. Thus the Self is "smaller than the smallest atom, greater than the vast spaces [...] invisible in the visible and permanent in the impermanent" (tr Mascaro 1965: 59). The concept of void is most prevalent in Buddhist philosophy; in Vedantic philosophy reality is characterised by the Upanishadic phrase *"Purnamidah Purnamidam..."*: all is fullness; when infinity is taken away, infinity remains.

5. The physiological and physical correlates of consciousness

Specifically referring to the techniques of Transcendental Meditation[viii] as a mental technology for the development of consciousness, Jayne Gackenbach reviews the scientific research on meditation as a tool for "qualitative advances" in physiological and psychological growth: "the integration of the intellect with the emotions as an advanced developmental state in a maturely functioning adult" (1988: 1).[ix] Her argument takes the model of consciousness beyond being merely representational to being the "driving force for development" (ibid). Gackenbach cites the research of psychologists Alexander, Chandler and Boyer who describe pure consciousness as "the silent state of inner wakefulness with no object of thought or perception", and as "a silent, content free inner-space". They significantly highlight moreover that

> Pure consciousness is conditioned not by cultural or intellectual conditions, but by fundamental psychophysiological conditions that are universally available across cultures. (1989)

The physiological correlates of this experience are available to anyone, and thus also enable us to move away from the prevailing understanding of pure consciousness as:

an inaccessible, ineffable or "mystical" experience. [...] Rather, we come to realise that the experience of pure consciousness is a natural consequence of unfolding the latent potential of human consciousness to fully know itself, that has profound utility for improving the quality of human life. (Alexander et al, ibid)

What then is the nature of the human mind? The human mind is characterised by thought, by the ability to move from one idea to another on what could be called a busy and never-ceasing "surface" level of activity. The mind seems to be, as Robert Forman puts it, "an enormously complex stew of thoughts" (1998: 1), which has as its main characteristic the subjective experience of constant change, constant activity. In such a state of constant "noise", there is little or no possibility of accessing the Self—the core of subjective consciousness. For this to be possible, Forman suggests that, "To understand consciousness in itself, the obvious thing would be to clear away as much of this internal detritus and noise as possible" (ibid).

Imagine, for example, a TV screen on which an image appears to be moving but which is in fact constructed due to the direction of a beam of electrons from the non-moving source at the far end of the tube. Or, like the blank screen in a cinema, where most filmgoers are only aware of the projections onto the screen, not the fact that behind the images lies a blank unchanging screen. So the mind could be thought of as merely the "screen" against which images of thought, sensory perceptions, memories and so on, are projected from a deeper, silent course. Yet, since it is impossible to analyse something larger from the perspective of something smaller, so it is also impossible to analyse the self through the intellect. If the intellect is not grounded in the self, its discriminating quality will be fluctuating—acting on the surface level of thought, rather than plumbing the deeper, as it were vertical, structure of the mind. As Daniel Meyer-Dinkgräfe notes:

> The immaterial cannot be *thought* about immaterially, because thinking is a function of the intellect, and the intellect, on the model of mind in Vedic literature, cannot grasp any more refined levels than itself, and thus cannot grasp the level of the immaterial, which is the level of pure consciousness. (2003b: 11, original emphasis)

Indian philosophy distinguishes two meanings of the concept of "mind": "It refers to the overall multilevel functioning of consciousness as well as to the specific level of thinking (apprehending and comparing) within that overall structure" (Alexander qtd in Meyer-Dinkgräfe 2001: 117). Underlying the subtlest level, that of the individual ego, and transcendental to it, is pure consciousness, "an abstract, silent, completely unified field of consciousness". Each subtler level is accessible to direct experience by the mind, which is itself able to "observe and monitor" the different levels (Alexander 1986: 291). In order to understand the ability of the mind to access these "deeper" levels, a working model of the mind is useful. Vedic Science proposes, "an architecture of increasingly abstract, functionally integrated faculties or levels of mind" (Alexander 1990: 290). This hierarchy ranges from gross to subtle, from highly active to inactive, from concrete to abstract, and from diversified to unified.

The expression of intelligence from the transcendental field of pure intelligence to the material world of everyday life is understood in Vedic Science to take place in four distinct stages. These are known as *Para, Pashyanti, Madhyama, and Vaikhiri*. Para is the transcendental level, the source of intelligence, the first sprouting of which is known as Pashyanti, and which as it becomes further expressed (Madhyama), reaches the surface level of the material world (Vaikhiri). The field of Para is influenced directly on the level of consciousness. Activities on the level of Vaikhiri must have the support of the infinite intelligence on the level of Para, the transcendental level. Ultimately, "the link between Para and Vaikhiri functions to bring fulfilment to human life – both individual and collective" (Clements 1996: 17). While corroborated by science, this structure is also described in the Bhagavad-Gita (3.42) where Krishna reveals the seat of intelligence in life by describing the hierarchy of the different levels of the knower: "The senses, they say, are subtle; more subtle than the senses is mind; yet finer than mind is the intellect; that which is beyond the intellect is he (the knower established in the Self)". Only through influencing the fundamental level of nature's functioning can the more manifest levels be changed. Thus, it is only from the level of the self that the mind, intellect and senses can be modified "away from the darkness of ignorance" (Maharishi 1969: 244). This development from unmanifest to manifest also takes place in the expression of language from the unmanifest through thought to spoken, expressed utterances. The levels of the mind are thus correlated to the levels of language:

The levels of the human mind

1. Senses – the level of mental performance
2. Mind – thinking and desire
3. Intellect—discrimination
4. Feeling—intuition
5. Ego—sense of limited individuality
6. Unbounded Self—unchanging, Real Self

The levels of language

1. Vaikari—the material world
2. Vach—audible speech
3. Madhyama—developing speech
4. Pashyanti—first manifestation of sound
5. Para—transcendental source

---

6. The literature of consciousness

In William Haney's work on the parallels between levels of consciousness and the levels of language, he elaborates on the difference between manifest language and language on the level of *pashyanti* or *para*, which "has no spatio-temporal gap between signifier and signified, sign and referent" and therefore creates an intersubjective wholeness, "a true intersubjective space beyond language and interpretation". This moreover involves the same process through which "the self in the drama of living undergoes a transformation of identity towards greater wholeness. This remedy and transformation can be individual (private) or cultural (intersubjective)" (Haney 2002: 97-8). This level of intersubjectivity, a breakdown of intrinsic/extrinsic, has obvious implications in postcolonial contexts, and echoes some of Homi Bhabha's notions of in-betweenness, liminality, and cultural hybridity.

This example is indicative of how, throughout this book, it will become apparent that some literary traditions in the world are centrally concerned with the nature of consciousness and in describing its characteristics as experienced in human life. The Vedic literature of India is one such textual reference point. While these texts may, by some, also be categorised within religious frameworks, it is most likely that they were incorporated into such use centuries after their first appearance. These works of literature were first part of an oral tradition, originating over five millennia ago, which were written down in more recent centuries. The works frequently referred to as "Indian Literary theory" are the works written more recently—within the past two millennia—to describe and theorise the impact and role of consciousness within the creative arts and performative expression.

At this point it is relevant to question why Indian academics in the field of postcolonial theory have not to date addressed the traditional knowledge of Sanskrit poetics, or Indian literary theory. I would ask why much, although certainly not all, of the interest in and work on Indian Literary theory and its ramifications has been written by European or American scholars, such as Meyer-Dinkgräfe, Haney, Malekin, Sheer and Yarrow. Why is it that the renowned Indian academics in postcolonialism have not accessed or utilised these indigenous texts? Gayatri Spivak, for example, appears wholly sold out to the Marxist western interpretation of reality, the *Weltanschauung* whose practical application seems to now be superseded if not actually discredited. While she actively endorses translation of texts from Indian languages to increase their accessibility to US-European readers, it seems that "ancient" Indian texts have been considered to be not worth studying and irrelevant today. The learned Harish Trivedi, however, has referred to the Indian literary heritage, but mainly in the context of elaborating the paradox whereby in the British Raj, texts from both civilisations were categorised and shared as classical narratives, so that even today in Indian universities Sanskrit classics and Homer and Euripides are taught alongside one another (2004). It seems that today the interchange of knowledge and texts between the traditions of Europe and India, in which each favours the other, continues. As a result of the suppression of these texts of Indian theory, and the gradual demise and distortion of the complete knowledge of consciousness, for countless generations the range of human experience has been limited to the states of waking, dreaming, and sleeping, and the human mind has been overwhelmed by boundaries.

7. Indian Literary theory and postcolonial studies

In general, postcolonial academics, shying away from any notions of "universal" truths that smack of totalising, and thereby "imperialist", narratives, have "othered" consciousness and the role of consciousness within literature, ignoring (or denying) the philosophical origins of much of its own discourse in indigenous Indian literary theory—one of the few literary theories that deals with (and is the source of) much of our past and current knowledge on consciousness and its role in artistic expression. The study of how language conveys meaning, and its philosophical and practical applications, has been a topic of detailed study in Indian thought for over three thousand years, a fact that has enabled a detailed and systematic explanation. Language in this system of inquiry is examined in relation to consciousness and "the fullness of reality which language in all its dimensions can manifest" (Coward 1980: 1). Moreover, language is understood as having both metaphysical and quotidian applications; the very nature of the Vedas, for example, elaborates the development of language, grammar, and speech in all their aspects, including the relationship between sound and creation of the cosmos. The Vedas, in fact, contain "in seed form the essence of later Indian thought on language" (Coward ibid: 6).

Postcolonial theory could well incorporate some of the ideas in Indian literary theory on language, aesthetics, performance, the role of writer/reader, and so on, in a more systematic and candid way. In the ancestry of postcolonial studies, the influence of Edward Said is unequivocal. He in turn based much on Foucault, who gained much of his inspiration from reading Indian texts on language and metaphysics, yet who failed to acknowledge the Indian philosophical and literary inspiration on which he based his thought. Foucault's conceptualisation of the co-existence of opposites, for example, or his exposition of the *phantasm* are influential concepts and ones that have been used by many writers since. Foucault proposes the phantasm as a way of accounting for some of the paradoxes, such as local relativity/universality, encountered in the problematic concept of history. Consciousness can be described as a co-existence of two contradictory values of intelligence: individuality and universality. The idea of the phantasm is one in which "neither the elements of totalisation nor difference can be definitely achieved or dispatched" (cited in Young 1990: 83-4), and his arguments are based on the Indian (Upanishadic) philosophy of the co-existence of opposites well known to Foucault although unacknowledged (see Schaub 1989: 306).

It is more readily feasible to accept this reciprocal interchange of knowledge if we recall, as Said writes, that

> like the history of all cultures is the history of cultural borrowings. Cultures are not impermeable; just as Western science borrowed from Arabs, they had borrowed from India and Greece. Culture is never just a matter of ownership, of borrowing and lending with absolute debtors and creditors, but rather of appropriations, common experience, and interdependencies of all kinds among different cultures. This is a universal norm. Who has yet determined how much the domination of others contributed to the enormous wealth of the English and French states? (1994: 261-62)

The west has long since bifurcated knowledge into what is factual and scientific as opposed to the un-objective and therefore unverifiable—in other words the non-rational. The study of linguistics is a fairly recent addition to the topics studies in the academy, and only really came to the foreground following Ferdinand de Saussure's ground-breaking work in the early twentieth century. The study of language in India, however, is not a recent phenomenon, but enjoys an unbroken tradition that goes back at least three or four thousand years. Profound and detailed as it is—and with remarkably widespread applications and consequences—Ferdinand De Saussure's work may seem superficial compared to the depth of knowledge in Indian theory. This may in part be due to its longevity, and also to the multifaceted dimensions and range of the theory. As Harold Coward explains:

> The Indian approach to language was never narrow or restrictive. Language was examined in relation to consciousness . . . All aspects of the world and human experience were though to all illuminated by language. (1980: 3)

The longevity of the theory is due to the fact that the grammarians like Patanjali were concerned to create a system that was of use in the everyday empirical world as well as in metaphysical study (Coward ibid: 4), similarly other great philosophers such as Bhartrhari were able to inquire into metaphysical realities while also exploring technical grammar points (ibid). The system of Indian language theory, or Sanskrit Poetics as it is also called, is so vast as to require several volumes of research just to enumerate some of its theories, which is obviously beyond the scope of the present chapter. Here, I shall merely touch upon some of the main concepts and topics as they relate to my overall delineation of the structure of human consciousness. [x]

8. A question of Hindu nationalism

Some critics ascribe contemporary political models to the millennia-old texts that originate in India. A common criticism of anything related to Vedic knowledge is often framed within the context of Hindu nationalist movements in India. Almost more insidiously than knowledge being denigrated as myth is its refutation as part of "Hindu nationalist propaganda", a plot to replace scientific method with an ultra-chauvinist decolonising of western rationality through "Vedic creationism" and "Hindu metaphysics" (see for example, Nanda: 2004). (While some agencies may be at work in this way, this interpretation is largely an argument of those who fail to understand the structure of the Vedic knowledge as being the mechanics of human consciousness rather than a "religion". To accuse the literature of psychoanalysis of being Zionist would be a close comparison.) Vedanta in fact presents both a theoretical framework of the structure of the mind and a way of catagorising and analysing subjective experience objectively. Later texts (6th-7th centuries AD) also provide an approach to the study of literature, the arts and aesthetics through the Vedantic tradition. Consciousness studies combines traditional knowledge from areas of philosophy, such as Vedanta and Buddhism (as well as the scientific research on the associated techniques of meditation) with quantum mechanical approaches to "reality", the quantum structure of the universe.[xi]

Vedanta is essentially a text of aphorisms (the Brahma Sutras) describing higher states of consciousness; it is not a treatise on belief but a study and systematic appraisal of the human mind. The Vedas are a set of texts that give a blueprint, as it were, for understanding the universe, the laws of nature governing the cosmos, and the relationship between the external world and the inner world of conscious experience. The hymns of the Rig Veda elaborate the profound relationship between language, sound, human consciousness, and the manifest creation. Another reason why this proper use of this knowledge has been lost is also because, as stated earlier, the home for complete knowledge is the human brain: Vedic study is not the intellectual analysis of ancient books, but rather the exploration of Veda and Vedic literature on its own level, enlivening the "laws of nature" (detailed in the literature) within one's own consciousness. If a political movement has used this literature to promote Indian nationalism, it is not because inherently those texts promote nationalism themselves. The bipolarisation of politics in present-day India has rejected the Nehru-ian secular philosophy, and the reconciliatory ideas of Gandhi, upon which the nation was founded after independence. Within this context both Hinduism and Islam have been politicised. Hindu nationalism is a radical political movement, not associated with a philosophy of consciousness, or the objective means of measuring structures of conscious experience. However, in every religion, the extremists claim their religious books to legitimise their political agendas. It has been wisely said that no text on earth legitimises or justifies antagonism between religions.

9. Veda, knowledge and experience: Seven states of consciousness

Based on Indian Vedanta philosophy, Maharishi Mahesh Yogi has proposed a theory of how language emerges from the silence of consciousness—in a state that is fully responsive within itself and from where it can express anything. Maharishi explains how Mahduchhandas, the first Rishi or cogniser of Rig Veda noticed the sequential unfoldment of language from unified wholeness to unified diversity. The theme of Rig Veda, and one that is elaborated through the sequence of sounds and words in the text is the sequential unfolding of the totality of nothingness into the whole multiplicity of manifestation. The flow of the manifestation arises from the alternation of syllable and gap—a sequential unfolding from gross to subtle, from infinity to a point, and from the point to infinity. This is the mechanics of the unfoldment of diversity from a state of unity. At every measurable point there is a return to the previous gap; every point of the manifest contains the silence that preceded it. In this way, every forward step of progress is always connected to the source. Thus, what is all-important is not the meaning of the words of the texts, so much as their overall inter-relating (or "self-referral") structure.[xii]

Vedic Science distinguishes initially between three basic states of consciousness, waking, dreaming and sleeping, and then continues to propose four further states of "higher" or more developed human consciousness. Transcendental Consciousness is the direct experience of the integrated wholeness of pure intelligence. This is why it is described as pure consciousness: it is the fourth state of consciousness, as described for example in the Mandukya Upanishad in terms of being "the pure Self alone", which is "known only through becoming it". It is neither waking nor sleeping consciousness, neither semi-consciousness nor unconsciousness; the fourth is " the awakened life of supreme consciousness" (Mascaro 1965: 83-4). It is the self-referral state of consciousness, the first stage in the growth of higher states of awareness. It contains the totality of intelligence. The Yoga Sutras of Patanjali refers to Transcendental Consciousness as the Self, the essential nature of the individual (I.3). All experiences of the waking state of consciousness are simply the fluctuations of the Self (I.4). The fundamental status of Transcendental Consciousness is expressed in an aphorism from the Upanishads: "know that by which everything else is known". Through the experience of Transcendental Consciousness every other experience gains its full significance.

Transcendental Consciousness is equivalent to the modern definition of the unified field of all the laws of nature; it is the integrated, unified totality of nature's intelligence. Haney (2002) has refined his discussion of consciousness within literature to establish the validity of consciousness as a fourth major state of human consciousness, one he describes as transcendental consciousness characterised by "a void in thought". Other documentation of consciousness includes the possibility of seven definable states of consciousness. Vedic science proposes higher stages of the development of consciousness. The permanent experience of pure consciousness (*turiya chetana* or Transcendental consciousness) with any of the other three states (dream, waking, and sleep) is called cosmic consciousness (*turiyatit chetana* or the fifth). This becomes refined cosmic consciousness (*Bhagavat chetana* or the sixth) through the refinement of sensory perception. Finally, in unity consciousness (*Brahmi chetana* or the seventh), one is able to perceive everything in terms of one's own transcendental self (Alexander 1990: 290). As every point of consciousness is connected to every other point, it is infinitely correlated, in other words, the part is connected to the whole: consciousness expresses itself equally in the point value and in the expanded infinite value—from individual consciousness to the universe of galaxies.

10. Reconciling Opposites: togetherness and participation

The practical application of this theoretical knowledge is contained in the Indian classical text The Bhagavad-Gita, which has been called a synopsis of the "thought and experience of India throughout the ages" (*The Encyclopaedia Britannica* quoted in Arnold 1993: v). The Bhagavad-Gita is a philosophical treatise, part of the *Mahabharata,* which itself if one of the two texts that comprise the Itihasa (the other being the *Ramayana*, the epic story of Rama and Sita). The archetypal epics of India are also found in the stories of antiquity in the Puranas (meaning 'ancient'), and these together with those in the Itihasa form the Upangas—one of the six systems of Indian philosophy. The Bhagavad-Gita is one of the discourses of the science of Yoga (union) and is also considered part of Vedanta.

The Bhagavad-Gita's eighteen chapters contain a "summary" of Vedic wisdom, as given by Lord Krishna to Arjuna. This teaching raised Arjuna from a state of confusion and despair to enlightenment.[xiii] The epic expounds that suffering is a direct cause of illusion, and that suffering and problems cannot be solved on the level of the problem, a deeper level must be reached to find the solution. It is a text that deals with the technology for raising human consciousness, from ignorance to full knowledge of the self—one in which ultimately Arjuna "remembers" the true nature of the self, his full dignity. The steps of gaining complete knowledge based on expansion of consciousness are expressed and elaborated throughout the text of the Bhagavad-Gita, which concludes that through the development of consciousness comes the restoration of Dharma—life in accord with natural law. (I discuss the text more fully in the next chapter.) In the current context, my intention is to refer to the text devoid of any religious implications, but to use it as a cross-cultural reference point in the description of the development of human consciousness—as well as it being a text that deals with my on-going concern with the theme of how human consciousness reacts to situations of violence, terror and trauma.

In terms of the relocation of consciousness and the literature of the Indian and African diasporas explored in this book, it can be argued that the imaginary—and thus infinitely deferred—location of the "real" home/land is the result of the fact that, for most of us, the extent of our diurnal experience is limited to the states of waking, sleep and dreaming. We have "forgotten" our real nature, knowledge of higher states of consciousness, the lack of which has resulted in a world characterised by loss and suffering of all kinds. Knowledge of and access to the "place of origin" (while in itself reminiscent of archetypal quest narratives) is only possible through—not a physical journey—but one that involves the growth of knowledge and inner experience. This process of inner development is reflected in a person's outer life, which begins to "flow naturally in the right channels of conduct" and all actions are "quite naturally right actions" (Maharishi 1969: 219). If one is able to accept the concept of developing consciousness then it might be possible to formulate a basis of theorizing inclusion rather than exclusion, a means of approaching moves beyond retribution, or suggesting alternative methodologies and paradigms in relation to displacement, violence and fear in the world today. Structures of self-other will always imply differentiation, whereas a viable and scientifically structured concept of Self-Self can only produce unity. Acting from the perspective of complete knowledge of the self in terms of the laws of the quantum mechanical universe—the intelligence of nature—could be one possible blueprint for the creation of peace in the world.

[i] "The limited understanding of the range of human consciousness has an effect on our knowledge of every aspect of nature. The whole of our modern educational system is based on the objective standpoint of modern science, in which subjectivity is condemned for its variability and unreliability. Yet where do all scientific discoveries occur? In the consciousness of the scientist. The whole of the modern approach to knowledge is thus based on a fallacy—that consciousness must be excluded from the field of knowledge" (Clements 1998). The application of technologies of the unified field in consciousness to all areas of education is elaborated in Clements and Clements (1985).

[ii] I am grateful to Dr Brian G. Blower for the discussion of this topic, which forms one of the themes of his forthcoming book *Thinking for Life*.

[iii] Here, I base much of my discussion upon the interpretation of Vedanta elaborated by the Indian philosopher Maharishi Mahesh Yogi over the past 50 years, which is the formulation most thoroughly documented and replicated experientially in the lives of millions of people around the world through the techniques of Transcendental Meditation and the TM-Sidhi programme.

[iv] See *inter alia* Nick Herbert's *Quantum Reality: Beyond the New Physics*: 1985.

[v] Where in the past misunderstanding, seekers of insight have attempted to "empty the mind" through meditation or contemplation, it is more accurate to say that a clear experience of the source of thought—the wellspring of infinite and dynamic possibilities—will rather "fill" the mind, which then overflows in creative expression.

[vi] An interest that is also an important theme of *Middlemarch*, both in Causabon's search for a "key to all Mythologies" and in Dr Lydgate's fascination in new scientific techniques in medicine.

[vii] It has received little critical attention, although it is discussed by Gilbert and Gubar in their classic feminist analysis of 19th and 20th century *The Madwoman in the Attic*. Gilbert and Gubar in fact find several biographical similarities between Latimer and Eliot (Gilbert and Gubar 1979: 447-8).

[viii] Transcendental Meditation is a mental technique that allows the attention, rather than being focussed out through the senses, to settle down and experience its own nature (comparable to the volume being turned down on a radio) until the finest level of thought is "transcended" and the mind is left in a state of inner silence, or Pure Consciousness.

[ix] New research on the health benefits of practising TM is constantly forthcoming: for example recent research by David Orme-Johnson indicates that TM reduces diseases of the brain. "Evidence that the Transcendental Meditation program prevents or decreases diseases of the nervous system and is specifically beneficial for epilepsy." *Med Hypotheses*. 2006 May 22.

[x] Throughout this discussion, I am indebted to Geoffrey Clements for access to the text of his unpublished lecture series, "Maharishi's Vedic Science V-VIII" (1988-1996.)

[xi] The Dalai Lama has also recently endorsed the scientific research on (Tibetan) meditation techniques, specifically the monitoring of brain waves taking place at the Harvard and Princeton university neuroscience laboratories. Preliminary results (such as the increase in high amplitude gamma synchrony) seem to confirm earlier research on TM, already published in four volumes of *Scientific Research on the Transcendental Meditation Program: Collected Papers* (eds Farrow and Orme-

Johnson 1996). See Susan Kruglinski, "The Dalai Lama Speaks the Language of Science" in *Discover*, February 2006.

[xii] It is because of this insight into the Vedic structure and language that Maharishi Mahesh Yogi's work is relevant to my discussion here. It is the most rigidly formulated theory of consciousness as well as being associated with a practical technique that has been empirically documented through hundreds of scientific research studies across a range of physical, psychological and sociological parameters.

[xiii] According to Maharishi's insights into the structure of the Bhagavad-Gita, the eighteen chapters are divided into three thematic sections, each sequence of six chapters relating to *Rishi*, the knower (chapters 1-6), *Devata*, the process of gaining knowledge (chapters 7-12), and *Chhandas*, that which is known (chapters 13-18). Similarly, each of these chapter sections sequentially illuminates the higher states of "cosmic" consciousness, "God" consciousness, and "Unity" consciousness (see Clements 1996).

Chapter Three
Trauma, Terror and the Impact of Consciousness

"The trick is not to transcend things but to *transform* them. Not to degrade them or deny them [...] but to reveal them more fully, to heighten their reality, to search for their latent significance. [...] To transform a physical entity by changing the climate around it through the manner in which one regards it is a marvellous undertaking, creative and courageous".

(Tom Robbins, *Even Cowgirls get the Blues*: 273)

1. The global world of trauma

In this global era, cultures can no longer be defined as separate entities but as a composite intermixture of one with other. While the origins of postcolonial study revolve around the concept and positioning of the "other", a new revolution—literally a "turning around"—locates the other as non-locatable within geographical space. Postcolonial studies were formulated to deal with theoretical issues impinging on literature and the arts—originally to do with resistance and theories of resistance—many of these issues have now been superseded in the interplay between local and global. The so-called "axis of evil", the epitome of xenophobic othering, is, by its lack of definition, paradoxically both omnipresent and unlocatable. As the postcolonial has by tradition negotiated and expressed the voice of the oppressed, problematising agency and freedom, so the current status of neo-colonialism must be addressed on a "new" level of understanding self and other. Where personal or ethnic "meaning" has been lost through experiences of migration, displacement, travel enforced through political or financial need, loss of homeland and so on, a "rooted-ness" in belief—regardless of what that belief system is—cannot be negated as a powerful means of accessing meaning for people(s) overcoming trauma.

It is largely recognised that global communications and terrorism inform each other. In a special edition of the journal *Interventions* on "the war on terror", globalisation is linked by Arvind Rajagopal with cosmopolitan terror and problems of cultural intranslatability, and terrorism itself is interestingly defined by Rosalind C. Morris as "premeditated politically-motivated violence against innocent people" (2004). The world and its peoples are being constantly translated and re-positioned, necessitating a new knowledge and a holistic understanding in terms of individual, racial and national identity. This "new world" of the 21st century, where the semantics of terror/war/terrorism has become fractured and in need of being redefined, also demands a reappraisal of what in fact constitutes "resistance" and how valid it remains in terms of global ethics.

In his essays *Five Moral Pieces* (2001), Umberto Eco has argued how the new millennium, with its shift in the definition of power, demands a rethinking of both war and fundamentalism, since the ethics of the past are inadequate to deal with the new realities of migration, immigration, racism and intolerance. Uncontrolled intolerance cannot be fought on the level of thought alone, and it is a perpetual and dangerous problem "because in daily life we are forever exposed to the trauma of difference" (100). Just as it is impossible to solve a problem on the level of the problem, so it is impossible to fight or correct irrational intolerance—"pure unthinking animality" according to Eco (103)—by recourse to intellectual argument. Eco argues (not without a *frisson* of self-reflexive irony one feels) that the fact that the Gulf Wars broke out at all "is a sign that the intellectuals' discourse has not been an unqualified success" (5). War, it seems, more now than even when Eco wrote his essay "Reflections of War" at the time of the invasion of Kuwait, has become for many an ineluctable necessity. In the face of this reality, Eco proposes, "we have perhaps reached the point in which humanity has become aware of the need to proclaim war a taboo" (15). He concludes, "War cannot be justified, because—in terms of the rights of the species—it is worse than a crime. It is a waste" (17).

Within this new global paradigm—characterised by the escalation of violence, the devastating ongoing wars that target civilians as much as armies—the future of postcolonial studies cannot be complete without reference to consciousness studies and recent work on trauma theory. Postcolonial needs trauma and both need to be based on consciousness. This chapter and the next will problematise the use of violence as a valid academic concept through concerns with the physical and psychological aftermath for those who have lived through trauma or are victims of violence. Paul Gilroy has argued recently that gestures of solidarity and the utopian political model based on the slogan "another world is possible"[i] could be viewed as today's version of the non-violent witnesses to the nationalist struggles of previous years conflicts, as written by Fanon and Orwell, both of whom took their part in the commitment to arms to overcome colonialist terror (Gilroy 2005). Other key figures in the commitment to the alleviation of suffering were deBois and Gandhi, who remain icons to the unarmed seeking for resolutions to social and national injustices. The new planetary humanism and acts of solidarity could be viewed as expressions of a raise in consciousness worldwide.

If Gandhi's lasting message was that the political and the spiritual can and moreover *must* coexist, as his life personified, then the spiritual forms a crucial part of the establishment of an alternative to the local-global conflict. Indeed, it is only though a consideration of consciousness and the "spiritual" (in other words a sense of surrender and loss of attachment to the limited small "self" or ego, and the development of a more profound notion of Self) that any trans-national connection can be viable. As Gilroy warns, if the connection is merely on the level of "democratic humanism", (or I would add, any other *isms*)[ii] it could merely be the moral excuse for a new imperialism, a new way of ignoring ethnic differences in a call to make everyone "the same", in other words, Western (2005).

The understanding of consciousness as the underlying substrate of human existence does not (as is frequently misunderstood) imply a universality of experience nor the eradication of individual difference in terms of needs, desires or "personality" expressed in each individual. Consciousness is: and it *is* before any *becoming*. The level at which consciousness expresses itself is at the junction point of matter and energy, where the unmanifest becomes manifest, where silence becomes sound.

2. Theorizing trauma and terror

Theories behind the documentation of trauma and terror are currently being expanded in terms of denoting both psychological and political experience. In her book *Hystories: Hysterical Epidemics and Modern Culture*, Elaine Showalter takes examples of different types of traumatic experience and argues how they have become central in American culture today—a "hot zone [. . .] of new and mutating forms of hysteria" (1997: 3). In the new millennium, this has become truer than she could have imagined when she wrote her book (most of them centralised around the rapid xenophobia due to the fabrication of a new national enemy).

As the use of trauma and terror (and terrorism) have become central to the future of human life on this planet, the discussions within the field of "trauma studies" are concerned to solidify the difference between perpetrators and victims, terrorists and the terrorised, inhuman atrocities and what may constitute legitimate retribution. They have highlighted a need to focus on various historical moments as well as projecting future outcomes. Many historians disavow the role of mimesis or repetition and theories of trauma are thus problematic.

Dominick LaCapra is concerned in particular with the dichotomy between event and experience, how the original experience is translated into emotional trauma through the role of memory. One main theme of his work is in formulating ways and means of "working through" trauma—emphasising the distinction between "working through" from "acting out". Performativity, or acting out of the trauma, may not be a working through of the events in terms of healing or closure. LaCapra also discusses the differences between historical and trans-historical trauma. Historical trauma can possibly be lived through and healed; trans-historical trauma cannot be healed, one just has to learn to live with it. Historical trauma relates to being a victim, trans-historical to being vulnerable: Historiography may provide a limited way of working through the past (LaCapra 2006).

The field of trauma studies is also concerned with the approaches of how personal testimony may be recorded and validated in the face of loss or fragmentation of memory (a typical response to a traumatic event), denial, and the passage of time. Although not associated with trauma theory as such, postcolonial literature has since its inception been concerned with the traumas that accompany and are intrinsic to both imperialism and the fight for liberation from colonial rule. As Edward Said points out, imperialism did not simply "end" but still has its lasting repercussions—such as India's link with Britain and Algeria with France (1993: 341). This lasting legacy is also widely seen in the situation of neo-colonialism—the ownership of countries by the

World Bank, the continued exploitation of land, peoples and resources by multinational companies, the association of arms deals with aid packages, the ruthless take-over of arable land by GM companies such as Monsanto, and so on. Just as a trading company once ruled India, the neo-colonial vice in which developing countries are held seems to have brought the situation full circle. Imperialism, now called by other names such as the desire to spread so-called "democracy", is still the most dominant form of political, economic and military power in the world today.

The trauma continues. The horror of the Gulf wars and the invasions of Afghanistan and Iraq have brought a chilling fulfilment to Noam Chomsky's prediction, written in 1982, that "the 'North-South' conflict will not subside, and new forms of domination *will have to be devised* to ensure that privileged segments of Western industrial society maintain substantial control over global resources, human and material, and benefit disproportionately from this control" (Chomsky 1982: 84-85, emphasis added). His discussion also pinpoints the necessity of the Western powers creating "a vast gulf" between the "civilised" West and the "barbaric brutality" of those who do not appreciate the benefits of historic commitment to principles of "dignity, liberty and self-determination" (ibid). The means whereby the United States devised a new enemy when the previous one had disappeared at the end of the Cold War need not be further elaborated here. (It is dealt with by, amongst others, Brian Eno, Harold Pinter, John le Carre et al 2006). Now the enemy is defined, however, as non-specific and ubiquitous; it is an enemy defined and perpetuated as much by Hollywood movies as by foreign policy; an enemy recognised (or rather presumed) by clothing, head-gear and skin-colour rather than by national or political affiliation.

While it may be possible to express theories of the "civilising" effects of terror as opposed to the anarchic effect of random acts of violence, it is still relevant to oppose both as unacceptable means of conflict resolution or political achievement. The fanatical dedication to the spread of "freedom" through any means is just as dangerous an absolute as its denial. The relative empowerments of the violent are a meagre alternative for those who are lacking the ability to fulfil their desires by socially acceptable means.[iii] If the old adage that "violence begets violence" holds true, neither governments nor individuals will ultimately gain from the gross violation of the laws of nature that is perpetrated in the name of "fundamentalist" (or "new") jihads or "democratic" crusades.

In response to the events in New York of 11 September 2001, Daniel Meyer-Dinkgräfe proposed an explanation of the root cause of violence and terrorism. He explains "any form of violence, thus including terrorism, has its root cause in people not being able to fulfil their desires." He continues to reason that since pure consciousness has been identified as the unified field discussed in quantum physics, pure consciousness is the field of human consciousness at which all laws of nature are active. Thus:

> A person who has established constant access to pure consciousness, characteristic of the higher states of consciousness (cosmic, refined cosmic and unity consciousness) as proposed by Vedic Science, will thus be acting always from the level of the laws of nature, and in accordance with them. He or she will not be able to make mistakes. Desires arising from such an enlightened person, a person in a higher state of consciousness, will also be in tune with the laws of nature; any action carried out to fulfil those desires will, by definition, never contain an act of violence against him or herself or any other element of life, including other human beings. (2003: 4)

While further delineating aspects of Indian literary theory to explain the role of consciousness in ameliorating the current expressions of terror in individual behaviour, Meyer-Dinkgräfe also usefully discusses the potentially redemptive impact of the arts "beyond an expression of grief, beyond irony, beyond the avoidance (at best) that comes with censorship" (2003: 1).

The incorporation of valid theories of higher states of consciousness is imperative to an understanding of production of and reaction to traumatic events, how a person reacts subjectively, and to the gaps and aporias in expression. It is well-documented how some individuals are able to go "beyond" a state of terror and can endure – classic examples being of those with faith during the Holocaust— those who were able to maintain positive attitudes, or an attitude of looking forward to the future, those who functioned from a level of consciousness where the self is not associated only with a superficial level of the body or attachment to the senses.

Literature is also a therapeutic device. Through literature we have a means of exploring the aftermath and implications of violent experience, often at one remove, where the text is written as an attempt to "write away" the trauma, to address traumatic memory or to seek healing. Memory, however, is itself problematic, as Zygmunt Bauman writes in the context of war victims, "Memory is a mixed blessing.[. . .] Memory *selects*, and *interprets* – and what is to be selected and how it needs to be interpreted is a moot matter and an object of continuous contention" (2003: 86, emphasis in original).

In this chapter and the next, I explore examples of trauma in a number of texts across a range of diasporic and postcolonial literature. I believe that to analyse postcolonial literature within the framework of trauma studies not only relates to the need of the time but also suggests ways of *solution* through applying an understanding of consciousness within this framework. These novels will range from such pivotal texts as Albert Camus' *The Plague* to J.M Coetzee's *Dusklands* and *Disgrace*, Michael Ondaadje's *The English Patient* through to Haifa Zangana's "fictionalised" memoir of imprisonment *Through the Vast Halls of Memory*. The novels I discuss in these two chapters dealing with trauma span a range of conflicts, including: the colonial "scramble for Africa", World War Two in Italy, the Vietnam War, and Saddam Hussein's Iraq.

3. Arab Women's narratives of trauma

In this masculinist world of terror and war, it is more often than not women who are the victims of national, international or community violence. In the Arab world in particular, women are targeted by both local and international communities—since it is inevitably the women who suffer the greatest impact of sanctions that limit the availability of education for children, healthcare and hospital treatment.[iv] Women are also often the targets of local patriarchal forces that locate women as the upholders of family honour. I have discussed the concepts of honour and shame, and the implications of violence against women in the Middle East and India under the guise of religious or nationalistic hegemonies elsewhere (Grace 2004). Here, I investigate the impact of national (political) sanctions against individual women, and their strategies for overcoming the trauma.

Exile, both physical and mental, is a recurring theme in postcolonial writing and one that especially epitomizes the location of secluded woman, whose access to public space may be restricted or curtailed. In third-world women's literature, the age-old problems of women in society and the quest of women for a true role and meaning in life are transformed in a variety of ways through the expansion of women's consciousness—socially, creatively and spiritually. The female authors and protagonists frequently overcome the seemingly insurmountable problems inherent within patriarchy—forging new realities and redefinitions of the self. The theme of woman's search for identity and fulfilment has been recognised by some critics as a spiritual journey.[v] For many Arab women writers, insurrection lies in understanding and empathy, not further division. In the light of a global feminist ethic, feminists from the Global North and South write in the context of a globalised revival of the human right for dignity and freedom from fear. Writers such as Charlotte Bunch voice their concerns over the continuing and escalating violence against women and abuse of their human rights, whether through politics, religions, fundamentalisms, social or economic structures.

In this chapter, I analyse to what extent writing is able to disclose the experiences and indicate implications of violent experience against women, and to what extent it may also be used for cathartic purposes. Here, the abuse of women is explored with particular reference to accessing documents that enunciate the trauma of women's experience of imprisonment, significant because:

> Prison literature is one of the distinctive areas of creative writing [. . .] and reflects the oppression exercised against thought. Prison, in fact, for hundreds of years has remained a part of our daily lives. But now this is more so than ever. It has become one of the heroes of contemporary novels (El Saadawi 1997: 205).

Like slavery with its symbol of the ship discussed by Paul Gilroy, the traumatic space of prison can be viewed as a symbolic shared experience of terror that lies at the heart of communities in Africa and the diaspora. The "cell" is a space of trans-national experience that transcends gender and religion: it is a place that—from the days of Nelson Mandela onwards —has become the site of trauma, terror and resistance.

Two Arab women writers of fiction and autobiography, Nawal El-Saadawi and Haifa Zangana, were jailed under the regimes of Presidents Anwar Sadat and Saddam Hussein respectively. Having both lived for many years in exile, they write about their traumatic experiences of exile, and utilize them in both fictional and autobiographic texts. Writing of the context of life in Iraq under the Saddam regime, Haifa Zangana explains, "Fear is our friend and our comrade, we grow up with it, it is closer to us than anything else. We have lived so long with fear, we cannot live without it"(2001: 9). The power inherent within Haifa Zangana's writing is that she is able to work through the trauma of recollection to expose and challenge her past experience. Trauma theory acknowledges the inadequacies of language to articulate such events; the experience of trauma is beyond language (Gilmore 2005: 102). In the context of Zangana's experience, it is the very denial of torture and the degradation of abuse that paradoxically confirms their occurrence. Yet, as Gilmore suggests, "speech of all sorts spills from the site of trauma" (ibid) and for Zangana the averted empty gaze of the abused man, or the banality of her conversation with her parents when they visit her in jail, speak volumes (2004). What happened is not as important as what the person feels they have become. Degradation, powerlessness and pain can render the documentation of event meaningless. Yet individual trauma transforms into the "deep scar" on collective memory (ibid).

Writers such as Haifa Zangana are not alone in their ethical concerns for our global society. Testimony, the power of remembering and retelling personal events, transforms apparent "victim-hood" into a powerful act of human connectivity. The whole past (with its quotidian repetition as present) is never totally recaptured by memory; if it were, as Baumann argues, "memory would be a straightforward liability rather than an asset to the living" (2003: 87).

In *Through the Vast Halls of Memory*, Haifa Zangana writes openly about the prison ordeal, including detailing her own physical squalor in the filth of her cell, and the horrific sight of her tortured friends and comrades, as they are brought in to identify her. Her memories create an enduring state of fear that overwhelms normal physical and mental function. "What do you do if you have inside you a wound as big as yourself. What do you do if the wound inside you is your very existence?" she asks (11), conjuring up the definition of autobiography as "a wound where the blood of history does not dry" (Spivak qt Gilmore 2005: 99). While she shares with the reader her experience of life in a hot and dirty cell with the other women "lifers", this is not specifically a "feminist" text, in the way that a campaigner of women's rights such as El Saadawi is often read, but an account of a vicious and sadistic regime that allowed no adversaries to survive, either male or female. Prison literature can express national liberation struggles or resistance movements and always has wider ethical, gender, and social implications. [vi] This type of document, however, in many ways must defy traditional narrative forms and is often a combination of fact and fantasy, autobiography and dreams. The interfusion of fact, fiction and dream is arguably both a deliberate narrative device and an artefact of the nature of memory. Zangana sees this fusion as necessary because of the unreliability of memory, and of the need of the adherence to truth where exact details of events may be blurred or forgotten. The nature of memory is both fascinating and problematic, in particular the selectivity of memory and how remembering can be triggered (Grace 2006).

Taking an example from Saddam Hussein's Iraq may seem a limited geo-historical perspective (especially in the hindsight of the revelations at Saddam's trial and its consequences) and yet the experiences of terror from the examples here can be universalised to a greater dimension of how individuals learn to live in environments of fear. Examples could equally be taken from Lebanon at the time of civil war, Afghanistan, or South America: all of these areas have been beset with times where imprisonment, torture and disappearances have become daily occurrences. (Frank McGuinness's play *Someone Who'll Watch over Me*, for example, remains a powerful drama of lasting political and psychological relevance, even years after the release of the Beirut hostages on whose experience the play is based.) The writer Hanan al-Shaykh's two novels set in Lebanon, *Beirut Blues* and *The Story of Zahra* (a controversial story about the Lebanese civil war) vividly depict how women's lives are torn apart by war and also provide insights into the strategies they develop to live in war-time border zones that have become "non-places". Since the norms of society have been shattered literally and metaphorically though the bombing and divisions of the physical city, these strategies involve basic survival as well as the renegotiation of sexual, family, and cultural identities. (These novels were banned across the Arab world, due to their outspoken and controversial portrayal of women and gender relations.)

Growing up in these circumstances leads to levels of stress in individual and community that overshadow consciousness. The Egyptian writer Nawal El-Saadawi comments on the situation of African writers, that even those who escape prison are very often haunted by a life-time of fear and by "the spectre of prison walls looming over the horizon, even if they have never engaged in political activity and never wielded anything but a pen. People in our countries are nurtured on fear"(1999: 205). These examples from writers are endorsed in the 2004 Reith lectures given by Wole Soyinka on the topic of the escalating "climate of fear" throughout the world, questioning and exploring what the role of the arts can be in the midst of a world that cultures fear.[vii]

How is the experience of being a subject of such an upbringing in fear or the victim of violence articulated in Arab women's writing? How is it possible to describe horrific experiences and their accompanying emotions? In her capacity as editor of many exiled writers' work, Jennifer Langer explains that "Generally, the silence of the women in this area is significant" (2005). She continues: "the omissions may be too painful or unacceptable to articulate, such as rape. Denial may be a way of dealing with atrocities too terrible to confront"(ibid). It is through the ability to articulate trauma that it is possible for the "knots" of traumatic experience to be released from both mind and physiology. The experience is gradually unwoven from the fabric of consciousness. The experience can change from being as it were one "written in stone" to being one "written in water"; and in releasing the experience it is shared with others, so that they too may benefit from a sense of communality of suffering. To write and share narrative is a two-way process and can heal both writer and reader. The healing process is often one of *identification*: the realization that one's experience mirrors a larger group experience can assist in overcoming a traumatic event.

Yet for the Muslim African woman, the writing of fiction or fact is equally fraught with problems. Highlighting autobiography as a common genre of self-representation, Fadir Faqir explains "within theocratic, military, totalitarian and neopatriarchal societies writing [. . .] becomes an act of defiance and assertion of individual identity" (Faqir 1998: 9). Women write to negotiate a "textual, sexual, and linguistic space" for themselves, while writing itself remains for many secret and subversive (ibid: 7). Miriam Cooke (1995) argues that women write autobiography as a search for a sense of empowerment either social or political, as a means of locating themselves within a master/male orientated narrative and language. As a genre, autobiography is not considered "literature" in Arab society, it is considered to be bold and indecent, especially when written by a woman, and easily becomes politicised. The Moroccan writer Leila

Abouzeid explains how, when she wrote her groundbreaking autobiography, *The Year of the Elephant,* she wanted to set down her experience as an Arab woman, and did not set out to challenge established Islam or women's position in society—although her writing became seen in those terms (Abouzeid 2005). [viii]

Nawal El-Saadawi's novels and lectures around the world have presented a forceful voice of protest from within the Arab world. Her fictions delineate the oppression and incarceration of women both physically and spiritually within patriarchal Islamic codes. Many of her fictional works also draw upon her own life experience. Nawal El-Saadawi uses fiction and autobiography to challenge and undermine both history and history-as-myth, and to expose everything she determines to be present-day violations of human rights. While emphasizing her outrage and sense of injustice, her protagonists refuse to be victims of patriarchal oppression, whether expressed in terms of religion or politics. El-Saadawi's two autobiographical works (1999 and 2002) address the social, cultural and political problems of her country, Egypt, while problematising both her own and Arab women's identity. Nawal El-Saadawi's extensive body of writing, both fiction and non-fiction, acts as a border-crossing to access and challenge topics and experiences that have previously been held as taboo or as "culturally" acceptable.

As a result of her confrontational writing and her outspoken political views, she was imprisoned in 1981 by the direct order of President Sadat, an experience she recounts in her book *Memoirs from a Women's Prison* in terms of a violation of human rights. Her prison autobiography reveals the heavy responsibility she feels in her writing, and the sacrifices that must be made as a writer. "Nothing in my life is more precious to me than writing but I think it requires even more courage than killing" (1997: 164-5). El-Saadawi writes about her incarceration, and the trauma of her experience, explicitly with the purpose of exposing the regime, in an attempt both to come to terms with it personally and to share it with a greater public. Incarcerated without charge and without trial, she describes her life in the jail and her relationships that were forged with the other female political prisoners, also there without charge or indictment for any "crimes". The Kafkaesque quality of her experience is highlighted along with the development of her relationship with the other women, who, despite their ideological differences, formed a close community behind bars. Sharing the unhygienic and depressing cell, the women support and care for each other, apparently overlooking contexts of class, education, upbringing, or religious conviction. El-Saadawi's text of her memoirs from jail emphasizes the community spirit and the interpersonal exchanges between the women.

Generalising her experience beyond the bounds of gender or race, and blurring fiction and reality, El-Saadawi's text acts to transcend boundaries and to "universalise" the prison. In her further explorations into autobiography, *Daughter of Isis* and *Walking though Fire,* El-Saadawi alternates personal detail of her quotidian life with episodes based on dream-sequences and her imagination, her projections of near-reality and might-have-happened, juxtaposed with graphic details of events and experiences that did, apparently, occur. These juxtapositionings both problematize and emphasize the narrow threshold between fact and fantasy, between memory and invention.

4. Defying/denying terror and trauma

Comparison of these texts with some themes within the writer and critic Salman Rushdie is valid here as he has also explored the ability of the human mind to distance and even deny horror through fictionalisation. Writers such as Rushdie and the South American magical realists, writing within contentious political contexts, employ the powers of the imagination to be able to express the inexpressible (Durix 1998). In *Midnight's Children,* when the protagonist-narrator Saleem Sinai, and his team of three young soldiers commit acts of appalling atrocity, he records the events as "things that weren't-couldn't-have-been true" (Rushdie 1995: 356). The horror of witnessing the atrocities that took place during the siege of Dacca forces the men into a state of denial:

> Many things which were not true, which were not possible, because our boys would not have behaved so badly [. . .] we saw the intelligentsia of the city being massacred by the hundred, but it was not true because it could not have been true. (ibid 375)

This denial of culpability and involvement demonstrates how traumatic reality can be manipulated by the mind, how violence can only be endured through the distancing effect of narrative and the defamiliarisation of fantasy. The narrator describes how "a person must sometimes choose what he will see and what he will not"(ibid). Similarly, the novelist Isabel Allende discusses in her memoirs how during the brutal dictatorship that replaced Latin America's oldest democracy:

> Chileans learned not to speak, not to hear, and not to see, because as long as they were not aware of events, they didn't feel as if they were accomplices . . . Ways were found to ignore—or pretend to ignore—violations of human rights for many years. (2003: 161)

Carol Gilligan's work on women and ethical responses based on connection offers a useful insight here, in accessing an explanation of this process of traumatic denial. She comments how, dissociation from our personal inner sense of true self:

> cuts through experience and memory, and when these cuts become part of cultural history, women lose the grounds of their experience and with it, their sense of reality. [This disconnection leads] people to abandon themselves and others: by not speaking, not listening, not knowing, not seeing, not caring, and ultimately not feeling by numbing themselves [. . .] against the vibrations and resonances which characterise and connect the living world. (1995: 125)

Isabel Allende analyses how the process of reconstructing the past through writing is to confront the trauma, and find a lasting meaning for it—a meaning that transcends the pain and terror of the actual events to become a lesson for the future. The final chapters of *In the House of Spirits*, in particular, deal with the violations of human rights such as rape, arbitrary imprisonment, and torture. Her (auto)biographical works *Paula* and *My Invented Country* also discuss the post 9/11events in Chile—although this was 9/11/1973—the year of the violent CIA-backed overthrow of President Allende's democratic government and the consequent wave of terror under General Pinochet's dictatorship—and she reviews how she came to terms with the murder and exile of her family members. The message of much of her writing (for example, the final chapters of *In the House of Spirits*, which deal with the violations of human rights such as rape, arbitrary imprisonment, and torture) remarkably remains one of reconciliation and forgiveness, an ethic of compassion more powerful than retribution, which would only perpetuate cycles of karma into the future.

Isabel Allende, like Michael Ondaatje, pieces together fragments of her family history through photographs (especially in her biography, *Paula*, and her novel *A Portrait in Sepia*) a technique through which to reinvent (or "re-member", to use Toni Morrison's phrase) the past through personal and collective memory. Morrison's novel *Beloved* also suggests that it is only through accessing collective memory that personal trauma can finally be healed. A work such as Michael Ondaatje's *Running in the Family* takes advantage of the illusive nature of memory and reinterpretation of events to create a fabric of "literary" if not "literal" truth of the past, as the author/narrator tries to come to terms with his family identity. This past, like the bottles of gin buried in the back yard by his alcoholic father, is one that has been lost through either deliberate or unintentional forgetting, through exile, and through death.

The literature of prison experience extends to include narratives such as the short stories written by writers in exile from around the world (Langer 2005). The story "My Teeth are Talking to Me" by the Iranian writer Nasrin Parvaz confirms how such documents of torture can be read transculturally. The experiences of shame, despair, and the fear of personal inability to bear further torture bear witness to human endurance—and are reminiscent of Zangana's experience in Iraq. Above all are revealed a sense of personal and interpersonal understanding, of the prisoner witnessing her own status, and of understanding the regime that enforces its religious and political beliefs through violence. In this story, for example, the character Pary relates in her narrative:

> Once you agree to be humiliated by doing what they want, you are defeated, and it will change your whole spirit. [. . .] Like a diseased person you will carry this personality until death, the very death you tried to escape from. (qt Langer 2005: 28)

In the account of atrocity and in the discourses of human rights, the novel, autobiography, and journalism overlap as narrative forms. Writers take on the role of witness bearers and documenters of their own traumatic experience as well as the wider socio-political implications of that historical moment to the community. The identity that is forged through such texts transcends gender and race, and despite inherent contradictions that are indicative of women's status throughout the Islamic world, as well as the search for a literal and literary place for the exiled writer, the women writers arguably form a trans-national group regardless of national identity or ethnicity.

To make another cross-cultural comparison, the US-Haitian writer Edwidge Dandicat also confirms the trauma of a woman's prison experience in her short story "Nineteen Thirty-Seven" (in Brown and Wickham 2001). In this story a daughter visits her mother who is in the infamous Port-au-Prince prison having been arrested and imprisoned for life on charges of witchcraft: "having wings of flame" and a skin that she takes off at night, feats that connect her to the island's *vaudou* culture. These abilities are both believed and feared by the prison guards (Graham Greene's *The Comedians* also refers to the belief among the common people in vaudoo and particularly in zombies, the living dead). The daughter brings a statue of the Madonna for her mother to hold, and food for her to eat; but she remains unable to speak because of the trauma of watching her mother die before her eyes. This is reminiscent of Haifa Zangana's comments in her journalism (2004), especially where she explains how impossible it is for a prisoner to speak of her experience; here in the story, the mother is unable to admit to the shaming conditions of her prison life, although physically able to speak:

> "They have not treated me badly", she [the mother] said. She smoothed her hands over her bald head, from her forehead to the back of her neck. [. . .] Manman pulled the meat and plantains out of her pocket and started eating a piece to fill the silence. Her normal ration of food in the prison was bread and water, which is why she was losing weight so rapidly. (449)

At the end of the story, the mother has been beaten to death by the guards, who believe they have further confirmation (her rapid weight loss) that she is a witch. It is with a sense of triumph and an affirmation of the female spirit, however, that her daughter and the other female prisoners await the public burning of her body. The daughter at last realises the truth in the seemingly fanciful stories told of her mother's survival on the night of the mass murder of Haitians. She is reconciled to the events of the past and recognises her mother's strength—especially at the time of her birth in 1937 when:

> On that day so long ago . . .in the Massacre River, my mother did fly. Weighted down by my body inside hers, she leaped from Dominican soil into the water, and out again on the Haitian side of the river. (455)

She appreciates how human lives and emotions are interconnected, how actions are related through a historical continuum of truthfulness that may also contain elements of the fantastic. The image of crossing the river is both literal and metaphorical. The simple survival of human beings is related to the survival of what it is to be human, a quality the mother upheld while in a situation that seemed bent upon dehumanising her. Endurance can in itself also be resistance.

5. Working through the fragments: Ahdaf Soueif

"Morally and emotionally, mankind has not changed from 7000 years ago," Egyptian novelist Ahdaf Soueif argues, "and it is naive and arrogant of man to think so". She comments that she can see no forward progression in mankind; the end of the twentieth century looked "very much like the end of the nineteenth in terms of politics and human nature" (1999b). Interestingly, this would serve as confirmation of the theory that for the last hundred years mankind has been living in a state of repetition (Barthes 1977). Michel Foucault also points out that twentieth century poststructuralists were plagued by the possibility they were merely repeating the nineteenth century (1978: 3-13).

Life's traumas, Soueif suggests in her journalism and her fiction, can be overcome through "making sense" of the present and the past—but this cannot be done by the intellect alone. [ix] The role of women and the meaning they seek in life can be transformed in a variety of ways through the expansion of women's consciousness— socially, creatively and spiritually. They are the preservers of culture and the community. Soueif cites women in Gaza who continue to create art, hold music concerts, research traditional embroidery and keep up their appearance; by responding to the brutal world around them in this way, they "are no longer its victims" (2004: 122).

In her article "Staying Alive" (2004: 119) Ahdaf Soueif meets with some of the women in Baghdad to find what they are doing in these "critical times" (the article was originally written in 2003):

> They are doing what they've always done: toughing it out, spreading themselves thin, doing their work, making ends meet, trying to protect their children and support their men, turning to their sisters and their mothers for solidarity and laughs. There was a time, I guess, when women's political action was born of

choice, of a desire to change the world. Now, simply to hold on to our world action is thrust upon us. (119)

The novel *A Map of Love* (1999) holds out a vision of reconciliation, and asserts the repetitive patterns of human behaviour *through* history, breaking down cultural/national boundaries as well as those of space/time. The text of the novel interweaves narratives of past and contemporary stories of European and Egyptian women who reformulate their identities through their cross-cultural relationships with men. These transformations involve repeating patterns of history and meaning: reconstruction and resurrection of fragmented personal identities and texts. The second, contemporary plot of *The Map of Love* reveals the current ramifications of Egypt's colonial past. Although one central episode in this latter plot relies on magic realism/mysticism for its signification, the novel overall maintains the conventions of historical romance. The women in the novel, whose lives together span the twentieth century, act to work out some problems of relationships and creativity that are trans-cultural age-old problems of women in society (such as cross-cultural marriage, children, divorce, creative fulfilment, loss, and love.)

A central concern of the narrative of *The Map of Love* elaborates how the past is re-structured through text. The discovery in an old trunk of the letters from the turn of the twentieth century allows for a gradual re-construction of the narrator's family history and thus enables the (re)assessment of both the narrator's own identity and Egypt's. The texts found in the trunk gradually reveal a love affair that bridges language and culture, and they symbolise a reciprocity and reconciliation across generations and countries. Together with the letters, the discovery of a fragment of tapestry suggests how both history and meaning (here indicated by the few embroidered words of an incomplete sentence) must be reassembled. The underpinning of the Egyptian mythology of Isis and Osiris is used allegorically to mirror the novel's theme of the deconstruction and reconstruction of personal and historical identity. (The goddess Isis has to reassemble the parts of her brother/husband Osiris in her fight to re-establish a literal body of truth in order to combat the personification of un-truth, Seth—a figure who evolves into the Muslim *Shaitan* and Satan. Later, the cult of Isis itself transmogrifies into that of the virgin Mary.) The three panels of the tapestry must be reunited in order for the total reconstruction of family genealogy, history (and karma) to be assimilated and understood. Soueif's novel asserts the repetitive patterns of human behaviour *through* history, breaking down cultural/national boundaries as well as those of space/time. Strength comes in moments of revelation, emotional or even mystical illumination arising from a more fundamental level of existence, which the intellect often cannot "work out".

Midway into the novel, the realism of the narrative is shattered by the mysterious reappearance of the final panel of the tapestry. Suggesting that all knowledge of the past cannot be "found", here the book challenges the totalising mastery of realistic discourse. This moment, in which the reader must suspend critical thinking and reason, is one where the minds of both the character and the reader must make a leap into the intuitive, more expanded, alternative forms of gaining knowledge. In a moment "out of time", the protagonist meets an old sheik in the courtyard of a mosque she is visiting. When she returns home, she finds the missing piece of tapestry in her bag, although she has no memory of how it could have got there. This transcendental moment of revelation suggests how text can be either cognised through the intellect (*smriti* in Indian literary theory) or divinely "heard" (*shruti*)—it is "found" in the gaps of manifest language.

When she tries to return to the mosque, she is unable to find it. The mystery surrounding this "revealed" text and the meeting with the old sheik is again in keeping with the mythology of Egypt, the land of the goddess Isis: the representative of how the illusory nature of reality covers the reality beneath. (Above the temple of Isis the inscription famously reads, "I am all that is, that was, and all that will be, and no mortal has lifted my veil".) It is also the land of El-Kadhr, the immortal trickster who, arising from the rhythmically flooding river, delights in surprises and ironic inversions (the relevance of whom I shall discuss again in chapter 6). There is no rational explanation of this event; it remains Soueif's mysterious "Malabar caves" episode, left for the reader to determine what exactly happened (however frustrating that may be for the reader). Indeed, the challenge to the reader to bridge this "gap" in realism parallels the leaps of faith required by historiography, or the gaps in the veracity of history crossed by the imagination.

Despite the detailed realism of her journalism and literary reviews, Ahdaf Soueif's fictional work includes the locus of the mysterious and mystical—reflecting the importance of these as features of traditional Egyptian life. In her first novel, *Aisha*, the eponymous heroine visits the shrine of the saints who are said to help women and give miraculous cures;[x] the narrator remains a shadow identity mirroring these traditional beliefs and removing them from the realm of superstition. This mysterious narrator of the final section of the stories undermines, and expands, the reader's sense of "reality" in addition to distancing and dislocating the narrative, making the reader question her own relationship to textual veracity. The mysterious narrator acts as a witness to Aisha's actions, in the same way that Ondaatje's English patient in his role as the "jackal god" Anubis watches and records the life of Katherine. The novel closes with the implications of death and re-birth, harking back to the beliefs inherent in the ancient Egyptian cult of preservation and return—or indeed, to Almasy's attempts in the cave ritually to preserve the body of the woman he loves.

The Map of Love is a novel that invokes the possibility of solutions through an alternative reality where cause and effect can only be appreciated through higher "expanded" awareness. Only wide-awake consciousness can have a full and clear understanding of the world around us. Restricted or limited consciousness can only create a partial or fragmented view of the world. The intellect appreciates knowledge, but is not its source. The source of knowledge is in experiencing consciousness: hence the injunction above the gateway to the oracle at Delphi: "Know thyself by which all things are known".

6. Feminist ethics and consciousness: Sebbar and Djebar

Historiography, as we have seen, can be a valid, if partial means of healing through narrative transcription of past trauma. The two Algerian writers, Leila Sebbar and Assia Djebar, are concerned with writing as a means of liberation and of celebrating a shared experience among women. Both living diasporan lives, they write from a liminal position, from the border of French/Algerian cultural heritage, which today continues to be a site for contested individual identity—an articulation of self that is even more problematical for women, as can be seen for example in the ongoing contestations over the wearing of the veil in France. Personal statements of identity have increasingly gained social significance and cultural controversy.

Djebar is an author and film-maker, for decades living in exile, who as a colonised subject expresses the struggle of locating the language for the enunciation of both freedom and protest. Djebar admits that she uses French as one of the "spoils of war" (1980: postscript) and Leïla Sebbar expresses the tensions inherent in the choices of language, which is even more burdened with socio-political implications in the situation of a writer in exile:

> I write fictional texts because my native land, Algeria, the land of my father and of my childhood, forsook me . . . I write because I didn't have the language of my father, Arabic, the language of his land which I never learned. I write because I feel that I am in exile, an exile that moves and perturbs both body and soul, even if France is also my country, the country of my mother and my sons, the country of my mother tongue, the language in which I create, French, the only language I have ever mastered. I never tried to learn Arabic, but I wanted to hear it; I wanted the voice of Arabic and not the meaning. (2005)

For Sebbar here, it is the *sound* of the language of her homeland that is so redolent with associated meaning. As we saw in the previous chapter, the levels of sound emerging from silence correspond to different levels of the mind. Thus, the finer dimension of a language corresponds to or triggers an emotional rather than a rational dimension of thought. The level of emerging speech, the sound of language prior to meaning, corresponds to feeling or intuition. (The sound of Arabic, more than any other language other than Sanskrit, has the additional dimension of being a sacred language of divine revelation, the oral recitation of which has multifaceted significance.) Sebbar's novels deal predominantly with the contemporary problems of the Arab community in France, for which she relies upon her recreation of her homeland –one that rigorously avoids sentimentality and exoticising, "an Algerian imagination" created from the memory of sounds and places. She grew up aware of colonial conflicts, and French-Algerian or Arab-French antagonism, that were later to inform her fiction:

> My writings are marked by Algeria—Algeria and the Maghreb in exile in France—and by France, through the contact between the Maghreb and Europe, East and West. I would not have recreated a world of interaction, of love and violence, in my novels had I stayed in Algeria--that Algeria of monolithic thought, of the single and controlled body. Algeria without the Other would not have inspired me. (2005)

Leïla Sebbar's novels (especially the *Sherazade* trilogy) bring issues of Arab women's identity and freedom into a contemporary context, in which women seek to define themselves as more than a colonial or patriarchal "other". In the struggle for women to gain cultural and personal meaning, the importance of language has both literal and metaphorical dimensions. Assia Djebar argues that for women to free themselves from the patriarchal moral strictures endorsed and expressed through nationalism, they must "retrieve a voice that has been driven into silence"(1985). Once women have spoken out, they move away from being "generalized woman" to being woman as an individual.

Djebar rewrites nationalist history by emphasising the role of women within that nationalist concept, in order to give a voice to all the forgotten and silenced women in history, women suppressed by the combined oppression of religion, colonialism and patriarchy. She does not claim to "speak for" the women of Algeria, but to "speak next to" the words that would be spoken by "incarcerated bodies" as they first gained their freedom (1980: 2). (This suggests a possible solution to Gayatri Spivak's famous argument that "the subaltern cannot speak": that the suppressed colonised figure in the third world has been deprived of a voice.)

It has been argued that, regardless of location, the power of the patriarchal order depends for its regeneration on a disconnection from women, and a process of dissociating women from what they intuitively know is right. The process of inner division that has been inculcated in women "makes it possible for a woman not to know what she knows, not to think what she thinks, and not to feel what she feels" (Gilligan 1995: 123). As Valerie Orlando (1999: 32) comments, Djebar's novels, although written in exile, establish and elaborate new feminist parameters for all women of the Maghreb—and arguably beyond. They demonstrate the importance of communication between self and other by a quest for collective and individual identity through reconstructing the lost voices of women in history. Djebar herself comments that her style of juxtaposing her own narratorial voice with that of the testimonies of other women's voices are:

> an interested and inexpert examination, by a postcolonial woman, of the fabric of repression, a constructed counternarrative of woman's consciousness, thus woman's being, thus woman's being good, thus the good woman's desire, thus woman's desire. (1985: 299)

Her works validate woman's presence and experience through the complexity and ambivalence of conflicting views on the predicament of women torn between tradition and modernity—often symbolised by the veil—and through these charged images she exposes and problematises colonial history. Her own ambivalent attitude towards Algeria remains unresolved. Like Fanon before her, Djebar sexualises the country of Algeria, seeing it as woman—violated woman, the woman whose hand is amputated, thus unable to write or express herself. In her novel *So Vast the Prison*, following more recent events in that decade, she refers to Algeria as a monster, "do not call it woman any more . . . not even a madwoman" (1999: 356). She sees Algeria now as a land of tears—and blood. Djebar's recent non-fiction work *Algerian White* (*Blanc de L'Algerie*) also documents the horrors of recent decades (2000). Concerned with the lost compatriot voices of journalists, intellectuals, playwrights, and poets (from Frantz Fanon, Albert Camus to more recent Algerian writers) who have died prematurely as a result of suicide, assassination, or illness, Djebar movingly recreates conversations and events to honour the bravery of their lives and writing. She catalogues the atrocities in the contemporary "Algeria of blood", serial murders wrought by the "madmen of God" (2000:127): a religious fundamentalism that "has decided to take power at any cost" (226).

Works of historiography such as Assia Djebar's *Fantasia: An Algerian Cavalcade* demonstrate also how narratives of women's political prison experience and torture expose the ethics of the colonial forces. In her versions of women's historiography, events are re-written to include the women's role in the war of the 1830's and the war of independence in the 1950's, seen through women's eyes. Djebar's focus is on the experience of compassion and care between women, and of the need for women to overcome the sense of rivalry that has been instilled by the patriarchy. Djebar also proposes an escape from "male" space into a place that women can be free from the male gaze and communicate without boundaries, a place out of time and space: one that amounts to a space of female consciousness.

The story of Cherifa, reconstructed by Djebar in *Fantasia*, retells the horrors of the French atrocities of the 1950's war of independence from a woman's point of view. Abandoning her family and education, Cherifa joins the men fighting in the mountains at the early age of 13, working as nurse, messenger and sister to "the Brothers". Her bravery goes unremarked upon, part of the way of things. She is captured by the French, imprisoned and tortured, but she continues to both defy their authority over her and to spend her time in captivity—no matter how frail or hurt she is—in helping others in the jail. After years in prison, the French interrogate her once more. She tells them she was in the mountains fighting for her ideas, for what she believed in.

" 'And now you're a prisoner . . . what have you gained?'", they ask. She answers, " 'I've gained the respect of my compatriots and my own self-respect. Did you arrest me for stealing or for murder? I never stole! My conscience is clear!'" (140). In one stroke, she defines her own morality while exposing the flawed morality of the colonialists.

Ethics in the developing world has to do with the simple survival of human beings and of humanness; ethics in fact has been argued to be at the heart of human survival (Sen 1988: 4). For women to be free to communicate, they must also be free to remove the veil of anonymity and fear that have been forced on them—to go, as Assia Djebar demonstrates in her novels, beyond barriers of language, culture and history.

Change in society impacts changes in gender relations: in the wake of the fast-changing dynamic of historical process and recent events, "In the Arab world today, the human rights of women are indivisible from those of men" (Soueif 2004: 120). Arab women are now fighting or protesting to defend their men. In the new world of arrest and unofficial detention of thousands of men, the women are now also history keepers: those who record, document and remember the "demolitions, expropriations, arrests and killings". She continues, "Keeping the children alive. Keeping culture alive. Preserving history and telling the story—these seem to be at the heart of our women's concerns right now" (ibid).

Carol Gilligan writes that "the moral imperative" that emerges from a woman's perspective is "an injunction to care, a responsibility to discern and alleviate the real and recognisable trouble of this world" (1982: 19). Moreover, as Sidonie Smith comments in the context of the testimonies by women sex prisoners in WW11, women writers "testify to the embodied connection they feel to one another, a connection that carries the ethical force of collective witness"(2005: 128-9). Women as the nation's story tellers, like Haifa Zangana, Assia Djebar and Ahdaf Soueif, amongst others, are now at the heart of the postcolonial literatures of human rights and of healing: literature as a force for reconciliation and cross-cultural understanding.

The connection between individual consciousness and national consciousness is well known. Frantz Fanon makes the connection in political terms of the struggle for freedom through the development of national consciousness, an enlivening of national heritage and the means to stabilise a sense of national self: "National consciousness, which is not nationalism, is alone capable of giving us an international dimension"(1963: 179). For Fanon the growth of national consciousness is connected to cultural consciousness, a facet of, for example African-ness, so that individual, national and cultural consciousnesses are all interlinked and "fragile" (ibid). Thus in terms of the development of individual consciousness the wider dimension of the social quality of consciousness is also affected.[xi]

Yet crucially in this regard, Maharishi Mahesh Yogi explains that "as natural law continues to decline through the passage of time, man's ability further deteriorates" as does his ability to maintain ethical and social responsibility (1993: 219). By the time natural law is expressed in its lowest level, the world has accepted the inevitability of suffering, so much so that, according to Maharishi, "The acceptance of suffering by religion is the indication of the complete decline of Natural law in daily life." He continues however to explain that this trend, although inevitable, is reversible, for at the point where values of integrity are at their lowest: "Thence comes the point of return. The beauty is that at this point in time the total value of natural law is in its pure potentiality; it is fully awake within itself [. . .] and begins to express itself in daily life" (ibid: 220). This he refers to as the "great leap" of Natural Law, the great swing of time, from zero to one hundred per cent –and this is said to occur within one generation (ibid).

This formulation is pertinent here to understand the cyclical nature of time, and how the breakdown of human life in accord with natural laws of the physical universe is the result of the loss of enlightened consciousness. Thus society as we know it today is based on disharmony and fear, but the understanding of consciousness suggests it need not always be so. The next chapter continues to analyse literary expressions of the trauma, and concludes by offering one text as a solution to understand the state of human stress and its amelioration.

---

[i] As evidenced by its appearance on many posters in Cuba, the slogan "a better world is possible" apparently originates in a speech by Fidel Castro.

[ii] Postcolonial theorists are also guilty of reducing the rich world of varied experience and narrative to "isms": jargon that in itself is the imposition of "western" ratiocination.

[iii] As some graffiti on a wall at Sussex University once read: "Terrorism is the war of the poor; war is the terrorism of the rich".

[iv] In her essay "The Right to Rule Ourselves", Haifa Zangana explains how:

> Most Iraqi women try to cope as best they can with the predicament of dealing with the occupation and the rise of reactionary practises affecting their rights and way of life. For a long time Iraqi women were the most liberated in the Middle East; now the US-led occupation has largely confined them to their homes. (In Eno et al 2006)

[v] See for example the discussions in the work of Carol Christ.

[vi] The late Egyptian feminist and political activist Latifa Zayyat comments, in the making of literature into art, "what matters is whether the specific personal experience is confined to the level of the subjective and the particular, or transformed to the level of the general, the impersonal and aesthetic [whereby] a meaning to this experience is discovered" (1997:2). Zayyat, like El-Saadawi, was imprisoned by order of President Sadat, an experience that led her to realise her "inherent human potential" and discover the "human ability to shape the self and create beauty" (ibid:16). Zayyat's writing is her way to "reinvent" herself and her society, and her concerns with social and political oppression form the basis of her fictional stories such as *The Owner of the House* (1997). Here, the terror of literal imprisonment informs the internal dynamic of the protagonist's fear-based relationship with her husband and his friend, one where her entrapment is both political and terrifyingly personal.

[vii] In his 1849-1872 memoirs, Giuseppe Garibaldi wrote: " 'Reciprocal fear rules the world', a friend of mine used to say—and he was right. Yet it is also true that the least frightened populaces are usually the last oppressed" (2004:19).

[viii] In general, autobiography as a genre is perhaps best suited at collapsing the existence of the binary opposition that distinguishes history from fiction. While postcolonial theorists have grappled with the idea of "truth/untruth", the writer of autobiography is at liberty to manipulate their construction of a past out of the fragments of memory.

[ix] Much of Soueif's work in journalism has also dealt with the role of women within conflict and in times of national upheaval (just as her novel deals with the early debates in Egyptian nationalism and the uprise of anti-colonialist feeling.)

[x] Mahfouz's Cairo Trilogy also mentions the importance in women's lives of visiting saints' shrines, as does Fatima Mernissi in other countries of the Maghreb, where she locates them as an important alternative "female space" (1977).

[xi] This sensitive interdependence of physical phenomena and consciousness could also been described in terms of the patterns of order seen in (inaptly named) Chaos Theory. See for example, L.R.Vandervert (1995) and recent work by Rupert Sheldrake. Some scientists regard chaos theory to be the other memorable discovery of the 20th century along with theories of relativity and quantum mechanics.

Chapter Four
Empire, Violence, and the Writing of History

Freedom and liberation are never-ending tasks. Let this be our motto:
"Do not forget".

(Umberto Eco, "Ur-Fascism": 1997)

1. Querying History

Postmodernism and postcolonialism have been haunted by
memory—memories of disaster, genocide, war, and by the trauma of
memory itself (Middleton and Woods 2001: 81)—a haunting that has
been worked out in the textuality of memory in literature. Yet just as
the past is constituted by its remnant shards, it is in these layers of
thought and memory that sense must be made from incoherence. Thus
history, as Hayden White famously puts it, is as much invented as
found: it is a prose narrative consisting of various "lived stories"
individual and collective, just as is much of fictional literature.
Historical narrative can be argued to be simply a process of form-
giving, bestowing order and coherence to fragments (White 1987).

The concept of historiography challenges classical notions of the
past as accurate and reconstructable as a coherent narrative; history as
mimesis becomes an impossibility as something is always left out.
Dominick LaCapra questions whether literature and literary criticism
can perhaps fill the gaps and compensate for the "lacks" and aporias in
history (cited in Spivak 1999: 204). Gayatri Spivak suggests that "the
reading of literature can directly supplement the writing of history
with suspicious ease" but worries that both archive and history are "a
crosshatching of condensations" where the authority of the author as
well as the historian is challenged since both have the desire to
"construct" history (ibid). Locating the theme of experiences and
resolutions of violence within postcolonial and diasporic authors
addresses problems of cultural conflict and political and economic

imperialism, as well as implicating gendered violence (as discussed in the previous chapter).

This chapter will explore how the problem of violence has been approached in a variety of contemporary novels from a range of cultures, European, African and Asian. Novels by the South African writer J.M. Coetzee will be discussed in order to explore the postcolonial concern with the violence of the project of imperialism, as well as with the epistemic violence inherent in the documenting of imperialism as history. Coetzee, however, together with the Sri Lankan novelist and poet Michael Ondaadje, create their narratives well aware of this problem. This chapter will chart the course of how these writers seek to problematise and reclaim what has been left out or forgotten by the memory that reconstructs historical narrative.

Critics such as Frederick Jameson refute that history has any validity since the death of experience in postmodernity (1991), and Baudrillard further problematises the concept through his questioning of distinctions between "real" and "media" experience in a hyper-real world (1983). Even while in the process of devaluing the coherence of historical narrative, much postmodern/postcolonial fiction has given structure to, as well as being structured by history. Works such as Rushdie's *Midnight's Children* especially plays with this concept of history being a bricolage of images, and narrative being, as Rushdie famously puts it a "chutnification" of history (1981). The gaps and aporias in memory experienced in trauma in fact become a feature typical of the postmodern experience of incompleteness. Yet significantly, in postcolonial terms, it is the gaps, the in-between spaces, that carry "the burden of the meaning of culture"(Bhabha 1994: 2). Of course, history is being made and written every day, and we are all, whether we like it or not, part of that process and part of the self-deception. In his article "The Arduous Process will Continue", the novelist and playwright Hanif Kureishi discusses how the availability of violence in video games distances young people from actual violence, and through the idea of virtual war, the concept of "real" death is avoided. The Iraq war has become a virtual war, according to Kureishi, born of "many lies and much dissembling"; the public were told it "would be quick and few people would die" (2005). The distance between public and war would somehow remove any culpability; the violence could not exist. This sense of video-game distancing has affected the politicians, who believe, "we can murder others in faraway places without the same thing happening to us, and without any physical or moral suffering on our part". Kureishi continues:

> This is a dangerous idea. The only way out is to condemn all violence or to recognise that violence is a useful and important moral option in the world.[. . .] If we take this position we cannot pretend it is morally easy and seek to evade the consequences. (2005)

Much of this continuing debate on the ethics of violence is the concern of the next two authors I consider here: J.M. Coetzee and Albert Camus. From South and North Africa respectively, together their writing covers some of the major conflicts of the latter half of the twentieth century to the present.

2. Taking issue with violence: *Dusklands* and *Disgrace*

The South African writer J.M. Coetzee has denounced "realism" and history as modernist discourses, and his early novel *Dusklands* in particular challenges the mythic status of history, and the reliability of narrative. The two novels taken from early and later in his career, *Dusklands* (1974) and *Disgrace* (1999) address concerns with the documentation of the colonial project and the moral aftermath of colonialism. Like *Heart of Darkness*, *Dusklands* locates itself within the trauma of the colonial process. Written by Coetzee while he was in America at the time of the Vietnam War, it is his attempt to come to terms with the violence of imperialism, and with the historical process of imperialism-as-history. In two adjacent narratives he addresses the "Vietnam project" and the project of the original colonisation of South Africa in the 1760's. Both narratives deal with the problem of colonisation as discourse: in other words on how and who records of "what happens next" are constructed.

The first of the novel's two parts is narrated by Eugene Dawn—a name resonant with connotations of eugenics and false atomic dawns. He is engaged in writing a report on what happened in Vietnam, and above all with an aim of disproving that anything "went wrong". There are clear parallels here to Conrad's Kurtz in *Heart of Darkness*, who has been entrusted to write a report by—as Marlow the narrator tells us with intended irony—"most appropriately, the International Society for the Suppression of Savage Customs" (83). As explained with great enthusiasm to Marlow, the text gives "the notion of an exotic Immensity ruled by an august Benevolence" (83) –just as Eugene is attempting with equal excitement to write such a justification with his report. He is engaged in fact in a giant fabrication of history, or truth as he sees it—a moral justification of an immoral world-view. Within the narrative he is constructing, brutality is normalised. While Kurtz writes his terrible postscript, "Exterminate all the brutes!", Eugene has the photos to prove they have done just that: appalling atrocities are in fact merely American boys having a good time away from home. Villages, Eugene reasons, cannot be wiped off the map if they were never marked on it in the first place: through accurate bombing they can be returned (in an ironic reversal) to be like Conrad's blank white spaces on the map of Africa. Conrad suggests in his novel that it is the colonizers who bring the darkness to an otherwise light/white continent; it is they who *write* the darkness onto the tabula rasa. (Conrad has Marlow quite clearly comment that the "blank space of delightful mystery", the "white patch for a boy to dream gloriously over" had "*become* a place of darkness" (22, my emphasis) *since* contact with the Europeans.) The depiction of Kurtz's and the other colonizers' violence in the name of progress and trade far exceeds any incidence of violence (or "savagery") done by the natives *to* the white invaders. Like the ring of staked heads surrounding Kurtz's hut, Eugene's photos/holiday snaps of raped women and beheaded Vietnamese men are the totems of superiority of a world-view turned horribly insane.

The mythic status of the Law of the Father, both as psychological hegemony and as the "paternalistic" civilising mission of imperial conquest—with all its implications of religious as well as patriarchal violence—remains at the forefront of Eugene's convinced attempts to order the chaos of rapine and ethnic cleansing. The gradual breakdown of Eugene's sanity parallels the breakdown of all ethical standards of justice and equality, arguably part of a world situation Linda Hutcheon (1989) sees as a postmodern trend. Yet Dawn denies blame, "I am a tool in the hands of destiny," he says and elsewhere he insists, "I have nothing to be ashamed of, I have merely told the truth" (Coetzee 1974: 31).

The second account in *Dusklands* focuses on the narrative of one Jacobus Coetzee, an early explorer of the South African continent, put forward as an ancestor of the author. Both (unreliable) narrators display a total inability to perceive the Other as human, and as the text reveals the "dark underbelly" of the colonial project, so the men become more and more savage in the name of global civilisation. Again, the Jacobus character is closely comparable to Kurtz in the way they both willingly assume the role of "savage", the otherness that they both despise. Dealing with issues of shared culpability (made more so due to the sharing of the author's name), the text demonstrates disintegration of meaning of self, history, narrative— just as Eugene disintegrates, Jacobus descends to a state of "barbarian" violence that is again normalised by his society as they deem him a great hero of conquest and founding-father of white civilisation. What is the reason for this depiction of wars fought on the basis of greed and revenge, the text asks—how far are we all responsible for "the horror, the horror": the dehumanisation of self and society? Just as with Conrad's *Heart of Darkness*, the trauma, with all its ethical ramifications, is one that lingers with the reader.

Coetzee's novel *Disgrace*, written three decades after *Dusklands* again tackles the trauma of the colonial situation, but this time in the aftermath of apartheid in South Africa. This novel was severely criticized for being "racist" as it deals with the problems of black violence against white South Africans, focussing on the trauma of revenge-motivated rape and the repercussions of colonial violence. While *Dusklands* deals with the "mythologisation" of apartheid, *Disgrace* deals with what happens after the collapse of such myths of power. Both novels deal with the writing of self and ask what it means, and what is takes, to be human in this world—the first through a clear demonstration of acts of anti-life and anti-existence. The second addresses a man's struggle to find meaning in face of atrocity and personal loss of faith, the damage of both physical and spiritual self. It is a novel dealing with "white" anxiety, however, and one that silences the voice of the colonised since their version of the situation—what amounts to a continuation of decades of grievances and conflict over land and resources—remains unheard. Relevant to this situation is Edward Said's explanation that:

> To think about distant places, to colonize them, to populate or depopulate them: all of this occurs on, about, or because of land. The actual geographical possession of land is what empire in the final analysis is all about. (1994: 93)

Thus the narrative of self cannot be divorced from its political and geographical framework in landscape in as much as in government. In *Disgrace*, all the trauma revolves ultimately around the ownership of land, and by extension, a gendered violence based on similar masculinist concepts of the ownership of women—and the patriarchal right to use, trade and violate both at man's convenience and to satisfy man's greed.

When there is no concept of a wider framework of reference, the telling of the (limited) self is always in terms of the personal and the political. The fragmentation of the self—the loss of wholeness—is taken up in this novel on the level of the political becoming the personal, even when the protagonist, David Lurie, is initially characterised by his cynical detachment from either politics or any social responsibility at all. Fired from his job as a university lecturer for having an affair with one of his students—and above all for refusing to be repentant for doing so—middle aged Lurie leaves town to live with his daughter on a small farm in the country. His escape to apparent tranquillity is shattered when the farm is attacked and his daughter raped by a group of black youths. This is an act of revenge for the past white land claims, a form of "rent", as much as a violation based on lust. Forced at last to take some stand on life and human responsibility, he fails to know how to act, and it is Lucy, his daughter, who must help him regain a sense of human value. She refuses to take the attack personally or to participate in a sense of trauma—she is just part of the aftermath of all the wrong done before them. Although he initially refuses to share her disinterested point of view, the shock forces him to re-evaluate himself and his values, and he is able to locate himself as a real being sharing with others through this trauma.

What can this mean in terms of consciousness –how can this loss of everything really relate to knowledge of the Self? The politics of hatred seems a strange climate in which to learn the continuum of self: the consciousness of self-respect and respect of other-as-self. Yet *Disgrace* does end in an affirmation of self. The baby that Lucy has conceived is, as David says, "after all, a child of this earth" (216). Just as Helen Schlegel's child at the end of *Howards End* is a symbolic reconciliation of classes, so this child will be the reconciliation between races. Similarly, one could compare Lucy's fate to that of Leonard Bast: they are both necessary sacrifices of innocence to ensure a peaceful resolution of conflict.[i] Amidst the changes and sadness of their shattered lives, David still resolves to be "A good person. Not a bad resolution to make, in dark times" (216). The final recognition that the "ordinary tasks" of life will be their redemption is an affirmation of life and the endurance of self:

> With luck she will last a long time, long beyond him. When he is dead she will, with luck, still be doing her ordinary tasks among the flowerbeds. And from her will have issued another existence, that with luck will be just as solid, just as long-lasting. So it will go on, a line of existences . . . .. (Coetzee 217)

The final scene of the novel is one of tranquillity after trauma, a moment of "utter stillness which he would wish prolonged for ever", that David feels both within himself and in nature. He recognises the moment as sublime, one worthy of Wordsworth, but now devoid of cynicism accepts that "even city boys can recognise beauty when they see it, can have their breath taken away" (217). He has reached a pure moment of transcendence, of the suspension of breath and thought, a moment of pure consciousness. He is silenced, not through violence, but by the vast grandeur of Africa itself, both its landscape and its history. The moment is one comparable to Wordsworth's, in his Lines written above Tintern Abbey where the poet enters:

> . . . that serene and blessed mood,
> In which the affections gently lead us on,
> Until, the breath of this corporeal frame,
> And even the motion of our human blood
> Almost suspended, we are lain asleep
> In body, and become a living soul:
> While with an eye made quiet by the power
> Of harmony, and the deep power of joy,
> We see into the life of things. (1798, 1969: 89)

This moment of transcending thought is not an experience of a void: it is a moment of supreme clarity, expansion and sense of wonder, a moment beyond words that can only be described once the moment has passed. It is the affirmation of permanence and possibility in the gap *between* words and experience, a thrill of the infinity inherent and latent in the silence. As Wordsworth described so eloquently, it is a realisation that "the basis of the external world is also the basis of the knowing individual" (Ramachandran 1980: 33). Of course pantheistic experience is nothing new; what is new is the dimension I am suggesting here in terms of the reconciliation of time, history and trauma. It is the shift from a focus on outer to inner phenomena, a shift away from the intellect to the emotions—which, according to Indian literary theory, is a move beyond nature and man to a more penetrating aesthetic quality of *bhava*, or "soul", its "real essence" (ibid: 11).

This moment experienced by David can in some ways be compared to Homi Bhabha's extrapolation of the uncanny, a moment at the border that impacts upon and disrupts normal waking-state binary oppositions. (Although unlike Bhabha's "uncanny", here the elements of trauma and anxiety are not so much evoked as resolved.) Thus, David is left no longer thinking of the violence inherent in "them and us", so much as contemplating the continuum of history as a long process of moments, of change within the non-changing. Similarly, in the opera of Byron and his mistress Teresa that David is composing, "There is no action, no development, just a long halting cantilena hurled [. . .] into the empty air" (214). John McLeod describes how the uncanny moment serves as a reminder of all who have been forgotten or erased by the process of history, as the logic of discourses of colonisation and patriarchy is challenged by the "unhomely" presences (2000: 220). In the re-writing of the African landscape, with the new boundaries and thresholds being contested and re-established, there is a shifting sense of identity for both communities. New uncertainties become opportunities for experience beyond the rational and objective.

Here, in *Disgrace*, the historical figures of Byron and Teresa are being re-enlivened just as David sees his daughter Lucy's existence (as a white land-owner) is being erased or written out. The fact he laments Teresa's fate—that he has "brought her back from the grave, promised her another life, and now he is failing her"—is a direct and ironic parallel to how he feels about his daughter. He, however, has taken the path from an outer to inner view of reality: a path that can ultimately lead to a realisation of the *sat* (existence) *chit* (consciousness) and *ananda* (bliss)—or eternal bliss consciousness—at the foundation of existence, the "doctrine of ultimate reality found in the Upanishads"(Ramachandran 1980: 34). He has surrendered his ego, and through this absence of egotism has reached a condition of pure joy, if only for an instant. Yet in his life, through this moment of greater illumination, he has ultimately been able to connect the Byronic with the Wordsworthian—the passion and the prose.

Finally, by accessing meaningful social relationships and a relationship with his Self, David Lurie has "worked through" the trauma. The traumatising event is no longer held as a traumatised affect. He has worked through both the personal *and* the collective past. If, as Jameson argues, the postmodern world makes real experience impossible, it is nevertheless possible to experience ultimate or "ideal" moments in which history is put into perspective as a genuine encounter, through a timeless moment of transcendence in which "history" as the past is simultaneously both meaningless and meaningful. The making of history is not over, but now, having surrendered the past, David only looks to the future. His new work of putting stray dogs "to sleep" engages in the seemingly irreconcilable ethical opposites of taking life, of using violence, to bring about peaceful death. But he has gone beyond the irony of oppositions. He has gained the wisdom of living purely in the present moment, and in residing only in the "now" he is able to transcend or even negate the multi-layered mutilations of time and history.

3. Working through trauma: *The Plague*

A humanist and existentialist who still believed in the value of "beauty and truth", Albert Camus reveals in novels and plays his concern with the threat of destruction of civilisation by the madman and the fanatic, and the constant threat to every human of the loss of self. "Now that God is dead" writes Camus in his essay "Helen's Exile", all that is left is history and power" (1995: 50). Connor Cruise O'Brien sees Camus as the most able European writer in confronting moral and political issues between the West and the non-Western world; he argues that "The inner drama of his work is the development of this relation, under increasing pressure and in increasing anguish" (1970: 103).

His classic novel *The Plague* (1965, originally 1947) deals with the physical, mental and moral crises that people face under the terror of immanent death. Often regarded as an allegorical work, it is also a philosophical one, and one that deals with dichotomies of hope/despair, healing/disease, love/death. Above all it can be read as concerned with issues of human culpability and the role of compassion as the only valid response. The novel can be analysed as a way of living through and working through trauma—both physical and spiritual. Camus uses the plague as synonymous with the evil wrought by imperial regimes and the misuse of power. Yet as a symbol, this trope can be taken a step further, out of its historical limits and given a wider, mythical power and relevance by analysing the "injustice and outrage" that befell the people of Oran in this novel. For the evil, represented by the disease, is, as Camus stresses, always present, it can rise up again at any time "for the bane and enlightening of man" (252).

The plot of *The Plague* has long been regarded as a metaphor for the tyranny of terror, especially the spread of Nazism, and more recently it has been argued that it "can be read as part of the debate about culture and imperialism" (Said 1993: 208), as anxiety over violence associated with the demise of the French empire in Algeria. Although Camus was born in the Algerian town of Oran of French parents, Camus was caught in what would now be termed the state of "hybridity", belonging to two worlds and two cultures.

The Algerian war of independence, which did not reach its conclusion until after Camus' untimely death, is a conflict symbolised by the plague eating away at the orderly and ordinary lives of the people. The narrator, at the beginning of his account of the plague, stresses the ordinariness of life in the town; suffering, he comments, takes place amidst the banality of life, in a town where "everyone is bored" (1965: 2). (Why bored? One can only conjecture that *ennui* was a problem of the French population alone.) As the people begin to realise their predicament, Oran is sealed off from the rest of the world, becoming a microcosm in which the very worst and the best of human characteristics come to the fore. Greed, pity, hope, fear, treachery, courage all become the faces of everyday life as the people come to terms with their exile and the "incorrigible sorrow of all prisoners and exiles" (62).

Prisoners in their own city, the inhabitants face the experience simultaneously of exile from the outside world and imprisonment within the walls. In his groundbreaking work *The Wretched of the Earth*, Frantz Fanon argues how the European colonizing powers (especially referring to the French in north Africa) devalued the nation by seeing its culture and history as a void. For Fanon, this predicament of the "other" proceeds from his (the gender specificity is within

Fanon) traumatic condition of colonial positioning and silencing. He sees people as power, and urges the native African to reclaim the past as a step towards eroding the colonialist ideology—just as here we can see the importance of the besieged people reclaiming their past through memory, nostalgia and imagination: "In short, we returned to our prison house, we had nothing left us but the past" (61). We can, here, read *The Plague* as more than just an anti-totalitarian diatribe: but as being about the dangers of misuse of power in Algeria and "the injustice and outrage done to [the people]" (251). Edward Said argues how all the characters, like the author, are white French Algerians; the politically and morally dubious presence of the French in Algeria is according to Said "outside the narrative" (1993: 217). Yet to read *The Plague* from a purely postcolonial, historical perspective ignores the moral and global perspective. Camus' concern is with a wider perception of individual and group trauma, with the inner self of being human. Although this standpoint is vehemently refuted by Said (ibid: 217), one might question why, as a philosopher, Camus would *not* be thinking of "the human condition". Said does, nevertheless, concede some respect to Camus by crediting him with the stance of being "a moral man in an immoral situation" (ibid: 210).

Camus is often criticised for being a supporter of French rule, and as Said argues for "hiding things about Algeria in his fiction" (212-3). Said questions why Camus chose to locate his three major works *La Peste, L'Etranger* and *L'Exile et le Royaume* in Algeria (211), concluding that Camus is surreptitiously justifying French rule. His play *The State of Siege* (1948), however is set in Spain, a fact ignored by Said. Camus claims that of all his writings this drama was the one that "most resembled me. I focussed my play on what seems to me the only living religion in this century of tyrants and slaves—I mean liberty" (1948: ix). By transferring the setting of this elaboration on totalitarian state violence to outside Algeria, Camus *was* able here to portray his thoughts on the French occupation of Algeria, and perhaps his vision of the terror and the misuse of power that would be involved in a war of independence: hence his reluctance to sanction it.

In *The Plague*, as in Camus' later play *The State of Siege* in which the town of Cadiz is similarly threatened by the Plague, here as a tyrannical personification, the sense of rebellion is spiritual as well as physical. Whereas in *The State of Siege*, Camus focuses on a more political warning—that even after a deadly battle of innocence against tyranny and totalitarianism in which heroic individuals are sacrificed for freedom to be successfully achieved, at the end of the revolt the old corrupt regime of Nada ('nothing' or nihilism) is reinstalled—in his novel, the message appears a more focused on ethics. The long combat with evil culminates in a discussion between Dr Rieux and his friend Tarrou about the nature of morality and culpability. The main plea of Camus' protagonist Dr Rieux is for "comprehension" as a code of morality (109), a faculty that Camus himself may have been struggling for in his understanding of the conflict within the heart of his homeland, Algeria. As the character Tarrou expresses, the nature of "plague" is not the sole property of any one nation or race, "I know positively that each of us has the plague within him; no one, no one on earth is free from it. And I know too, that we must keep endless watch on ourselves lest in a careless moment we breathe in someone else's face and fasten the infection on him" (207). Man has only a choice between murderer or victim. Tarrou is in many ways a saintly figure who sacrifices himself for others and whose final martyrdom heralds the end of the plague in the city and the lifting of the state of siege. Just as the protagonist of *The Outsider* places himself outside society by killing, here the opposite stance has an equivalent result. Tarrou's vision and stance of empathy places him outside normal society—and to return would be impossible. "I know I have no place in the world today", he tells Rieux, "once I'd definitely refused to kill, I doomed myself to an exile that can never end" (297).

The clearly related *dehumanising* effect of violence and involvement with killing, as found in *The Plague* and *The Outsider*, reveals another option in regard to Camus and the situation in Algeria: that of the search for non-violent means of conflict resolution. In the play and the novel that deal with the Plague as symbol of "the evil that men do" in whatever shape (totalitarianism or colonialism), the Plague is ultimately defeated through acts of self-abnegation and a refusal to become a victim of fear. Those who stand against violence, such as Tarrou and Diego in *The State of Siege*, are those who are sacrificed for "the greater good"—yet Camus also makes them the symbols of goodness and morality in a world where honour, justice and love swiftly become meaningless concepts.

At the end of the novel, the disinterested voice of the narrator reveals himself to be Dr Rieux, the central and most *involved* character in the events of the novel. But, as he stresses, his desire is above all for detachment and impartiality from the account he has written. One could argue that this impartiality is an enlightened one, since it incorporates compassion:

> All the same, following the dictates of his heart, he [the narrator] has deliberately taken the victim's side and tried to share with his fellow-citizens the only certitudes they had in common – love, exile and suffering. Thus he can truly say that there was not one of their anxieties in which he did not share, no predicament of theirs that was not his. (246)

This account is indicative of the fourth state of consciousness that witnesses but is uninvolved. The doer of action does not partake in the results of his action—a stance of being "unattached to the fruits of action". This is Krishna's teaching in the Bhagavad-Gita, that on the battlefield of life one must transcend and perform action from the field of pure consciousness. The seeming coexistence of opposites demonstrates Camus' philosophy as he expresses it in his essay "Existentialism is a Humanism" that "A priori, life is senseless [. . .] but its up to you to give it meaning". The very ambiguity of Camus' position in his works is in itself at the core of his writing, thus: "one can be sure of nothing" is a basic tenet of his philosophy. Roger Quilliot comments, "Camus is as uncertain today as he was yesterday. This, doubtless, is why he has not ceased to exist" (qt Bree 1962: 168). This uncertainty also generates an exciting dynamic for all possibilities to exist.

The works of Camus can be read in terms of an unenlightened man struggling with the problem of what is right action with regard to concepts of morality and violence. This is comparable to the situation of Arjuna on the battlefield in the Bhagavad-Gita: he must face battle, the certain shedding of blood, and the abandonment of ethics—the battle of Kurukshetra, was, after all the event that signalled the start of Kali Yuga—our current age defined by suffering and ignorance. In *The Rebel*, Camus formulates his concept of the ethics of violence or "rebellion": the fight against "falsehood, injustice and violence" that refuses to give in to despair. "Rebellion is the very movement of life and it cannot be denied without renouncing life," he argues (1953: 271), again pairing oppositions that are typical in attempts to define colonial uncertainties.[ii] Yet rebellion actually affirms human dignity: as Camus put it, "I rebel, therefore we exist" (ibid: 22). In contrast to Fanon's advocating violent revolution as one of the essential stages of nationalism, Camus' concept of rebellion is one of moral questioning, one where the ethics of compassion rather than revenge comes to the fore. Following in the legacy of Edward Said who became conciliatory in his tone (in for example, "The Question of Palestine") is reconciliation/peace an option? One must ask if there is a place now in postcolonial theory for a foregrounding of Camus' insistence on revolution as "moderation", humanity and love?

Yet it is obvious that if the future is to include a moral approach to violence and the settlement of disputes, one must ask, by whose code of morality? Is there such a thing as a "global ethics"? On an outward level, almost all of the world's religions sanction against killing, and endorse that murder is a sin. Again, however, this is circumstantial and depends upon the situation: a killing in the context of a traditional, orthodox, jihad (which disallows suicide) affords the killer a place in heaven with all the promised attendant *houris*. Similarly, the concept of a patriotic fight for homeland involves rhetoric of glory, duty, and honour, and bestows a concept "hero" upon those who take part and are killed. The rhetoric is not new, and neither is rejection of such vocabulary as morally unacceptable, as the following extract from Ernest Hemingway's *A Farewell to Arms* (written in the context of the 1914-18 war) shows:

> I was always embarrassed by the words sacred, glorious, and sacrifice and the expression in vain. We heard them, sometimes standing in the rain almost out of earshot, so that only the shouted words came through, and had to read them, on proclamations that were slapped up by billposters or other proclamations, now for a long time I had seen nothing sacred, and the things that were glorious had no glory and the sacrifices were like the stockyards at Chicago if nothing was done with the meat except to bury it. There were many words that you could not stand to hear and finally only the names of places had dignity.
> [. . .] Abstract words such as glory, honor, courage, or hallow were obscene. (Hemingway 1927)

At the end of the plague, the people of Oran are to commemorate their survival with a monument. One old man is cynical, "'All these folks are saying, We've had plague here. You'd almost think they expected to be given medals for it. But what does that mean—'plague'? Just life, no more than that'"(Camus 1965: 250). Camus points out that individuals like Rieux who are seeking a greater meaning to life, beyond the desires that can be apparently fulfilled merely through romance or human love, are doomed to a greater understanding, an awareness of the depth that ordinary people are spared. "But for those, who aspired beyond and above the human individual towards something they could not even imagine, there had been no answer" (ibid: 245). This apparent negation of transcendent meaning however is in the context of the philosophy of non-attachment, where the purpose of life is fulfilled whatever the individual experience. This is the realisation that defines the true perception of action in the relative world: "And he alone really sees, who sees all actions being performed by manifest intelligence alone, and the Self as the non-doer" (*Bhagavad-Gita*: 13,29).

It is important to note, however, that the renunciation of attachment to the results of action is not the surrender of principles, but, as the mystic Rumi best puts it in his poem "The Seed Market":

> This giving up is not a repenting
> It's a deep honouring of yourself. (Tr Barks and Moyne)

In many ways, Camus' novel on the exile of the human spirit and the ultimate solitude of the human mind is a search for a unity that transcends the meaningless or trivial—the day to day, the boring, the normal. Through the trauma of the plague and the struggle involved in fighting it (or terror, or evil, or totalitarianism, or injustice) the human mind is shaken out of complacency and we are able to take a new "leap into freedom" (Camus 1953: 273).[iii] Through the radical swing of awareness from a life characterised by boredom to one of terror, a shift in consciousness takes place: the state of consciousness changes from the fluctuations of waking/dreaming to the stability of living pure consciousness alongside the waking state. More than an indictment of terror, the novel can be read as a working out or healing of trauma through the development of consciousness.

In the volume of short stories, *Exile and the Kingdom* (1966), Camus explores further the implications of involvement/detachment, belonging/exile, and love/loneliness in terms of human consciousness. Within the framework of implicating the alienation of cultures, Camus explores the more profound meanings of human alienation because of the separation of limited self from universal Self. Janine, the protagonist in the story "The Adulterous Wife", is perhaps the only Camus' character allowed the liberation of transcending to experience her own pure consciousness, and it can be read as significant that she is the only central female character in his fiction. (In his other works, female characters are insignificant and the overall concern with man does seem to be a gender-specific debate.) In a moment out of time and place, she escapes both past and present; there is only infinity and peace—an escape to the symbolic kingdom of freedom and certainty: "the kingdom which coincides with a certain free and bare life and which it is up to us to refind in order for us to be reborn" (Camus, qt Said 1994: 214). In another essay, *The Myth of Sisyphus*, Camus emphasises the importance of the "impulse of consciousness [which constitutes] a definite awakening ... for everything begins with consciousness and nothing is worth anything except through it" (1955: 10).

4. Traumas of displacement: *The English Patient*

One of the major traumas of the modern diaspora is the sense of loss of identity. Many writers are concerned specifically with the "migrant condition" and the sense of alienation inherent within relocation. Just as in *The Wretched of the Earth* Fanon insists that a sense of national identity—a national consciousness that gives form to "that revolutionary capital which is the people"—is required, so a new loss of that identity can be the foundation of trauma. The predicament of exile can in itself be accompanied by the sense of oppression, and of injustice (as seen in the discussion of *The Plague*).

The politics of country and home is a dimension that has been explored in many facets of the work of the Sri Lankan writer Michael Ondaatje. The sense of home is a lingering presence in many of his novels, a presence that can be both disturbing and liberating. As Chelva Kanaganayakan discusses, in most of his works (with the obvious exception of *Running in the Family* and his most recent novel *Anil's Ghost*) Ondaatje avoids direct reference to Sri Lanka, and yet all his novels could be interpreted to be about coming to terms with his status as expatriate writer. His novels, particularly *The English Patient*, which I shall discuss here, are about outsiders:

> about those for whom identity is elusive and home remains a site of conflict and uncertainty. Here [. . .] one encounters the concern with allegory in those who seem to establish a niche that transcends marginalisation. (Kanaganayakan, in King 2000: 207)

In *The English Patient*, the space of exile is the war-torn landscape as the allies move up into northern Italy at the end of the

Second World War. It is a place of exile equally for Hanna, a Canadian nurse; Caravaggio, an Italian thief; Kip, an Indian sapper with the British army; and the dying English patient himself. In different ways, they are all traumatised. They all seek a new form of awareness, of self-identity, with which they can face the reality of their experience outside the derelict villa in which they live in self-imposed exile, protecting themselves from the outside world of horror, loss and death. In terms of Homi Bhabha's formulation of Third Space (which is an "in-between state", a state of suspension of time, space and identity), the characters should, in this in-between location that is neither home nor having arrived somewhere else and thus a place of transit, be able to negotiate new identities. This state of both physical and temporal in-between-ness in which the characters reside in the villa should by definition be a transformative space. The villa, after all, acts as a meeting place between old and new cultures (the physical structure of Renaissance Italy clashing yet coexisting with the violent destruction of the 20th century) as well as national identities; but it also acts as a postmodern non-place [iv], as "an external catalyst for emptying consciousness of its intentional content" (Haney 2002: 65). Jonathan Shear writes that the experience of trauma "explodes" the cohesion of consciousness and this is clearly depicted in this novel.[v]

Memory is also trauma: the characters have cut themselves off from the past as well as the future. Only at the end of the novel, when the revelations of the past and the present come together in the detonation of the bombs over Hiroshima and Nagasaki that finally end the war, can the barrier between outside and inside realities be shattered and a release made possible. The characters cannot face themselves or the world: the English patient literally has lost face, he lies unrecognisably burnt and helpless—a symbolic victim of the annihilation of territory and text and the ascendancy of terror.

In their discussion of consciousness and theatre, Malekin and Yarrow (1998) outline their theory of how a writer is always seeking some form of transcendence. This transcendence can be defined in terms of locating new or renewed knowledge. Vedic science also speaks of the "purifying" influence of knowledge, of how gaining knowledge is to rise above both ignorance and the limitations of self. The artist or writer is able to annex liberating forms of knowledge in various modes of existence: as questor, as hero, as martyr, as lawgiver, as magus or as exile the artist seeks, achieves, codifies, and champions new knowledge (Malekin and Yarrow 1998). *The English Patient* is a text where we can find many of these modes of transcendence; like the building blocks of old books with which Hanna reconstructs the stairs of the villa, it is a narrative densely layered with meaning and with transcendences.

Ondaatje as author could be argued to be as much on a quest for meaning and for his own identity as the English patient or Hanna or Caravaggio. As the time- and place-fractured narrative unfolds, the reader is similarly drawn into the quest to discover the identity of the patient, and, like the characters, to unearth whether the "I" of identity can be maintained in the aftermath of trauma. Each character is, like many following the trauma of war, a shell: inert, dead to the interior life and the significance of outer experience, seemingly like the unexploded bombs everywhere in the landscape around them, that must be located and rendered harmless.

Perhaps of all the characters only that of Kip, the Indian sapper, reaches any conclusive reclamation of identity. Like his alter ego Kim in Kipling's novel (and significantly *kim* means the question 'what?' in Hindi), he has been torn between the worlds of east and west, claiming allegiances with both, and ultimately fighting on the side of the British. (The name Kip also of course pays homage to *Kip*ling.) His search for knowledge is through the skill taught by a wise, fatherly Englishman (as in both novels) finding his way through the wires of the booby-traps and mines left by the retreating Germans, tracing a path though the invisible maps within his mind. Figuratively, this is the same exploration undertaken by Almasy, the same accurate charting of territory, and the same maps that Almasy spent his life tracing across the unrecorded deserts of Egypt –for the British and then the Germans: maps that proclaim "Knowledge is power". Through their knowledge both Almasy and Kip are able to cross the boundaries of logical space that others are bound by; they function as nomads across the territories they are mapping. They both transcend their cultures and nationalities.

The role of Almasy in the novel is as questor to answer "what is the self?" once the arbitrary social, national, and temporal labels of self have been cast off. "All I desired was to walk upon such an earth as had no maps" (261). He becomes as close to "himself" as he can become. The English patient himself reaches a state where he has almost completely lost any physical existence: his face is the mask of "no-identity", unrepresentable identity or, as according to Homi Bhahba, an identity of "no presence" (Richards 1994: 294). Certainly, he has "gone beyond the senses" in that he is almost without sensory ability to communicate—he is reliant on an ancient hearing aid, and at the mercy of others like Kip, who may for their convenience snip the wires that keep him attached to the outer world. Like a bird he is kept barely alive on the little that Hanna is able to feed him. Yet he is the most "alive" presence in the novel for us, created as he is through sutras drawn from history and the sense-impressions, threads of identity that sew his being into a whole. Freed from pain by constant morphine, he lives entirely within the world of his imagination and his memories "imploding time and geography" (161). There is no time-space dimension to his thoughts, and his mental narrative is the one that we as readers share—the one that we must navigate our way through to make sense of his mental terrain.

It is this formless terrain beneath the black mask that in fact is the Third Space, the "nonspace" of cultural difference embodied by the man who seems to be without nationality and culture, or to combine so many. Here is the possible terrain for formulating his self-hood. His hybrid, multiple, cultural identity intimates a mode of consciousness that is non-linguistic, which can be compared to Bhabha's discussion of the hybrid moment "outside the sentence". His experience replicates Bhabha's description of this moment, which is "not quite experience, not yet concept; part dream, part analysis; neither signifier nor signified" (1994: 181).[vi] It is an existence of almost pure consciousness, where the potential to express has not yet manifested into language or form. It is a liminal space between, as Haney puts it, "the intentional mind and the nonintentional consciousness" (ibid: 64). There is clearly within the consciousness of the English patient a state of awareness of self that is *constant* regardless of shifting national, linguistic or political identities. It pre-exists these definitions of identity; it is the constant non-changing *always* in the notion that "everything is always changing". He has let go of the rational that constitutes ratiocination, he has realised a state of consciousness unmixed with intentional content. The patient's identity becomes like the desert he so loves--without boundaries, seemingly empty and yet full of limitless potentialities. " 'Who is he speaking as now?'" asks Caravaggio significantly.

Human beings, claims the novel, are all driven by the need to know, to understand "how the pieces fit" (121). By the end, the English patient claims that identity is communal and composite: implying that consciousness is innate to all people regardless of their cultural background. Consciousness is the all-pervasive ground to intentional knowledge. Moreover, "access to this ground is not only an innate capacity but also promoted by the excesses of a world that compel us to let go of our fixed attachments" (Haney ibid: 66).

This realisation of the patient in a more limited sense also has its ethical perspective; it lays the ground for Kip's horror and placement of moral blame on all in the west for the responsibility of the war's final genocide. The patient lies dying, having virtually gone beyond his attachment to desire, and yet wishing that his body could be marked by every event he remembers, as if the body itself can bear testimony to conscious experience (which of course his ironically does). His body has become one with the landscape; his body has become the "body of history".

The equally human desire (in addition to that of knowing) is the desire to forget. The tragedy of war, and especially of WW2, lies in the denial of memory, the repression or inability to express what had occurred. Throughout *The English Patient*, various attempts are made by the characters to forget or to remember. Hanna blanks out much of the trauma she has witnessed as a nurse, a negation that includes attempts to annihilate both memory and her physical self, while simultaneously trying to put evidence together to determine what had happened to her father. Kip eventually "regains" his identity as Indian and following a metaphorical rebirth by near drowning in a river (in a parallel episode to that in *Kim*) returns to his own country, an older and wiser man. But this "national" and racial identity that Kip finds flies in the face of Fanonian politics and is not the whole story of "self". Kip learns that "the only safe thing is himself" (218), but what is the self he has found when he can no longer trust himself or others?

The reformulations of identity in the text are fragmented and dubious: both the English patient himself and Caravaggio are by profession liars and the keepers of secrets, and both are revealing identities forged as much though morphine as through memory. Significantly, when the reader and the characters do seem to have discovered the "true" answer to the identity of the patient, and the fact that he is certainly not "English", the question is no longer relevant.

The self of the patient as revealed through his own testimony of text and hypertext—through the imaginative recreation of an identity—is finally essentially a mythical one: the jackal god Anubis. As this jackal god of death and preservation, the character has acted as omnipotent narrator and as *witness* to events, he has been able to observe and record across time and space. He witnessed Katherine in Oxford, the Miltonian fall of the flaming angel, the plane crashing in the desert, the events in the cave. As god of death he symbolically preserves his memories of Katherine from oblivion just as he literally attempts to preserve her body. Finally he witnesses, and embalms, his own life's story.

One aspect of the true nature of the self, the text reveals, is as witness. This is why the sense of time and space can be overcome, fractured, compacted. At the end of the novel, the present crashes into the future. An action in one part of the globe receives a reaction in another. Like the frequent references to Herodotus's history, narrative and "truth" are both blurred and mythologized; the past is constantly being repeated in the present. Why then a quest for individual self if the past is what is repeated? For then the "participants" in that narrative must be a continuum of witnesses not actors. This is what the English patient discovers for himself—that the body is merely an inscription of past action, the self meanwhile free to gain knowledge from memory, to know what one has always known, and thus be released from culpability, or karma.

In Vedantic philosophy, in the state of enlightenment where pure consciousness is lived as a permanent reality, silent consciousness (Kaivalya) is the silent witness to action. Action is identified as being within the absolute, that is to say, within the eternal field of no action. In Vedanta the field of action *is* the field of the absolute, all action eternally takes place in infinite silence. Maharishi Mahesh Yogi explains the mechanics of witnessing in higher states of consciousness in terms of the two qualities of intelligence within human consciousness: the aspects of *purush* (the silent but wakeful quality of intelligence) and *prakriti* (the creative quality of intelligence). These two qualities of intelligence silence (Purush) and dynamism (Prakriti)—the field of pure life within everything in creation—co-exist as the basis of very grain of creation (1993: 109). A further quality *purushottam* is the holistic value of all the various values of Purush in the universe—it is the silent organising power of the whole universe, the totality. (A metaphysical parallel to the unified field of quantum physics.) It is the level of intelligence that witnesses the two aspects of nature, silence and dynamism, at the same time, the witness of both purush and prakriti. The aspect of Vedic literature called *Nyaya* refers to Purushottam as "the lamp at the door", and explains that this quality of intelligence is available to the human mind in its settled, self-referral state of awareness, transcendental consciousness. Thus, when the mind becomes settled in the fourth state of consciousness (pure consciousness), the quality of witnessing the other states—waking, dream and sleep—is a possibility. Witnessing in this state is an experience of non-attachment, or of watching from a distance without being involved in the actions or events in which we are taking part. It is as if the person's intelligence is aware of the blank screen, the unchanging immutable field of pure consciousness, on which the actions of life are projected.

In postcolonial literature the questioning of the reliability of discourse, the rewriting of self, identity and the nation are connected through attempts to make sense of the past and through re-membering. Just as the past is refigured on the blank canvas—the tabula rasa of the English patient's body burnt dark and featureless—the fragments of history are contingent upon fragmented and subjective incursions of "reality" recorded and defined and revised. "Am I just a book?" wonders the English patient. But subjectivity is equally contingent and fluctuating according to postmodern thought. It is subject to negotiation, it is gendered, sexualised, localised and nationalised. The concept of a stable transcendental self is absent. It is no wonder then that the quest for "self" after the advent of postmodern and postcolonial criticism is problematical—and trivialised.

What do we need to discover and understand the Self? This is a question also asked in Ondaatje's *Running in the Family*. Postmodern indeterminacy again seems to rule out the possibility of re-discovering his father, either as character or as narrative legacy. All that is possible for Ondaatje, as for his English patient, is a collage of memory and images. He is able to create a mythology, but not a history.

5. Postmodern masks of self : *White Castle*

The themes of trauma, war, fragmented identity and the search for self all come together in the novels of the eminent Turkish postmodern writer, Orhan Pamuk. Amongst his novels that address questions of relationships between individual and nation, I will look here at two of his historical novels rather than novels set in contemporary Turkey. Both Pamuk's novels *White Castle* and *My Name is Red* present history as unstable, a "fiction" constructed by multiple voices and multiple selves. Both character and narrative are fluctuating and non-stable, especially in the display of multiple fragmented—often inanimate— narrators in *My Name is Red*. The perception of self is always from the perspective of others. Similarly, the perspectives in both novels involve the contrast between "western/European" and "eastern/Asian" approaches to gaining knowledge: scientific knowledge in the former and artistic knowledge in the latter. Both concern the search for "higher truth" and how it can legitimately and authentically be represented. While the multitude of narrators of *My Name is Red* do at least declare their identity (as in the title), the single narrator of *White Castle* is fascinatingly unnamed, ambiguous and left open to interpretation. Is the narratorial "I" at the end of the book even the same as the voice of "I" who begins? If not, at which point does it change? As discussed earlier, Yarrow and Malekin argue that a writer is always looking for a way to gain some form of transcendence—of going beyond self, history and time to find new kinds of knowledge. *White Castle* in particular (Pamuk's first novel to be translated and read in Europe) modifies and changes concepts of self and history through a quest for knowledge. The novel concerns itself with the protagonist's search for knowledge within the "clash" of traditions of knowledge between sixteenth- century Italy and Turkey. Reality and imagination within the narrator/protagonist's account of events become so enmeshed and distorted that the concept of identity and self are utterly confused. This novel also fits within the framework of postcolonial concerns since it explores in detail the concept of self as opposed to other, as well as the clash of cultural interests between two imperialistic civilisations. Where are the boundaries? How far in determining the other, are we looking at our own mirror image?

The novel begins with the narrator, a merchant, being captured onboard his ship sailing from Venice, and he is taken as a slave to the Ottoman court in Istanbul. There, after showing his ability to heal people of plague, he quickly becomes known for his learning and "western" knowledge. He is taken before the Sultan and given as a slave to a man he refers to simply as *Hoja* (a title of respect given in

Turkey, meaning 'teacher'). With Hoja he becomes engaged in an intellectual debate to determine whether the eastern or western approach to knowledge is superior. In the meantime, the Turk eagerly wants to be instructed in everything that the Italian knows—about astronomy, science, the arts, and above all about weapons. The narrator, however, never loses hope that one day he will escape back home to Italy and his family, and he steadfastly refuses to convert to Islam, gripping to his faith as if his Christianity were the last remnant of his self-identification. The novel delineates the gradual transformation of the Venetian. His construction of identity is based on his writing, on analysing his dreams, and on his appearance. In a moment of self-analysis or even narcissism (an episode that is delightfully reminiscent of Wilde's Dorian Gray), he looks in his reflection in the mirror, and sees the "horror of uncanny resemblance" between himself and Hoja (83). (Significantly, Freud's notion of the uncanny also involves the doubling of self.) " 'Why am I what I am'" he asks (58) in a detailed moment of introspection. His desire to gain knowledge over the other, and to defy and control the other, results in a battle for existence between the two men. They have become literal opposites, like the face and its image in the mirror (59-60). (Significantly, the word 'introspection' has its roots in the same Latin word *introspicere* 'to look inside' as the Italian *speccio* 'mirror', as does the word 'spy'.) As with Dorian Gray, in the similar incident in Wilde's novel, this moment of self-reflection has both uncanny and unsettling consequences.

After many years, the two men, rivals yet mutually dependent friends, have constructed a weapon capable of laying waste to any city. When the country goes to war with a neighbouring enemy, the two now middle-aged men, the Hoja and his slave—neither is ever actually named—must join together to take this weapon to defeat the besieged Castle Doppio. The expedition to war becomes parallel to the narrator's personal search for liberty and truth. It also culminates in Hoja's violent extraction of the villagers' "sins", just as in their battle for existence he had earlier been obsessed with fabricating them, and just as the narrator has been obsessed with formulating the exact nature of sin. The name of the castle (*doppio* meaning 'double') itself suggests the final twist of the plot, in which the lives of the two men become interchangeable. Hoja is the narrator's double, his Doppelganger.[vii] The word *doppio* in Italian also means 'deceitful', 'duplicity', or 'double-dealing': thus the castle they are trying to gain also represents the duplicitous nature of life. The narrator describes the castle as "on top of a high hill [. . .] purest white and beautiful. I didn't know why I thought that one could see such a beautiful and unattainable thing only in a dream" (143). The castle represents the dual nature of life itself: appearance versus reality; dream consciousness verses enlightened awareness. Slowly he realises that the invincible castle symbolises the life he had lost in his old country and of the future he would never live: a life that his Doppelganger will now claim for himself. The inability to fulfil his desired goal of return to his home and finding again his sweetheart is an indication of his confused state of awareness—like Dorian Gray or Faust he has traded his soul for knowledge; he has survived but at what cost? He takes Hoja's clothes, as Hoja slips out of the tent to make his way towards Italy. Consciousness here is truly "relocated", as identities and homelands are exchanged.

In wishing to conquer the inviolable "Doppio", the men who have lived so long side by side and yet in antagonism—literally on opposite sides of the table—desire to unify diversity, but fail. As readers we become aware that the identities of Hoja and Venetian have changed; and it is also at this point that we realise we are not aware at *which* moment in time the switch took place. Was it that moment as they stood before the mirror? Was it earlier or later? Was it the Muslim Hoja who was obsessed with sin, or the Christian? Perhaps the characters can be interpreted to be the same person or two aspects of the same narrator—complementary aspects of man perhaps, such as in the novel *War and Peace*, where Andre represents action and Pierre the intellect. The narrative here is also further destabilised by the shift in time frame, the frequent foreshadowing juxtaposed with the remembering of events from a distant point in the future. In the moment when the narrator first sees the white castle, symbolising as it does purity and unassailability, pure consciousness, he experiences a instant of unbounded awareness. It is at this moment that he gives up his battle of striving for self-knowledge through an outward, rational mode of exploration. He is himself purified, rehabilitated (literally re-clothed) by exchanging identities. He gains transcendence from war and violence as he switches to an internal mode of self-searching. Yet in postmodern style his search is fraught with indeterminism and the slippery nature of self and meaning: signifiers can only produce an endless chain of more signifiers, and he seems unable to reach a transcendental signified.

As the narrator loses his identity, he questions the validly of both internal and external ways of gaining knowledge and rejects introspection. He remembers the Sultan who felt that "To search within, to think so long and hard about our own selves, would only make us unhappy." In tune with postmodern trends of self-reflexive narration, a narratorial/authorial voice explains, "This is what happened to the characters in my story: for this reason the heroes could never tolerate themselves, for this reason they always wanted to be someone else" (Pamuk: 155). The problem of writing is also addressed, for "by searching for the strange within ourselves, we too, would become someone else" (154-5). The narrator of *White Castle* finally resolves the siege of his identity by resorting to the world of the imagination, to similar phantasms that the people of Oran in *The Plague* cherished in order to allay their terrors. He explains, "I wrote stories so as to forget Him, so as to distract myself with those terrifying people and their terrifying worlds of the future (156). Like Foucault's phantasm, which was constructed to make sense of the contradictions of history (such as local relativity versus universality) the two opposites co-exist: the Italian and the Hoja. The opposite, the other, is referred to only as "Him". (This is also reminiscent of the style of poetry in the Sufi tradition where the Lord is usually only referred to as a longed-for absence, as Him, the Beloved—and in keeping with the Rumi-Shams relationship, certainly the homoerotic connotations of the novel cannot be overlooked. Yet this is also a reference to the longing for the spiritual revelation that comes with enlightenment. The poems of Rumi and others use this conceit. The evocative and wistful verses to the long-lost lover in this tradition are certainly reminiscent of the tone in which the narrator here thinks of the long-departed Other/Hoja. Perhaps this also refers to the longing for the ultimate other, the transcendental signified, so much denied in the materialistic post-modern world of violence.)

The uncertainty remains: together with the question: which is he, and which "Him" is the other. The concept of identity and self is confused, merged in mire like the swamp beneath the white castle that swallows up their "ultimate" weapon, which after all, is the manifest achievement of their years of intellectual pursuit. At the end of the narrative, the narrator—freed from any specific identity—stares out at "some infinite point in the emptiness" (160). He has reached a state where the mind experiences the field of pure consciousness, a self-referral, integrated state of consciousness, a field of silence, beyond the impulse of a thought.

Pamuk's two novels are interesting to compare in their explorations of self and other, and the human search for higher knowledge. While a postcolonial perspective elucidates how the other is defined and depicted, with all its connotations of the uncanny or the unwanted, it also becomes clear that what is left more ambiguous is not the other, but the self. Knowledge of the "I" is lacking. To define the "I" in contrast to the other obviously remains grossly inadequate not to say inaccurate. Moreover it is fear of the other, whether racial or gendered, that is at the root of much if not all of violence in the world today. Without recourse to the unbounded self that underlies the other four levels of the mind–the levels of senses, mind, intellect and ego—there cannot be a non-changing objectively-verifiable knowledge. Hence the search for self by authors or characters in these novels can never be complete—although a vision of that completeness may be glimpsed (as in the revelation of wonder on first seeing the white castle). This glimpse of reality underlying the appearances of everyday life is the same moment of illumination in the quest for the grail—the moment when the grail is clearly seen, only to be lost once more when consciousness returns to the normal waking state—or the moment of unveiling when the face of the goddess is finally revealed.

6. A commentary on overcoming trauma: The Bhagavad-Gita

The Bhagavad-Gita is the core of the epic text, The *Mahabharata*, a tale that was compiled over several centuries and ultimately transferred from oral to written form. It opens with a situation that epitomises a state of trauma: the decision of whether or not to go to war. As Arjuna surveys the field of battle, where he sees his own people and the enemy—his own kinsmen—as great armies lined up and ready to fight. The battle is one of supremacy between two groups of royal cousins; one the one side are the five Pandava brothers, including Arjuna, and on the other are the Kauravas, or Kurus. The Pandavas are joined by another cousin, Krishna, who is an embodiment (avatar) of Lord Vishnu. In grief at having to make the decision, and "possessed by extreme compassion", Arjuna is filled with concern not only for himself but for the others involved. It was due to this concern that he initially accepted the challenge of duty and honour before him, but now he is caught between the claims of his head and his heart, between duty and love. Arjuna is paralysed, caught between ethical considerations and the fear of yielding to evil; he turns to Krishna, his charioteer and explains:

> "Seeing these my kinsmen, O Krishna, eager to fight, my limbs fail and my mouth is parched, my body quivers and my hair stands on end. Gandiva (the bow) slips from my hand and even my skin burns all over; I am unable to stand and my mind seems to whirl". (1, 29-30)

This description reveals Arjuna's confusion and his resulting inability to act. The scene is set amidst the great noise and clamour of the battlefield. With so many of his kinsmen on both sides of the battle, he does not know whether he should fight or simply lay down his arms, or what possible good could emerge from such a battle. Arjuna's awareness is fragmented, his physiology in a disturbed state, and in this classic state of terror, he is unable to act or comprehend the situation from a moral point of view; as he explains, "I see adverse omens, O Keshava (Lord Krishna), nor can I see good from killing my kinsmen in battle" (1, 31).

Interestingly, in his commentary on the Bhagavad-Gita, Maharishi Mahesh Yogi suggests that even though Arjuna thinks here from a heightened state of consciousness, he must realise—as Lord Krishna will expound to him—that "the answer to every problem is that here is no problem" (Maharishi 1968: 65). The only way that it seems possible to accept this declaration from a normal waking state of consciousness is provided in Lord Krishna's advise that all action must be from a level of consciousness that is beyond attachment to action. This in turn necessitates the knowledge of a technique to make this transcendence possible, one that may alleviate suffering. From this point on in the Bhagavad-Gita, when Arjuna has identified the depth of his despair, the recovery from trauma begins as Lord Krishna begins to instruct him. Arjuna turns to knowledge as his only recourse in his state of confusion and despondency. The only prerequisite is that Arjuna actually requests Krishna to help him:

"My nature smitten with the taint of weakness, confused in mind about dharma [duty/righteousness], I pray Thee, tell me decisively what is good for me. I am thy disciple; teach me for I have taken refuge in Thee". (2, 7)

As Lord Krishna begins his discourse to Arjuna, it becomes clear that Krishna does not deal with the specific problems that Arjuna has enumerated, that is to say, how he is going to deal with the situation on the battlefield. Krishna deals with the situation using the principle of the "second element": since the problem cannot be solved on the level of the problem, a deeper level must be reached to find the solution. Krishna's first advice to Arjuna is to establish his awareness in the field of pure consciousness. This is the first and most fundamental stage in gaining complete enlightenment: Krishna instructs Arjuna *"nistraigunyo bhavarjuna"*, to 'go beyond the three gunas', the field of eternal change and difference, to the eternally unchanging field of pure consciousness.[viii] (The "three *gunas*" referred to here are *tamas*, 'sloth' or 'darkness'; *rajas* 'energy' or 'heat'; and *sattva*, 'purity' or 'light': these elements, either by themselves or in combination, are the constituent parts of all manifest creation.)

The result of being established in pure consciousness is then elaborated when Krishna says to Arjuna: *"Yogastah kuru karmani"*, perform action established in the field of pure consciousness, and thus become balanced in success and failure, "for balance of mind is called Yoga" (2, 48). These two verses establish the importance of the transcending process and of performing action established in the field of transcendental consciousness, the Samhita (togetherness of the knower, known and process of gaining knowledge). Krishna defines the true perception of action in the relative world: "And he alone really sees, who sees all actions being performed by Prakriti alone, and *the Self as the non-doer* " (13, 29, my italics). This establishes the relationship between the field of action and the Self. As Geoffrey Clements explains, the eighteen chapters of the Bhagavad-Gita:

contain the wisdom for any person to step on to the path to complete enlightenment. By following Lord Krishna's advice to transcend and perform action from the field of Pure Consciousness, any individual can attain higher states of consciousness and fulfilment in life. (1996: 25)

The main code of conduct advocated in the text is to perform action while remaining non-attached to the results of that action, to perform action remaining in the Self. This ability skilfully to act from the level of non-action also encodes an ethic of "what ought to be done and what ought not to be done"(Bhagavad-Gita: 16, 24). Thus, Krishna's advice is a move away from adherence merely to scriptural texts and practices and towards locating ethics and consciousness within the self—a move more in line with a gnostic tradition than one of religious dogmas and piety. Knowledge is to be found within the self of the individual, "the hearts of men", and is the "refuge" of peace from the mistaken perception of illusion (Arnold: 97). In terms of consciousness, the ultimate goal of Krishna's teaching is for full enlightenment to be reached, not just by one individual, but for the whole world. This is expressed in Krishna's words that he has come to restore Dharma—life in accord with natural law—characterised by goodness, victory, glory, and unfailing righteousness (Chapter 18).

In the content of this ancient text, it is interesting in comparison to re-examine Fanon's essays "On Violence" and "On National Culture" (1963). In the context of desiring national liberation and the overthrow of colonial powers, Fanon calls for the creation of a "total" man, a situation where humanity can take a step forward to reach a new level (1963: 239). According to Fanon's vision this can only be produced through violence, and through war, and through rejecting models and institutions of society created by Europe and America (ibid). While advocating the use of violence as a creative means of liberation, he also paradoxically enumerates the psychological problems associated with being the target of violence, oppression and racial victimisation, especially some of the mental disturbances after torture (1963: 207). From Fanon's words written in rage against the plight of the colonised peoples of the world, it is evident that people both as groups and individuals can define themselves by their hatred, by their self-identification as "other" and as the objects of hate, as well as *their* location of the other that is the target of their hatred. The belief that some are not equal for racial or cultural reasons is self-endorsing. The "violent, unanimous demands of the revolution" endorsed by Fanon (ibid: 90) refuses compromise, refuses to be duped by placatory approaches of conciliation: "Enlightened by violence, the people's consciousness rebels against any pacification" (ibid: 52). In reading and analysing Fanon's work almost half a century after it was written, the reader is faced with a similar ethical quandary to that faced by Arjuna: while most would surely endorse the need "to fight against colonialism, against poverty and underdevelopment, to fight against debilitating traditions" (ibid: 52), his advocating violence to achieve these goals may now, from a global perspective, appear unrefined and ethically (and academically) problematic.

Roberto Calasso's scholarly rewriting of Indian "mythology" provides some illumination to this contemporary problem. He highlights that the world at the time of the epic *Mahabharata* was about to plunge into a new era, *Kaliyuga*, characterised by *adharma,* the distortion or loss of *dharma,* the Law of right action. Once these values came into effect, sacrifice and war became "two sides of the same coin. Sacrifice became the failed war" (2001: 327). What began as a war over righteousness ends as a massacre. Ultimately, according to Calasso, the *Mahabharata* "can be seen as an overwhelming demonstration of the futility of conflict. Of every conflict. [. . .] The only irreversible inequality is the one that only now became clear, detachment, the doctrine that Krsna [sic] passed on to Arjuna before his hostile relatives, lined up for battle" (2001: 329-331). "Right", or natural, skilful action demands a balance between dynamism and silence, the code of conduct of performing action while remaining in the Self, the fully awake self-referral state of intelligence. This is the "action in the state of non-action" advocated in the Gita as the model of conduct for both an ideal man and an ideal government, behaviour that upholds the principles of the ever-expanding universe (Maharishi 1992: 106-7).

Yet together with the lesson on detachment, Krishna also brought another notion with which to survive kaliyuga, the quality of *bhakti,* devotion. Moreover, Krishna gave this lesson first to the *gopis* (the milkmaids of Vrindaban, all of whom were in love with the young avatar) before he gave it to the warriors (Calasso ibid: 334). Both *bhakti* and *dhyana,* 'meditation', are techniques of the paradoxical path of non-self, which when followed one-pointedly is the route to develop consciousness, the higher Self. Meditation is a technique of self-exploration; the way "to avoid sorrow and delusion" (Iyer 1977: 4).[ix] Thus, as we have seen in this chapter, development of consciousness is linked with expansion of the qualities of both mind and heart. For many, the seat of consciousness *is* the heart. Both intelligence and emotion are purified through meditation, as Pandit Iyer emphasises: "Happiness, understanding and wisdom—these are not unworldly aspirations, but man's birthright" (ibid: 10-11).

---

[i] Comparisons to this novel are not without relevance, since in addition to its critique of English class issues, Forster's novel is also recognised as having anti-imperialist sentiments. The Wilcox family's wealth and social status is founded on the Imperial rubber trade. Forster's subtle irony undercuts the validity of this business, without overtly challenging empire. As Said points out, Forster highlights how this imperial background effects changes occurring in England, which in turn impinge on the lives of the Basts and the Schlegels (1994: 77). See also, Jameson's essay "Modernism and Imperialism", in Seamus Deane (ed) *Nationalism, Colonialism and Literature*, Minneapolis: University of Minnesota Press, 1990 (43-66).

[ii] Homi Bhabha in particular discuses what he calls "the articulation of nonsense" – and recognises the problems inherent within the "contradictory place" of postcolonial arguments that try to formulate the colonial choices available between nature and culture, being and meaning, subject and other, which are ultimately "neither one nor the other". Colonial discourse is thus caught between the language of universality and a repeated "translation" of meaning. See *The Location of Culture* chapter 7.

[iii] In the wake of *The Plague*, and events of more recent decades, it is perhaps ironic that Che Guevara's speech at the Afro-Asian conference proclaims Algeria as a prototype of a utopia for the oppressed peoples of the world, and proclaimed the newly independent capital city of Algiers as "one of the most heroic capitals of freedom". See Ernesto Che Guevara, "At the Afro-Asian conference in Algeria", in David Deutschmann (ed.): 1997 (301-312).

[iv] See the discussion by Marc Augé, *Non-Places* (1995).

[v] This can be explained in terms of lack of coherence in the functioning of the brain— the opposite effect of meditation in which brain-wave coherence increases. Experience in the waking state of consciousness has its basis in the functioning of the five senses and their corresponding structures in the brain: hearing, sight, smell, touch and taste. Trauma experience disturbs normal balanced functioning of the brain and hence the senses, leading to experience of a loss of control over both self and environment. As research indicates, those practising Transcendental Meditation and the more advanced TM-Sidhi programme have access to "the brain reserve", a holistic value of brain functioning that supports the partial values and processes of the senses. (See research by Lyubimov cited in *Maharishi Vedic University: An Introduction*, Maharishi 1992: 352).

[vi] A concept also discussed in terms of semiotics in Haney's analysis of Bhabha; see *Culture and Consciousness*, 2002: 64.

[vii] In postcolonial theory, the concept of otherness includes doubleness, both identity and difference, "so that every other, every different than and excluded by is dialectically created and includes the values and meaning of the colonizing culture even as it rejects its power to define" (Lye 1998).

[viii] "Be without the three gunas, O Arjuna, freed from duality,
ever firm in purity, independent of possessions, possessed of the Self". (2,5)

[ix] Meditation consists of experiencing thought at subtler and subtler levels until the finest level of thought and language is transcended, and the state of pure awareness is reached. The techniques are laid out in the Yoga Sutras of Patanjali, and chapters Two and Four of the Bhagavad-Gita.

Chapter Five
The Self-Reflexive World:
Consciousness and Social Responsibility

Man is not merely a possibility of recapture or of negation. If it is true that consciousness is a process of transcendence, we have to see too that this transcendence is haunted by the problems of love and understanding. Man is a *yes* that vibrates to cosmic harmonies. Uprooted, pursued, baffled, doomed to watch the dissolution of the truths that he has worked out for himself one after another, he has to give up projecting onto the world an antinomy that coexists with him. [. . .] the white and the black. Stubbornly we shall investigate both metaphysics and we shall find that they are often quite fluid.

(Frantz Fanon, *Black Skins, White Masks*: 8.)

Globalisation and theories of transformation remain a crucial strategy for the future of postcolonial studies. In the current world of political, religious and cultural uncertainty and upheaval, postcolonial writers of fiction must look beyond concepts of nationalism and rational space-time in order to access today's sense of belongingness within hybrid, ever-shifting "mongrel" communities. Robin Cohen explains how diasporas involve "dwelling in a nation-state in a physical sense, but travelling in an astral or spiritual sense that falls outside the nation-state's space-time zone" (Cohen 1997: 134). The migrant's sense of being rootless, of being between worlds is symptomatic, it seems, of the growth of globalisation. In the face of racial tensions within countries such as the United States and Great Britain, a vision of a working paradigm of consciousness is more necessary than ever in the quest for an end to violence between individuals, communities, and between nation states.

The failure of religions to pacify rather than incite violence is not new. The stark and brutal realism of writers such as Rohinton Mistry elaborates on this failure together with showing how whole social groups are manipulated and controlled though the exploitation of religious doctrines by governments and national leaders. The Indian writer Saadat

Hasan Manto highlights in his stories how it is a return to social and spiritual humanity above all that is needed in our interpersonal relationships—a humanity that transcends class and caste. In his short story "*Sauraj ke Liye*", the outward show of religious observance is condemned as having transformed spirituality into a mere sham. The signifiers of religious observance have become the fixed mask concealing any signified "meaning" (Hasan: 2005). Manto speaks through the central character Ghulam Ali:

> Human beings should remain human beings. If you want to do good deeds, is it essential to have your head shaved, put on ochre robes or coat your body with ash? You may say that one is free to do as one wills, but I say it is because of such erratic conduct that one misguides others. Such people, flying high in the belief that they have found a superior level of awareness, forget that while in time their character, their ideas and their beliefs will evaporate into thin air, their shaven heads, their ash-covered bodies and their ochre robes are all that will survive so far as simple people are concerned. So many reformers have been born to mankind but what they taught has been forgotten. However, crosses, beards, sacred threads, metal wristbands and underarm hair are all that survive. We are wiser than the people who lived a thousand years ago. Why does it not enter the heads of our didactic counsellors that they are distorting the human personality? I often want to stand up and start screaming, "For God's sake, let man remain man. You have already distorted his face. Now take pity on him; do not try to invest him with divinity because, as is, he is losing his humanity". (Tr. Hasan 1997)

As Khalid Hasan argues, this story reveals how "the rise of religiosity, which its adherents mistake for religion, is not a recent phenomenon but it is more visible than it was, say, a quarter of a century ago". Outward symbols, "be they beards or metal wristbands or sacred threads [. . . or] the hijab, which has been gaining ground among Muslim women" are all "outward manifestations of a spirit that is no longer there"(2005: 1). In twentieth century literature, some authors can be read as attempting to provide answers to the questions created by compassionless existence and the failure of organised religion, and to provide alternative "spiritualities" to this loss of both the original message and purpose of religions to provide paths to higher consciousness. The problem within the areas of life purportedly associated with spirituality is that real knowledge of the self has been lost and life is dominated by the fundamental mistake of the intellect—*pragyaparadha*—in which differences are not experienced in terms of their underlying unity and wholeness.

Even within postmodern and postcolonial contexts, concepts of alternative spiritual or sacred space play a part in deconstructing the failed social structures and reconstructing out of the void. In terms of cultural and political change, Fanon expresses it in terms of a "zone of nonbeing, an extraordinarily sterile and arid region, an utterly naked declivity where an authentic upheaval can be born" (1967: 8). This gap between realities is also one that provides a Heideggerian shift in creative process: it is a void within which all possibilities exist. Heidegger (1977) suggests that strife, a "violent concept-metaphor of violation", emerges out of the violence of the rift between earth and space. A work of art is created from the dynamics of this thrust, from the dynamic interaction in the conflict comes the making of a text. To place this into the context of consciousness studies, it can be compared to the internal dynamics of the gap. According to Vedic Science, the whole process of manifestation is an alternation between sound and gap, a continual oscillation within the unmanifest between point and infinity:

> Consciousness first locates infinite dynamism in itself and then projects this infinite intelligence and dynamism to create the whole Universe. In the sequence of expression from one sound to the next, the key element is the coexistence of infinite silence and infinite dynamism, which is the definition of perfect wakefulness. Pure wakefulness, in perfect sequence, unfolds its infinite status to itself as the infinite progression of all finite values. In this process, in every finite value, infinity is located; infinity is never lost (Clements 1989: 6).

In the state of full enlightenment, the awakening of every level of the manifest creation is found to be nothing other than the awakening of the Self. This is a realisation that the infinity of one's self is eternally identical to the infinity of the Self of the whole Universe. It is the loss of this realisation that has arguably brought about the sterility of religions and their loss of real social significance.

2. The diaspora and alternative approaches to social space

Both Chitra Banerjee Divakaruni and Salman Rushdie are authors concerned with migrancy and trans-national concepts of ethnic identity in the diaspora and with trans-cultural experiences of exile and belonging, alienation, and the hope of reconciliation. While approaching such ideas from vastly divergent perspectives, these authors use constructs of magic or the "esoteric" to transcend traditional notions of geographical borders, boundaries of time and space, and limitations of identity. They propose magical spaces (and people) with which to redefine human abilities and communication, and to re-examine issues such as intercultural violence, ethnic identity, and an individual's responsibility for war. Sacred, or what I will discuss in the context of the novels in this chapter as "magical" space, allows for alternative readings of both past and future. As Don DeLillo commented in the wake of the 9/11 attacks, "when we say a thing is unreal, we mean it is too real, a phenomenon so unaccountable ... that we cannot tilt it to the slant of our perceptions" (2001).

Compared to Homi Bhabha's "Third Space" (that allows for the renegotiating of individual hybrid/migrant identity), the magical space I propose here is one that allows for a repositioning, re-writing, and re-*inventing* of not only individual but also national/cultural/political identity. This re-*location* of cross-cultural existence implies negotiation not negation of cultural difference, cultural integrity based on a unity of diversity. While writers cannot merely opt for an alternative culture, nor write in a utopian vein classified as "science fiction", the use of magical space alternates social realism, especially in a postcolonial context, with the positioning of contemporary post-modern reality *as* illusion.

Several critics have examined Rushdie's novels in terms of their use of magic realism, and Divakaruni also admits to using magic realism as a technique to "bridge boundaries", and uses "realism" as a concept also linked to mythology (Morton 1997). In *Mistress of Spices*, Divakaruni creates a mythic world paralleling this one, in order to contrast the harsh realities of inner-city life, a place whose magic overlaps into the "real" world. Tilo, the mistress of spices, moves back and forth between one existence and another. It can be argued of course that this is analogous to women's position that is always on the edge of society, a central part of society but one marginalized by men, a positioning that can make black women doubly marginalised. The role of the writer is to expose but also to reposition woman within this dichotomised existence, with the aim of bridging divides and accessing empowerment. Divakaruni explains:

> A writer should push boundaries, and I wanted to try something new, take risks ... all this risk-taking ... involves bridging barriers, doing away with boundaries: not only boundaries between life and death, the everyday world and the mythic one, but with the thought that perhaps the boundaries we created in our lives are not real. I'm talking about the boundaries that separate communities and people. (Divakaruni 1997)

Similarly, Rushdie's use of magic places in *Midnight's Children* makes accessible territories, which, like his narrator Saleem, are both "in-the-world and not in-the-world" (356), spaces where memory, meaning and history become fragmented and problematical. In both novels, as I shall discuss here, magic space mediates between the physical and spiritual worlds. Both these novels articulate new territories of transitional or transnational space, and thereby offer a vision of a new global citizenship and the increasing need for a global, rather than local, patriotism.

Since this postmodern age negates any claims to any such complete, totalised explanation of the world, the fictional novel itself, "the form created to discuss the fragmentation of truth", as Rushdie argues, starts from the assumption that "reality and morality are not givens but imperfect human constructs" (Rushdie 1991: 422). Reality, then, can be reshaped by the novelist, questioned, subverted and challenged: and while there may be no answers, magic space provides the terrain for this exploration to take place: "the elevation of the quest for the Grail over the Grail itself" (Rushdie ibid).

3. Magic realism/magic space

Magic realism is defined as involving absurdities, non-rational, dreamlike elements injected into an otherwise realistic, rational world with the purpose of a subversive rejection of the dominant rational culture (Harrison 1992: 55). Use of magic space, I would argue, contains elements of subversion and satire, while also being rooted in a mythological dimension that serves to expand its implications beyond the immediate cultural location. Magic space is used as a means of the migrant's reconciling to exile in what is often a bewildering, alien world. "Migrants of necessity make a new imaginative relationship with the world", Rushdie comments, "The migrant suspects reality, having experienced several ways of being, he understands their illusory nature. To see things plainly, you have to cross a frontier" (Rushdie 1991: 125). While magical realism involves a juxtaposition of fact and fantasy, magic space can be all pervading, a space of an alternate reality that informs and influences "our" reality—"other" but equally valid. Like Tilo in *The Mistress of Spices*, one can choose between worlds. Rushdie's use of magic space also demonstrates a country's endless capacity for "constantly renewing, rebuilding itself" (Rushdie qt

Harrison: 59). This sense of renewal extends to the migrant lost in a labyrinthine tangle of history/memory and political uncertainty who is able to reformulate his own sense of reality versus illusion. In both novels, then, individuals and societies are able, through magic space, to rise again like the phoenix from the ashes of self-destruction to strive towards a more optimistic vision of the future where individual and class/caste, or colour and ethnicity conflicts are subsumed in a wider, more tolerant and caring society. Rushdie proposes in this situation: "Unreality is the only weapon with which reality can be smashed, so that it may consequently be reconstructed" (1991: 122).

In first discussing Rushdie's *Midnight's Children*, I focus on the last section of the novel, avoiding a repetition of extant critics of the so-called magic realism of the Midnight's Children Club or other magical coincidences that link the (unreliable) narrator/protagonist Saleem with the history of India. Here, I wish to analyse Rushdie's use of magic in the episode of the Sundarbans, the "dream forest" beyond the boundaries of both civilisation and history. Rushdie's use of magical space, the "enchanted forest" on the edge of war-torn Bangladesh, allows for a devastating critique of the horrors of war, which "cannot have happened". Magic space, I shall argue, provides the terrain for an alternate version of the politicians' official "truth", much as literature " is in part the business of finding new angles at which to enter reality" (Rushdie 1991: 15). From Bangladesh, Rushdie's novel progresses back to India to illuminate/parody the events of Mrs Gandhi's Emergency of 1976-7. Central to this story is the magicians' ghetto and the "magical" character of Parvati-the-Witch, who, with her magical powers, also offers alternate modes of deconstructing and subverting both history and identity.

Peter Brigg sees the magical elements of *Midnight's Children* as "the escape from the chaos of reality into the ordered artistic creation of fantasy" and as "a continuous and subtle investigation of the relations between order, reality and fantasy" (in Fletcher 1994: 290). The making of an alternate reality in the case of the Sundarban jungle is, however, a retreat from one kind of fantasy to another. Rushdie describes the episode as a "descent into hell". The forest is a magical, unfathomable, unpredictable—and terrifying—space, which is comparable to the mythical "enchanted forests" of western myths of the Waste Land, the sterile landscape of spiritual death, of the forsaken Grail and the wounded Fisher King.[1] By "The Sundarbans" episode of *Midnight's*

Children, the protagonist, Saleem Sinai, has lost his memory and has been drafted into the Pakistan army, using his prodigious power of smell as a sniffer-dog to track down and kill the "undesirable" subversive elements who are fighting for the independence of (what will become) Bangladesh from Western Pakistan. After he and his team of three young men witness (and commit) acts of appalling atrocity, "things that weren't-couldn't-have-been true" (356), Saleem leads his team by boat down the river Ganges. Ironically questioning the glorification of war "heroes", Saleem, deserting from the war, embarks on a journey into the heart of darkness, leaving the "unreality" of the conflict for the apparent "reality" and peace of the country. Saleem himself shatters this rural idyll when he rapes a farmer's wife and his companions shoot the husband, who with his great scythe resembles Father Time. This murder of time, like the Ancient Mariner's slaying of the Albatross,[ii] marks the transformation of the countryside from benign to evil. They enter the great jungle of the Sundarbans, a labyrinthine mass of salt-water channels that "closed behind them like a tomb" (360). At once they begin to "succumb to the logic of the jungle", the unreality of a jungle that grows incessantly in "size, power, and ferocity" (361). Abandoning their now-useless boat, the four men take refuge in the sundri trees, where they give in to fear, blood-sucking leaches and diarrhoea. Like heroes on a mythical quest, they soon forget the purpose of their journey: "the chase, which had begun far away in the real world, acquired in the altered light of the Sundarbans a quality of absurd fantasy which enabled them to dismiss it once and for all" (363). From now on, they "surrendered themselves to the terrible fantasms of the dream-forest" (363).

Events in this enchanted forest bears comparison to Jason and his Argonauts, or Odysseus undergoing the trials and tests of the exile struggling to return to his homeland. The forest sends its magical punishments: visions of men they had killed, the accusing eyes of women, the screaming of fatherless-children; they regress into a frightened childhood, haunted by misdeeds of the past. The magical jungle conjures up the lamenting voices of the "undesirable elements" the team had exterminated, until, tortured by the sounds, the three young soldiers fill their ears with forest mud. Only Saleem, like a latter-day Jason, leaves his ears unstopped, and so avoids the permanent deafness the poisonous mud brings. They come to a Hindu temple dedicated to the goddess Kali and shelter there, falling into a deep sleep. Upon awakening, they find four young girls "of a beauty beyond speech" (366), recalling for the men the four *houris* that traditionally await them in "the camphor garden" of Paradise. Like Odysseus's sailors in Circe's cave, forgetting everything, the men made love to the girls, who come to them every night in the temple. Time in the Sundarbans follows "unknown laws", so that the men are unaware how long they remain, until at last:

> the day came when they looked at each other and realised they were becoming transparent [. . .] In their alarm they realised that this was the last and worst of the forest's tricks, that by giving them their heart's desire it was fooling them into using up their dreams, so that as their dream-life seeped out of them they became as hollow and translucent like glass. (367)

This realisation of their fate—the invisible equating with the unreal—allows the men to escape the forest of illusion. Joseph Campbell's discussion of the classic hero's journey includes a description of the arrival at the temple, where the hero undergoes a metamorphosis, he dies to time and is "returned to the World Womb, the World Navel, the Earthly Paradise"; he must cease to exist for the outside world before being initiated into the knowledge he will eventually take back for the renewal of the world (Campbell 1949: 92). Here, fiction is not intended to "mirror" reality, but to allegorise, distort, and re-align our perceptions. As one critic explains, "The fantastic serves to question the tyranny of the logos [... and] comes as a necessary corrective to narrow conceptions of the real" (Durix 1998: 81). Rushdie's use of magical space thus challenges the validity of "reality" and perception, for if the forest of illusions (*maya*), the temple and its houris could not have existed, then neither could the field "leaking bonemarrow" (372) nor the atrocities of the siege of Dacca.

Based upon the archetypal perilous journey of myth throughout the ages, the episode of the magic forest utilises the classic story of the hero summoned out of his society into an unknown fateful region. Represented by a forest, or a secret island (as we shall see in the *Mistress of Spices*), this is always a place of strange beings, "unimaginable torments, superhuman deeds and impossible delight" (Campbell 1949: 58). For Rushdie, the forest represents man's struggle of memory against forgetting. In the monomyth, once the hero has answered the call to adventure—which is always a passage beyond the known world into the unknown—destiny will aid and guide him through the dangers of this zone of magnified power. The forest region of the unknown, is, Joseph Campbell suggests, an area of projection of unconscious content: of violence (as with the tormented consciences of the soldiers), as well as dangerous delight—projections of demons and "sirens" of mysteriously seductive, nostalgic beauty (the four *houris* in the temple). Once this magical threshold is survived and the hero emerges back into the world—in this case, ejected from the jungle on the crest of a tidal wave (368)—the hero symbolically passes into a sphere of rebirth, "symbolised in the world-wide womb image of the belly of the whale" (Campbell 1949: 90).

This rebirth takes place for Saleem in his meeting with Parvati-the-witch, first when he regains his memory as she calls him by name, and secondly when he "dies" to the world when she makes him invisible in her magic basket, womb/tomb experience he describes as being "insubstantial; actual, but without being or weight; I discovered, in the basket, how ghosts see the world" (381). Like the hero at the end of the mythic quest of self-discovery, Saleem finds the key to the question, "Who what am I?" and experiences an expanded realisation of his true self (383). Like Whitman, who was also shocked into an awareness of self by the horrors of war, this time the American Civil War, Saleem's "I" contains "a multitude":

> I am the sum total of everything that went before me, of all I have seen done, of everything done-to-me. I am everyone everything whose being-in-the-world affected was affected by mine. (383)

As the Indian army pours into the newly-formed Bangladesh, Saleem becomes "the willing captive of [the] Indian magicians" (379), found by another of the Children of Midnight, Parvati-the-Witch. Unlike the others in her group, Parvati employs real magic, enabling her to spirit Saleem in her magic basket out of Bangladesh to Delhi. During this disappearing act and his invisibility inside the basket, Saleem learns what it is like to be dead. His only means of holding on to reality in this ghostly time-and-space is to cling to his silver and lapis-lazuli spittoon, the Grail-like chalice that has ensured his survival.[iii] The character Parvati, like Saleem, functions as both indicator and instigator of historical process. As Saleem lives happily with Parvati in the magicians' ghetto in Delhi, Rushdie provides a vision of harmony amongst difference: the multitude of the poor, the bizarre and the freaks living together in alternate society of the ghetto. These sections of the novel vividly demonstrate the futile nature of inter-group conflict.[iv] This idyll is shattered by the arrival, first of Shiva, Saleem's rival and alter ego, who fathers a son by Parvati (a child—the Ganesh of Vedic tales— who represents the novel's hope for the future) and then by Mrs Gandhi's forces of destruction in the form of her mass "city beautification" and sterilisation campaign (Rushdie ibid: 431). Parvati is to lose her life in the destruction of the ghetto, and Saleem (along with all the other children of midnight) loses whatever power he had, magical or otherwise, in his castration. In itself, the magicians' ghetto can also be seen as an alternative "magic" reality—magic through the harmony and alternative choice it represents. The magicians, while being "Communists almost to a man, reflect the many divisions and dissensions of the world at large" (Goonetilleke 1998: 39). Yet together, Rushdie seems to say, they could change the world. They are illusionists. They offer a possibility of spiritual renewal.

4. *The Mistress of Spices*

The Mistress of Spices is also a novel concerned with how quotidian reality can be reformulated through alternate reality, magic space. A novel of the Indian diaspora in America, *The Mistress of Spices* lacks the subversive edge and the deconstructive satire of Rushdie's magic realism. Unlike *Midnight's Children,* which juxtaposes magic and history, the world of Divakaruni's novel is written without irony but with the wonder of magic and myth intact. Magic is utilised to postulate positive social change, not to undermine political events with an alternate history. Magic drawn from an alternate, parallel world is accessible, utilisable as an alternate mode of living. In *Mistress of Spices,* the postcolonial expatriate experience of cultural displacement is personified in the character of Tilo. She must straddle two cultures, two worlds—one real and the other magical, as well as the "diametrically opposed worlds of India and America". Here, rather than fantastic serving to protest against the "tyranny" of fact, the magical elements serve to incorporate a sense of old values and beliefs (including stories of the Indian epics) into the modern world. Magic has a socialising rather than subversive function.

Chitra Divakaruni describes how the novel was written with the aim of showing "that the art of dissolving boundaries is what living is all about", elucidating the "breaking [of] ethnic barriers, showing people of different races at war and in love" (Divakaruni, 1998). Tilo, the mistress of the spices, is "the quintessential dissolver of boundaries, moving between different ages and worlds and the communities that people them" (ibid). She gains her wisdom from the magical world of the Spice Island she has left to take a seemingly immortal human form. As a migrant in both space and time, she is able to fully participate in neither world, nor able to return to the magic world of total power and freedom of the island. Again, the magic island—like the forest—serves a similar function to that discussed by Joseph Campbell (1968: 58-79), a zone of magnified spiritual power, which acts as a transitory realm of initiation into self-knowledge for the mythical hero.

Tilo's magic lies in her knowledge of the secret powers of the spices in her shop in Oakland, together with her intuitive reading of the problems and needs of her customers. The mythical world of the spice island (7), whose sacred knowledge constructs both ethics and magic, is juxtaposed to the harsh realities of inner-city life. Tilo moves back and forth between the two worlds, divine and human —at least in her awareness—since the path back to the island is closed to her, as is full participation in human life (since she is forbidden by the power of the spices to ever leave the shop). Similarly, Joseph Campbell comments how it is the function of the *writer* to move in two worlds:

> the inward of our own awareness , and an outward of participation in the history of our time and place. [. . .] Creative artists are mankind's wakeners to recollection [. . .] Their task is to communicate directly from one inward world to another . . . not a mere statement, but an effective communication across the void of space and time. (1968: 92)

Boundaries, however, whether real or magical are to be transcended. The novel reinforces on many levels that whether between separate communities or peoples, "the boundaries we create in our lives are not real" (Divakaruni 1997a). The novel and its characters are a metaphor for the struggle between social responsibility and personal happiness (Divakaruni, ibid). The rebellious Tilo eventually must decide between the world of magic and that of human love. Transgressing the rule of non-involvement with the people she helps, she falls in love with Raven, a bitter and disenchanted part-Native American. He himself seems to have some extraordinary power of insight, since he alone recognises the young woman Tilo really is beneath her old woman's body. He urges her to run away with him to live a pastoral life away from the problems of urban America in an "earthly paradise". Raven's dream of the earthly paradise is again a reference to archetypal myth: the Earthly Paradise being a metaphor for the transcendent reality (discussed at length by Campbell 1968: 625-678). It is also the end of Dante's purgatory, where he again finds his earthly muse, Beatrice, who in life had opened his eyes to earthly beauty (Campbell 1968: 106).

The cross-cultural and cross-world relationship here addresses the problematic issues of ethnic diasporic positioning, where communities meet within the host country. While Raven is eventually identified himself as being outside mainstream American culture,[v] both in terms of race and class, their relationship is fraught with the possibility that their attraction is based on, "Each of us loving not the other but the exotic image of the other that we have fashioned out of our own lack" (310). When Raven calls her his "mysterious Indian beauty", Tilo realises that Raven has loved this Orientalised image:

> [...] for the colour of my skin, the accent of my speaking, the quaintness of my customs that promised you the magic you no longer found in the women of your own land. In your yearning you have made me into that which I am not. (290)

She recognises that once she loses this imposed exotic persona, her "power . . . mystery", she runs the risk of losing his love also. Tilo does lose her magical powers as a consequence of choosing human love and a fully *human* identity: she must finally choose between worlds. She passes "through a trial by water, then a trial by fire, and finally the trial of earth-burial to emerge transformed, each time with a new name and a new identity" (ibid). When Tilo makes the decision that transitory human love is worth more than the eternal power of magic, she changes her name to Maya—the Hindu term that defines the everyday world of perception, pleasure and pain as illusion.

Midnight's Children involves a reassessment of "the real"; here Divakaruni centralises the problematic of magical—and cultural—space. Questioning which world, and which laws, are illusory, the magic or the material, Divakaruni's Mistress of Spices is able to manipulate social space through her experience of magical realms beyond normal experience, in order to create new multi-ethnic moral and emotional configurations within the interracial communities of urban America.

While culture has long been defined as the force that defines and delimits societies in terms of fixed spaces, the recent intensification of globalisation means that it is no longer possible to imagine the world as a collection of disparate, autonomous regions. Understanding the relationship of culture to space is one of the challenges set before contemporary "world citizens". The issues of overlapping ethnic and cultural communities in America raised in Divakaruni's novel, the violence inherent within human incapacity to empathise with or understand "the other"—even when the other is one's close neighbour— addresses this challenge. The concept of hybridity or syncretism discusses the evolution of commingled communities that are different from the parent cultures (Cohen 1997: 131). The hybrid and changing character of diasporas—such as the Oakland of this novel—indicates two contradictory tendencies:

> On one hand the drift of globalisation is towards homogenisation and assimilation. On the other, and perhaps in reaction to globalisation, is the reassertion of localism—notably in the form of ethnicity, nationalism and religious fundamentalism. (Cohen 1997: 131)

Group identity, as we see here with the different communities in Oakland, may remain strong and even strengthen in response to the shrinking of space between peoples (ibid: 134). Yet as Robin Cohen (1997) questions, for the migrant and refugee in the postmodern world, what is home and what is exile? –A question that Tilo must also address and resolve. The characters in the novel, mainly of Indian descent, struggle to both adapt to the expectations of a new environment and maintain their cultural identities. For example, problems of arranged marriage, expectations and acceptable behaviour within marriage are all questioned in the light of the impact of American mores, as is the necessity to understand the kind of racial and tribal violence to be met on the streets of America.

The migrant's sense of being rootless, of being between worlds is symptomatic, it seems, of the growth of globalisation. Divakaruni's magic space, in this light, takes on an increasingly important role in the solution of the problems of globalisation and ghetto-isation. Tilo, who through her magic seeks initially to solve the problems of the people who she meets, eventually succumbs to a similar emotional and physical crisis. Almost killed in the earthquake that devastates the Bay Area (a symbolic event comparable to the mythological "phoenix fire" [vi]), she learns that happiness comes from being *involved* in the human world, a lesson she also teaches Raven, who dreams that perfection only exists outside society. She advocates a philosophy of global citizenship, where all must care for all, and take responsibility for the good of all.

Reference to the possible diasporic Indian experience of exclusion from mainstream California society is explored together with the notion of a culture of "care and communication" within and across ethnic diasporas. Recent discussions of global citizenship emphasise obligations across borders, tolerance of other cultures, truly international communities that imply the ideal of a world community (Carter 2001: 5-10). Feminism has also engaged with the ideal of global citizenship, often emphasising the "feminist ethic" of care and compassion. Carol Gilligan writes that "the moral imperative" that emerges from a woman's perspective is "an injunction to care, a responsibility to discern and alleviate the "real and recognisable trouble" of this world" (1982: 19.) Following in this trend, Gita Sen claims that ethics in the developing world has to do with the simple survival of human beings and of humanness. She speaks of such an ethic not as a secondary or academic matter, but as the heart of human survival (Sen 1988: 4.) Significantly, Patricia Collins argues in *Black Feminist Thought* (1990: 215) that a feminist ethics of care has striking similarities to the African and African-American world-view, an argument that could surely be extended to other ethnic groups, such as non-resident Indian communities.

Critics have expanded the concept of global citizenship in terms of citizenship of planet earth, stressing our shared dependence on nature (Carter 2001: 4-5). Cosmopolitanism is also associated with the quest to end war between nation states and establish an international ethic of human rights transcending borders. The definition of the global citizen—although there are utopian elements in claiming to be a global citizen—denotes:

> a coherent understanding of a relationship between human rights and human duties and cosmopolitan beliefs, including a commitment to prevent increasing world poverty, and the destruction of ancient cultures and the natural environment. (Carter ibid: 10)

In the novel, the purpose of Tilo's existence and exile in America is to minister to others like herself—the vulnerable immigrants and people with no place in mainstream society. She speaks of herself as being, "[the] architect of the immigrant dream" (28). For, as Tilo explains to

Raven, in an episode where having escaped from an earthquake they look down from the Golden Gate Bridge on the decimated city:

> "there *is* no earthly paradise. Except what we can make back there, in the soot in the rubble . . .in the guns and needles [. . .] yes, in the hate in the fear . . . for in the end some things are more important than one's own joy". (315)

In the mythic quest of the hero, the earthly paradise, magic space, comes only through compassion and pure knowledge. Formulations of magical space project strategies of peace and co-operation beyond anger, xenophobia and civil strife. As Joseph Campbell comments, today the only "mythical forest zone" is the human heart (1968: 677), so Tilo reveals that the "deepest magic . . . lies at the heart of our everyday lives, flickering fire, if only we had eyes to see it" (51). All important in the apprehension or vision of this transcendent reality are the gaps between one state of being and the other. As Tilo discovers, in order to see into the hearts and minds of people who are constantly "asking more than their words, asking for happiness except no-one seems to know where", she realises, "I must listen to the spaces between" (780).

She finally leaves behind the magic island in order to return to ordinary life and utilise the omnipotence of total knowledge which it offers—a state that could be compared to the regular experience of the transcendent, which, even once the transcendent state is lost, brings its benefits into daily life. Like Tilo's experience of the island, with repeated experience, the ability of being in tune with nature and harnessing that power expands. Soon, Tilo significantly gains both *"the words"* and *"the sight"* (8, 98, my italics)—both the sound and the form (or *Shruti* and *Smriti*) become lively in her awareness. She is in the state of *samhita*, where the knower, the known and the process of knowing are all united. The *samhita*, the integrated wholeness of pure intelligence is also the state of transcendental consciousness. It is the first stage in the growth of consciousness, and it is this element of wholeness that is normally missing in the daily cycle of waking, dreaming, and sleeping. The experience of transcendental consciousness is the first and necessary stage in developing skill in the field of action. By going beyond, transcending the field of changing reality, the result is action established in the field of Yoga (unity), equanimity.

Yet this dual positioning, like the migrant who experiences living between two worlds, is not without its struggle or hardship, a fact that is evident when Tilo returns to the magic island in her meditations: "When

I close my eyes the island comes to me...so real I could weep" (147). Her current state of entrapment on earth is contrasted to the happiness and idealism of the new mistresses still on the island who think "we will change the world". She has been basking in the bliss of the transcendent state of being, and feels bereft once that bliss is lost in the quotidian world. This state of dissatisfaction, the difference between the real and the ideal, calls for the introduction of a more perfect technique for gaining knowledge, one that will overcome the "mistake of the intellect" –the mistake that difference exists:

> Every experience of transcending is a step of further awakening, in which the Self becomes progressively awake to itself. Every process in Nature, every step of evolution and every form found in the manifest world faithfully follows this perfect theme of awakening, which is the play of the Self within itself. Individual awareness discovers its basis, its Self, to be identical with the Self of the Universe. (Clements 1996: 25)

For Tilo, this process is made possible both by her own spiritual experience of the pure knowledge available when her consciousness accesses the "magic island", and the process itself of oscillation between positioning—gaps—the gap between relative and Absolute. Vedic Science describes how the growth to an enlightened state of consciousness is reached through the alternation of two opposite states, between here and there, point and infinity, or between self and other. These swings of awareness bring about the growth of total knowledge and the organising power associated with it:

> The sequence of sound to gap to sound to gap [....] displays the mechanics through which the Samhita, the Self of the Universe, sequentially awakens to itself. As individual awareness awakens to its infinite value, the specific impulses of consciousness are all absorbed in the infinity of the Self: Pragya Apharadha is transcended. The awakening of individual consciousness means that Pragya Apharadha, the mistake of the intellect, is dissolved. (Clements ibid)[vii]

The use of Indian theory here, particularly Vedic Science, is particularly relevant to this novel since Divakaruni frequently draws upon her Indian literary heritage, and the text is diffused with mythical and legendary cross-references, such as to historical figures such as Dhanwantari, "the foremost of healers" (83), and to stories from the Puranas. Avoiding an exoticisation of the "east" or its "mythology", these stories are retold within the framework of the mistresses and their spice-knowledge. Thus, for example, the Puranic story of the devas and asuras churning the ocean of knowledge in order to produce "the treasures of the universe" is told within the context of turmeric, the spice that "came after the poison and before the nectar and thus lie[s] in between" (13). Elsewhere the same tale of the search for the nectar of immortality is expanded to include the role of the god Siva, who drank the poison that first appeared from the ocean. "Ah," reflects Tilo, realising how insignificant her work is compared to that of the great Siva, "even for a god it must have been painful. But the world was saved" (298).

The Mistress of Spices is infused with the sense of being between two worlds of the sacred and the profane—but power comes from the sacred. The alternative magic island is contrasted to the "human world of harshness", with its odour of hate and fear (54). The enforced segregation of Tilo, who is required by the terms of her "contract" with the supernatural powers of the Mother to stay inside the domain of her store and not venture into the "real" world of Oakland, parallels the psychic separation often experienced by diasporic communities within the adopted country. In fact, Tilo's fear of going outside her "home" of the store she runs and the supernatural injunction against it, relate to Homi Bhabha's discussion of the meaning of the uncanny, *das Unheimlich*: where being literally 'outside the home' equates with 'out of control' (Bhabha 1994:10). Thus for the immigrant who permanently feels *unheimlich*, concealment means conformity, and to be exposed in society can reinforce a sense of being alien and "unnatural" (as we shall see in Divakaruni's next novel). The beyond, as for Bhabha, signifies "spatial distance, marks progress, promises the future" (1994: 4). Yet the act of *going beyond* is unknowable and unrepresentable and constitutes a break in the sequential flow of time, the border is both a spatial and temporal threat and can be (or become) an uncanny location out of normal space-time.

4.1. *Queen of Dreams*

Other aspect of Divakaruni's novels that confirms their important contribution to diasporic experience is the protagonists' powerful link of memory across space and time to "the home country", the acknowledgement of the emigrant living in one community accepting, "an inescapable link with their past migration history and a sense of co-ethnicity with others of a similar background" (Cohen 1997: ix). Divakaruni's recent novel, *Queen of Dreams* (2004), is again located among the Indian American community in the Bay Area of San Francisco and deals with the problematic identity of self and home. In a scenario obviously continuing the theme of *The Mistress of Spices,* the woman with extra-normal abilities is the (unnamed) mother of the protagonist, Rakhi, who is able to read other people's dreams and help them with her predictions. The mother, originally from India and a migrant to the USA, maintains a spiritual and emotional connection with her homeland, whereas her daughter belongs to the young generation of Indians born and raised in America, for whom the concept of motherland is but a vague, unknown, and often orientalised dream.

This younger generation, who do not speak any language other than English, and have no cultural or linguistic ties to anywhere but their local downtown community see themselves, as they legally are, as US citizens who love their country. Their world is suddenly threatened and their sense of home and belongingness are challenged by the upsurge of violence against them as a result of the World Trade Centre bombings— after which many people of colour, regardless of origin, became victims of violence and harassment across the continent. When Rakhi, her father and friend, who together run an Indian snack shop in Berkeley, are advised to fly an American flag and banner proclaiming "God bless America" outside their store for protection, Rakhi asks: "'Is this California, year 2001 . . .or is this Nazi Germany?'" (Divakaruni 2004: 293). The values of the so-called migrant community are tested by the intensity of anti-racial sentiment, and at the lack of understanding that they also are Americans. When the café is attacked by white youths, Jespal (a young turbaned Sikh) cries, "'Stop! We haven't done anything wrong. . . . We're Americans, just the way you are'" (296). The phrase "just the way you are" is met with the reply "'Looked in a mirror lately? . . . You ain't no American!'" and consequently Jespal is attacked.

This violence rekindles some postcolonial debates on the nature of literature as resistance set against the stereotyped, and arguably sensationalist, image of "third world woman" as victim. Yet here it is problematised by the fact that America is ostensibly first world and "the land of the free". Furthermore, Rakhi's new sense of alienation within her own country is exacerbated by what she feels to be a permanent inability to gain any understanding of or connection to her parents' roots in India once her mother dies. She is unable to understand the culture, language, or spiritual abilities of her mother, none of which she has inherited.

Another novel published in 2004, Jhumpa Lahiri's *The Namesake* also extrapolates the seemingly inevitable distancing of the younger generation born in America from a sense of belongingness to the homeland. Here, the protagonist tries to re-establish a link to his cultural heritage by re-identifying himself though a change in name, from the literary-inspired and alien "Gogol" to a name more essentially "Indian", Nikhil. Against the paradigm of negotiating the unfamiliar terrain of life in the USA, the characters search for a means of articulating self and selfhood, the strategies of self-rehabilitation –literally here played out in a 'reclothing' as in the frequent references to Nikolai Gogol's story "The Overcoat". The boy Gogol must suffer the agonies of his inappropriate Russian name before coming to terms both with it, the mind-colonizing literary tradition it embodies, and his society. The sense of being an outsider within the country of one's birth is a problem that challenges notions of physical assimilation and emotional belongingness. For Gogol's mother, eventually returning home after thirty years of living in Massachusetts feels "suddenly, horribly, permanently" lonely and India is "in its own way foreign"(2004: 278). America seems both "stubbornly exotic" (281) and ultimately home to her since it is "the world for which she is responsible, which she has created" (280), a significant realisation of the world being our own mental, physical and spiritual creation.

For Divakaruni's Rahki, it is eventually through her father's Indian recipes and songs, which are "authentic" (a frequently emphasised word, and again one that raises problematic notions of exoticisation and nostalgia of oriental essences) that she begins to appreciate her heritage as well as heal her sense of alienation from it. The mother's endowment as a "healer of dreams" is an ambivalent gift; while she is able to help others, she must remain distant and cold-hearted to her own family, resulting in an almost insuperable alienation from her daughter. She represents the first-generation migrant who is unable to settle and attempts, unsuccessfully, to return to her homeland, although she realises that such a return remains impossible. The mother's failure to negotiate and reconcile the personal and professional parts of her life, and her resulting unhappiness are surely due to the fact that she gained her knowledge and, most importantly, her sense of self from the *dream* state of consciousness. Dreaming, *Swapn Chetana*, the third of seven states of consciousness, is characterised by the fact that the mind is lively even while lacking connection to the channels of the physiological structure of the brain responsible for the senses of hearing, sight, taste, smell and touch (which normally characterise the waking state). While the waking state is often referred to as illusory (because of the nature of *maya*), the dream state can be said to be even more delusory. As knowledge is different in different states of consciousness, each state of consciousness has its own "world" and hence, "Your world is as you are". In the dream state, true knowledge of the self is unavailable: hence experience based on that level of knowledge is inevitably going to result in mental and emotional anguish and the inability to fulfil desires.

> For countless generations, the knowledge of life and of the range of human experience has been sadly limited to the states of waking, dreaming, and sleeping--in which the human mind is beset by boundaries and in which life is characterized by instability and change. (Clements 1988: 4)

In this novel, it is eventually her daughter who must "heal" interpersonal relationships by connecting and reconciling the past with the future, the old country with the new, the needs of society with those of the individual. She must accept the ambivalence of the concepts of home with all its associations of the uncanny (as discussed by Bhabha 1994: 10), with the intellectual and spiritual senses of belonging, both personal and patriotic. The harshness of life in contemporary America is healed through the female figures of Tilo, Rakhi, and others like them who, although flawed individuals, realise that "The magic is in the heart" (1997: 137). Significantly, the migrants and the dispossessed of America (here represented by the shadowy figure of Raven's native American mother) keep a secret place within them that remains a source of empowerment and sanity. As the Mother of the magic island argues, "When you fill your head with inessentials, the true knowledge is lost, like grains of gold in sand" (168). These wise women, like the oracle of Delphi, realise, "Turn inward for what you need to know"(168). Interestingly, the growth from the waking state to cosmic consciousness through the regular experience of transcendental consciousness is a process of progressive purification of the mind and the body, and the Upanishads speak of a state in which "all the knots of the heart have been released"(Clements 1996: 10). With the development of inner emotional fulfilment, stability becomes a permanent feature of life.

[i] The descent into the dark, pathless forest of fear, representing man lost in delusion, also forms the starting point for Dante's *Divina Commedia*: a work which has informed and inspired European literary imagination for centuries, see also my discussion of Lowry's *Under the Volcano* in chapter 8. In postcolonial terms, Dante remains a relevant figure since he was adopted as the representative of Italian identity in the nineteenth century fight for national unity and independence.

[ii] In S.T. Coleridge's poem, "The Ancient Mariner", which appeared first in the *Lyrical Ballads* of 1789.

[iii] Interesting for the discussion here, Joseph Campbell describes how the *lapis exilis*, the philosopher's stone of ancient alchemy, was also one term for the Grail. (See his discussion on the significance of the round table and the grail legends in *The Masks of God: Occidental Mythology and The Masks of God: Creative Mythology*). I am aware that Campbell's work and his promotion of understanding based on universal mythology have been rigorously criticised in the light of poststructuralism.

[iv] For Rushdie's discussion of the ethnic violence of India, see "The Riddle of Midnight" in *Imaginary Homelands*, 30.

[v] The name "Raven" is also that of the trickster figure in North American Indian mythology, so if the character here also plays this role, Raven has come to Tilo to shake up her reality and create the "play" of the universe that reawakens the psyche and suggests new points of view and possibilities in life.

[vi] See Campbell 1968: 257.

[vii] Indeed the whole structure of Vedic literature is parallel to the structure in the universe, as Clements (1996) describes: "The whole of the Vedic literature, from the beginning of Rig Veda to the entirety of all the 36 areas of Vedic literature, is found to be the alternation of finite expressions and the infinity of silence, the alternation of sound and gap."

Chapter Six
African Explorations of the Sacred and the Self

"From a certain point of view the universe seems to be composed of paradoxes.
But everything resolves. That is the function of contradiction."
"I don't understand."
"When you can see everything from every imaginable point of view you might
begin to understand."

(Ben Okri *The Famished Road*, 376.)

1. The world of African literature

Wole Soyinka has argued that Africa is "a culture where the
mystical and the visionary are merely areas of reality like any other"
and that in African literature the spiritual is an inextricable part of life.
"This impulse and its integrative role in the ordering of experience
and events leads to a work of social vision", he writes (1976: 65-66).
William Haney (1994) has already located parallels between
Soyinka's analysis of Yoruba myth and the functioning of
consciousness. He elucidates the relevancy of Sanskrit poetics to
Soyinka's vision of how African literature "not only reflects human
experience but also extends this experience through the social vision
of the author" (1994: 159). The African tradition is both mystical and
visionary, and, according to Soyinka acts as an "imaginative impulse
to a re-examination of the proposition on which man, nature and
society are posited or interpreted at any point in history" (1976: 66).
This re-examination encompasses dimensions of human experience
ranging from the sacred to the scatological, from the political to the
personal—all of which involve redefinitions of self, an exploration of
alternative states of consciousness to discover what Soyinka calls the
"metaphysical self" (ibid: 40). This metaphysical quest is accessed
through myth and ritual, through drama and language, as played out in
both the individual and society, individual growth being mirrored in

social transformation. In this chapter, I will explore how the mythological/spiritual and the sacred play a part as a means of accessing postcolonial expression in African literature, addressing the creative and aesthetic dimension of literature as a "revolutionary" experience—one that defies preconceived boundaries. Encounters with the sacred will be analysed as experiences of empowerment from the different cultural viewpoints and locations of supra- and sub-Saharan Africa. As Soyinka explores, much African literature addresses either notions of reconciliation and reconstruction or "an inward-directed demand for self-cognition" and can be regarded as a "realistic and essential dimension of the moral equipment required for the reconstruction not merely of society but of man (ibid: 75). Thus, in diverse ways "spiritual" or sacred experience will be seen to be part of the authors' vision of social change.

Africa is a space of transculturality. African culture cannot be spoken of as a bounded whole but as a mosaic of multiculturalism. It is also a space for the unseen and the unknown: a place for resistance and reconciliation. As Nadine Gordimer writes of her position in South Africa following the elections of 1994, "My country is the world, whole, a synthesis. I am no longer a colonial. I may now speak of 'my people'"(1996: 134). The writers I examine here are not chosen to be representative of any stereotypical African experience; indeed the fact that there is no definitive "African experience" or literature is a widely accepted argument. I also leave unexplored the problems inherent in the uses of colonial language, although this could be argued to be an important facet of consciousness articulating itself in literature. As consciousness expresses itself initially through the physiology and then through language, the development of an individual's physical body is in fact structured according to the mother tongue. Thus, the choice of language one uses does not only have superficial implications, nor only political consequences.[i]

While the novels are chosen to some extent for the similarities of their concerns, the hybrid nature of African response to the colonial experience is implicated. To analyse African literature within the context of an overall theme of diasporic literature, I adopt the general premise of Gilroy's "Black Atlantic": that the problems and experiences implicated by African literature cannot be divorced from the scope of concerns within wider geographical boundaries. He sees the dangers of a nationalistic approach to literary and cultural studies and advocates an "outer-national, hybrid blackness" and an "emancipatory black diasporism" (Chrisman 2003: 75). Within my discussion here, therefore, I shall take "Africa" to embrace theories of migration associated with the diaspora, especially since much contemporary literature (by Caryl Phillips, for example) draws upon themes of the physical and spiritual journey, migration, rupture and relocation of people, as indicative of the African legacy of the past centuries. Phillips's novel *Crossing the River* deals with wider explorations of marginalisation and racism as part of the "African" experience. Told by a multiplicity of characters' voices, the novel transcends fixed time and place, as the time-line extends over a century, even though the story purports to examine three children's dilemma of being sold into slavery by their father. The "children" inhabit places in America, Liberia, and England; their stories take place in various times in the nineteenth and twentieth centuries. Africa is thus a translocational space, where, according to Gilroy, individuals have traded roots for routes, imaginative and physical (1992). Thus narratives are constructed out of the imaginative and real crossings of migrancy, resulting in fractured and fragmented identities, multiple and transformative encounters with new knowledge. Thus, although some novels may take place solely within the geographical space of a particular nation, the themes are still those that deal with spiritual migrations, with the individuals' process of change within social change. The literature itself is a way of exploring these new avenues of cultural expression and of coming to terms with the fraught place of the human within seemingly vast, if not global, forces of irrevocable transformation.

In a number of contexts, I will argue with Gilroy that "Africa" (or indeed any place of "the homeland") is a "cultural condition" and a mode of thought rather than a geographic location. His concept of the Black Atlantic was initially formulated "though [a] desire to transcend both the structures of the nation state and the constraints of ethnicity and national particularity" (1992:19), and the concept is "a lesson not restricted to blacks" (223). Gilroy suggests the image of the ship as one that captures the specific experiences of ongoing suffering and "being in pain" (207), or travelling within and without national boundaries. This suggests a transcendence of categorisation, a going beyond sterile and artificially conceptualised borders. For me, the purpose of addressing a relocation of "the spiritual" within life is with an aim of finding solutions to that ongoing suffering and pain; is not a true "move to a new place" unless it involves a transcendence of preconceived notions based on exclusivity, or spiritual and cultural "endogamy" so to speak. A repositioning in consciousness involves a shift from ignorance to knowledge, a swing of awareness from limitations to unboundedness. [ii]

For Homi Bhabha in his virtuoso work *The Relocation of Culture* (1994), these new subject positions can be liberatory modes of being in the world, a chance to access the hybrid identity of being "in-between" cultures. Yet the ability to access such liberatory space is, I have discussed elsewhere (2003), often restricted according to gender and class: mental space is as important as that of physical space; they are overlapping realities and are often defined by gender. Thus, within this discussion one should not overlook that even within "new" potentially transformative locations, the distinction between (male) public and (female) private space is frequently enforced, limiting women's access to social, spiritual, and economic spaces and opportunities. New locations can also mean reinforcement of old ideas. The Bhabhaian concept of imaginative crossings upsetting received notions of identity and subjectivity may ultimately only be true for those who depend upon the enforced fixed positioning of their women, who may be actively discouraged from "elaborating new strategies of selfhood . . . that initiate new signs of identity" (Bhabha 1999: 4). A semi-autobiographical novel by Buchi Emicheta, *Second Class Citizen*, for example, reveals how for a Nigerian couple recently arrived in London, the "rules" of the new life are very different for the wife, who is physically bound through multiple pregnancies, and spiritually bound through an enforced subservience maintained by a patriarchal code of morality transplanted from Lagos. Physically and mentally abused and beaten, she works while bringing up her four children to provide her husband with the money required for *his* new carefree life as a student. When she attempts to voice her strangled identity and gain some sense of fulfilment through writing, her husband's reaction is not that of a transformed man open to new ideas of diasporic modernity:

"You keep forgetting that you are a woman and that you are black. The white man can barely tolerate us men, to say nothing of brainless females like you who could think of nothing except how to breast-feed her baby."

"That may be so," cried Adah, "but people have read it. And they say that it is good. Just read it, I want your opinion. Don't you know what it means to us if in the future I could be a writer?"

Francis laughed. Whatever was he going to hear next? A woman writer in his own house, in a white man's country? [. . .] He was not going to read Adah's rubbish and that was that. (1974: 178)

For Adah, the Nigerian wife, the fact that "he had said she would never be a writer because she was black and because she was a woman was like killing her spirit. She felt empty. What else was there for her to do now?" (178). As if performing a traditional sacrifice to maintain his spiritual and temporal power and masculinity, her husband burns her manuscript, with a smug smile on his face at his "heroic deed" (180). Chimamanda Ngozi Adichie's novel *Purple Hibiscus* is another recent example of how patriarchal "order" is maintained across generations through abuse and violence—here towards children. As a survival strategy, the children create an alternative world of language and communication—one that is ultimately devastated through the traumatic revelation of past truths. Although an elaborated analysis of the ways available to young women to achieve independence (often mirroring the independence struggles of their countries) is beyond the scope of this present work, the question of how far access to the sacred and the spiritual—frequently connected with access to language and writing—remains a gendered inequality is not to be ignored.

2. Africa and the Sacred

The positioning of Africa both as political and national construct and as an imagined terrain of the colonialist is widely discussed in terms of writers from the times of Rider-Haggard. Authors such as Chinua Achebe realise the problems and challenges of African writing in terms of western discourse, how literature is both a weapon and a mirror (Achebe 1994 and 2000). Sacred space can conflict or co-exist with terror; resistance with tolerance; indigenous civilisation with colonialisation. The literature I analyse here will be used to elucidate how these coexistences can be both confusing and liberatory, and how their very juxtaposition can implicate/ initiate shifts in consciousness.

In Emile Durkheim's early influential work in *The Elementary Forms of Religious Life* (1915), he differentiates between experiences of the "sacred" as opposed to the everyday or profane. For the western-trained mind it may seem that more traditional cultures do not place much emphasis on this distinction. What is more prevalent, perhaps, is a totem/taboo dichotomy, or Levy-Strauss's famous raw/cooked formulations. What becomes most important, as Mircea Eliade elaborates (1959), are the moments of the sacred being defiled, a state that the very nature of sacredness paradoxically contains within itself.[iii] For the spiritual adventurer or the priest, engagement with sacred knowledge is at once hidden, transient, and exclusive, containing within it the threat of danger, since "that which sanctifies is always potentially polluting, the divine infusion may become lethal if the dose is not properly regulated by the rules of art and ritual" (Young 1991: 379). Engagements with hidden knowledge, the role of the intermediary between man and gods, as we see in a novels such as *Things Fall Apart* and *The Arrow of God*, also expose the nature of the sacred, its validity across time and in the face of cultural change. Within literature, this area of discourse can also be expressed as the play between realism and nonrealism, often to test the effectiveness of these modes of exploration.

The role of the sacred, as distinct from the religious,[iv] is—both in terms of a largely denied human experience and as a tool of literary analysis—crucial to a complete understanding of "ethnic" experience in the modern world. It is also not unrelated to a problematisation of violence as the only means of accessing narratives of power. Addressing notions of violence perpetrated in the name of religion allows for a distinction to be drawn between theory and experience, between the religious and the sacred. The need today is for an expansion of contemporary postcolonial theory beyond the limited dimension of the dialectic of power-based-on-violence, to a more visionary exploration of experience explicating the creative and aesthetic dimension of consciousness as a "revolutionary" experience. While I concede some contestation exists towards the complacency of modernity to "the inhuman violence and brutality with which modernity is entwined" (Chrisman 2003: 74), little has been done to reconceptualise and implement viable alternatives.

V.Y. Mudimbe discusses how dominant colonial hegemonies and myths of "African primitiveness" created an illusion that Europe was the centre of civilisation—the "real" world, superior to other worlds (1994: 20). Based on the fear of anything outside the imperial concept of Sameness, Africa was forced into another dimension of reality. As elsewhere in the colonial world, history became transformed into myth, the sacred into the profane. Many African writers today are returning to address these problems. Some, like Ben Okri in *The Famished Road*, take up and challenge metaphors of the real world and create alternative, apparently illusory worlds within "real" Africa. Just as Levy-Strauss argues that the two parallel modes of gaining knowledge—science and magic—can coexist, so for Okri the harsh social realities coexist with a sacred world of bliss and freedom. Myths for Levy-Strauss, "think themselves" (*se pensent eaux-mêmes*): they exist independently and are universal structures through which we are able self-reflexively to observe ourselves and our own culture, so these parallel worlds reflect and clarify each other, annihilating the "mythology" of the Same and Other. Africa, in fact, provides alternatives to the search for "truth" (Mudimbe 1988: 41) and the question of what constitutes knowledge and *where* it is to be located.

Africa for the colonialists was a spiritual "terra incognita" (Mudimbe 1988: 10). Traditional African belief-systems today can still be a challenge to the rational approach of western academics according to Kwame Anthony Appiah who argues that the distinction between the rational and the symbolic is a problematic area when it comes to western academic incursions into African religion and ritual (1992). He cites, in order to refute, Durkheim's conclusion that traditional religion must be symbolically true since it cannot be literally true (187). But what if, we could ask, the beliefs behind ritual observances are literally true? This is a possibility that is proposed in *The Famished Road*, a novel I examine in this chapter, where the spirits and symbolic encounters with the "others" of traditional belief are literally manifested in the lives of the characters. Alternatively, a novel such as Achebe's *The Arrow of God*, never gives the reader privileged access to judge the reality or wisdom of the god—who remains silent in the moment of crisis, a deity who is tantalizingly offered as an alternative to the new Christian God but one who ultimately is deserted by his people.

In a challenge to western intellectuals who may think the beliefs of tradition are false, *The Famished Road* plays with the idea that appeals to the spirit worlds of magic, incantation and ritual may not be invalid, and it normalizes the spiritual as part of the social. As Appiah and Soyinka have both pointed out, the distinction between "sacred" and "profane" is not an aspect of African life: this dichotomy is largely a western creation. Against the background of western rationality, West Africa presents a system of beliefs that hold the community together. In the *Famished Road* one could argue that it is when this system is under greatest threat from western industrialization and the encroachment of destructive change (both ecological and social) that the spirit world is forced to manifest, to literalise itself from metaphor to reality. Thus, the characters of the boy Azaro and eventually also his father encounter the spirit world to be as real as the material social world: the demons that they fight are as real as the bulldozers tearing down the forest. Just as Appiah criticises the structuralist anthropologists who claim that all magic and religion is a symbolic language that can be translated and thus understood, so the manifestation of the beliefs into tangible visible figures are not merely those of language, they are not to be interpreted but experienced in all their rawness and unpredictability. The spirits that Azaro encounters are not to be understood: they are literally "free spirits", capable of endless translations of form and identity, who cannot be so easily referenced nor their behaviour controlled.

Appiah addresses how the "modern European or American" assesses the religious beliefs of other cultures from the perspective of their own. (The so-called traditional worldview that Appiah contrasts to the world's dominant monotheisms is, however, not conceptualized as such by its practitioners, for whom it is "current".) For these believers: "The evidence that spirits exist is obvious: priests go into a trance, people get better after the applications of spiritual remedies, people die regularly from the action of inimical spirits" (1992: 190). In his analysis of Soyinka and African literature, Haney points out how, without its spiritual heritage, Africa falls into a state of "self-alienation" lacking unity and coherence (1994: 162). He argues that Soyinka's remedy to this is not merely through resorting to a repetition of the past, but through its mythology, which "provides a means of self-purification, a means of crossing the gulf between the historical and the mythical self" (ibid: 163). We see this process being acted out in Okri's *The Famished Road*, where the boy Azaro is able to move back and forth between the physical and mythical worlds, to reformulate concepts of both sacred and the profane. His awareness swings between inner and outer, to establish expanded modes of consciousness; he withdraws from one world to communicate with other beings and with other realities. Crossing from the limitations of the "real" social world of Africa across the abyss of time-space, the character offers an insight into the functioning of an unbounded Self that transcends opposites.

3. Diaspora: Exploring problems and solutions

Within discussion of how to resolve the ongoing problems of identity both of individual and nation within the diasporic world, one of the issues that must be dealt with is how to maintain cultural integrity while still accommodating social change. Significantly Robin Cohen explains how diasporas involve "dwelling in a nation-state in a physical sense, but travelling in an astral or spiritual sense that falls outside the nation-state's space-time zone" (Cohen 1997: 134). This often-empowering experience is explored more fully in Ben Okri's *The Famished Road,* which I shall discuss here next, in conjunction with a consideration of other African novels taken from differing religious or sacred traditions, including *Season of Migration to the North,* and *The Arrow of God.* These novels are a sampling of the diversity of African literatures and are not chosen to demonstrate any particular universal structure or concern, but more as random examples of how the sacred can impinge on empowerment and formulations of identity within an overall paradigm of the colonial/postcolonial experience—explored and described in a variety of approaches. The sacred and the religious play an important part in the maintenance of social cohesion in the face of social change. In Achebe's novels, *Things Fall Apart* and *The Arrow of God,* the rites and ceremonies of the indigenous religion are placed in contrast to the religion of the white man; and it is through the ensuing conflict that the characters must align themselves to worldviews and to each other. In *The Arrow of God,* understanding the white men is a central part of survival in the new world order where roads are built connecting enemy villages, roads that run neither to markets nor to work places (and therefore useless). Similarly, the new religion initially seems to be unconnected and totally out of touch with the beliefs, social practices and needs of the Igbo people.

Appiah makes an interesting distinction in comparing Euro-American and West African worldviews that bears relevance here. Citing the work of Robin Horton, he explains how in traditional cultures, "nature, the wild, is untamed, alien and a source of puzzlement and fear. Social relations and persons are, on the contrary, familiar and well understood". On the other hand, in the industrial world, just the opposite is true: nature has been tamed and it is social relations that are "puzzling and problematic" (1992: 197).

By extension I would also suggest that the west views "diasporic" space to involve a movement between physical locales, since it is physical space that is all important, taking precedence over social or psychological spaces of reference. More significant re-locations are those that involve shifts in consciousness, the changing spaces from one state of consciousness to a higher state. The translation of experience between ordinary waking state of consciousness and cosmic consciousness has been compared to waking up after a long dream. Once that inner space has been crossed, there is no looking back. If alienation is held to be a "characteristic state of modern man" (Appiah ibid) where constant flux is the pattern of quotidian existence, it is only through an inner stability that alienation becomes an irrelevant concept. This is where Appiah's distinction between "the pre-colonial African world view" which he equates with the "pre and non-scientific thinkers" who are "inclined to suppose that events in the world have meaning" (ibid: 200) and the western scientific mind, which negates the concept of meaning, falls short: for it is the world of quantum mechanics that has confirmed the non-locability of the local within time and space. Modern science in fact has confirmed, rather than negated, traditional beliefs in the interconnectedness of all things, and the fact that the physical world is manipulated by the mental.[v]

The reclamation of self from relegation to "other" can be established though an encounter with an alternative sacred space. Traditionally, the sacred is associated with devotion to a deity, to a religious site or event, to something considered holy. It can also be connected with the idea of the mystical or epiphanic experience. In the novels I discuss in this chapter, the reforming of self through sacred encounter cannot be achieved without influencing or involving the larger community.[vi] According to Sufi thought, for those on the spiritual path or inner journey:

> Each of us should realise that we are a self-sufficient particle of the whole. Each particle is responsible for the evolution of the world, in proportion to the place it occupies in the cosmos. (Khan 2006)

My discussion here, however, goes beyond the function of mythology or the changes forced or required whereby the practises of religion "keep pace" with the fast pace of social change. The novel *The Famished Road* incorporates these perspectives and magnifies the process within the realm of experience as an inner trauma. The journey towards self-knowledge, and thereby the participation in a wider concern for the world, whether gained willingly and through an epiphanic experience or through traumatic encounter is my next theme.

4. Alternative spiritual spaces: *The Famished Road*

Ben Okri's 1991 Booker-prize winning novel *The Famished Road* addresses the importance of the power of "traditional" beliefs and religious practises and the impact of social change. In the novel, the small boy Azaro is able to traverse the world of the spirits and the world of man. He experiences the home of the human souls that exist in a state of bliss and fulfilment prior to their next human incarnation on earth. He travels not only within his mind, it seems, but also literally between worlds. This is due to the fact that Azaro is an *abiku*, a spirit-child. In the traditional Yoruba belief in the simultaneous existence of several layers of existence, the spirit worlds and the world of the living are separated by a gap that some are able to cross. Before their births, *abikus* enter into a pact with their fellow unborn spirits to die and return to the spirit world as soon as possible. Azaro, however, out of love and compassion for his mother decides to stay in the world of the living, and thus alienates his fellow abiku spirits, who throughout the novel attempt to lure him back to their strange paradise. Although Azaro is torn between these two existences and is tempted to return to this world, it is not one without hazards and fears associated with it. While it is tempting to equate the source of consciousness with the world of the spirits, the two are very different. This is because, without the experience of pure, transcendental, consciousness, even the extent of knowledge to which he has access means little to him; he is seemingly unable to utilise this knowledge for any constructive purpose. The novel, while attempting to create parallel worlds of man and spirit, a return to the theme of an African sacred space, or spiritual dimension, is lacking in its real insight into the field of the transcendent. However, some useful comparisons may be drawn, particularly in the way that the boy alternates his existence between the two realms.

In her analysis of West African novels, Brenda Cooper cites the use of magic realism as a means to "capture reality by way of a depiction of life's many dimensions, seen and unseen, visible and invisible, rational and mysterious." She claims that writers using this technique walk a political tightrope between capturing this reality and providing a utopian escape from that reality (1998: 32). "The idea of transition, change, borders, and ambiguity", she writes, occurs in alternate zones which exist "where burgeoning capitalist development mingles with older pre-capitalist modes in postcolonial societies" (ibid: 15). In *The Famished Road*, the social and economic hardships experienced by the inhabitants of the city ghetto, epitomised in the lives of Azaro's parents, are heightened for the reader by their alternation with the other reality of Azaro's spirit world. Yet the worlds are not mutually exclusive, they overlap, just as traditional values of social annunciation through oral narrative co-exist with "modern" visual text of the community reporter's photo-documentary. Even Nigeria shares this schizophrenic identity; it is delineated as an "abiku" nation: "Our country is an abiku country. Like the spirit-child, it keeps coming and going" (478). Azaro's personal story is symbolic of the nation's struggle to come into and remain in existence. As Thomas Martinek concludes:

> In postmodern fashion, *The Famished Road* challenges the notion of a single, coherent, empirical and "objective" reality. In the narrator-protagonist's consciousness, for instance, the world of the living and the spirit-world, waking-periods and dreams, history and myth are not differentiated. The result is a fictional reality that is frequently surreal, "magical" and astonishing to the reader. (2004)

In his discussion of intersubjectivity in theatre, William Haney explains this type of metaphorical co-existence in terms of sacred space, where the sacred and the profane "converge in a liminal zone of sacred experience, the in-between-ness or beyond-ness we transit whenever we encounter pairs of opposites: subject and object, history and aesthetics" (2006: 21). The result for the reader is a shift in thinking, the astonishment referred to by Martinek, or a "spiralling pattern that encompasses the sacred and the profane, ordinary mind and 'pure' consciousness without content or ideas" according to Haney (ibid: 22). It is an experience of encounter with the sacred, which is defined by Haney in Upanishadic terms of being "neither one pole nor the other, neither this nor that. The spectator oscillates between opposites toward a sacred wholeness that is not a fixed point of reference" (ibid: 24). Furthermore, Haney suggests that this liminal space is an intersubjective space, a "presence" characterized by the "absence" of external boundaries that dissolves the distinction between self and other. Victor Turner similarly refers to a threshold or liminal phase as "a no-man's -land betwixt-and-between the structural past and the structural future as anticipated by the society's normative control" (Turner 1998: 65), a concept that certainly depicts the social relevance of Okri's use of the alternative world of the spirits. Both in terms of individual and society, this liminal space is one of transformation and increased comprehension: the oscillation between worlds allows for a growth in clarity of consciousness. This is due to the experience of a "shift in consciousness", the transition from one state of being to another, which replicates the dynamic within consciousness as it oscillates from point to infinity, from the unified state of "is-ness" to its expression of "am-ness". Within the dynamic, the unified state of the subject (the knower) knows itself—it is a state of self-referral, a state of knowing*ness*. Thus, the swings of awareness taken by a character, such as the boy Azaro, enlivens his own consciousness, while allowing for his awareness to grow. The transcendental level that he gains is characterised by qualities such as increased empathy and compassion, qualities of the unified field at the basis of creation. By experiencing this field (the unified field of all the laws of nature), order in the universe is enlivened; entropy is transformed into orderliness. As Maharishi Mahesh Yogi explains:

> When individuals enliven the Unified Field of natural law . . . everyone in the environment shares the benefits. [. . .] Like a wave coming in from the ocean, the coherence generated from the level of the Unified Field by a few people enriches the lives of all and the population as a whole. (1993: 116-120) [vii]

When Azaro's awareness returns to the "real" world, he is able to compare one world to the other, to encounter all things strange in both worlds and be able to assimilate them into his frame of reference. Gradually he grows in his capacity of witness to events and his wider perspective of understanding them from a disinterested standpoint. Initially, the world of the before-life is presented as harmonious and as a place where Azaro is, as his character explains:

> happy most of the time because we floated on the aquamarine air of love. We played with the fauns, the fairies, and the beautiful beings. Tender sibyls, benign sprites and the serene presences of our ancestors were always with us bathing us in the radiance of their diverse rainbows. (4)

Once Azaro has decided to break away, the influence of that world changes; it becomes a constant source of menace—the former benign companions become a constant other, a constant threat.[viii] Witches, wise women, use of herbal medicine, use of prophecy through the stones, reading omens and entrails: all these aspects of "traditional" Africa are accessed by Okri to create an "exotic" positioning of Africa. This could be problematic, were it not for the fact that these traditional beliefs and rituals are weighted as more valid than the "alternative" world view glimpsed occasionally at the outskirts of their world—that of the whites, Christianity, and technology. These locales are set worlds apart: more distant in world-view and in accessibility than the easy crossings-over between the worlds of human and spirit. Thus, the real choice, if there is one (or rather, the real conflict) is not between spirit/human, since these are on a friction-free level of intimacy, where one can and does influence the other; but on the postcolonial level of tradition/social change, traditional/Eurocentric narratives, self-determination and agency versus exploitation and corruption, jungle/city, spiritual life/social death. Many of these polarised themes are portrayed through the characters' daily lives in the grim and rubbish-littered ghetto: in particular the wretchedness of father's work contrasted with the idealism of his politics (468). Critics such as John C. Hawley (1995) have argued that the postmodern aspects of Okri's novel play deliberately with crossing cultural boundaries, and intertextually parodying both African and European traditions.

The Famished Road can also be read as a parody of African myths and literature. Modern and traditional are juxtaposed, and both problematised, neither more elevated than the other, both are equally authentic. Of course, as Appiah points out, traditional beliefs can always be shifting and, since they are based on oral memory, no written record exists to define and freeze that meaning. Traditions are open to change through constant incorporation of new evidence and experience. The very concept of African identity is one that "draws on other identities central to contemporary life in the sub-continent, namely, the constantly shifting redefinition of 'tribal' identities to meet the economic and political exigencies of the modern world" (287). This is reflected in the novel in the constant transformations of identity—man to beast or bird or dog—suggested as possibilities of other states of conscious being. Parallel traditional versus modern identities also jostle for importance in Azaro's life: the witches, and shamans, healers with local knowledge of herbs, co-exist with the journalist with his camera, the man whose role of witness and recorder of history is able to change the fate of the ghetto. When not recorded by the photographer, it is as if the traumatic events had not happened: "It was if the events were never real. They assumed the status of rumour" (214). The photographer's oppositional stance to the colonial regime and its corrupt followers—together with brief mention of Bible and Christianity and the rule of the whites—are placed textually outside the main narrative. They form another universe out of Azaro's central narratorial experience, which is more at home in the world of the spirits. These alternative visions of the spirit world are contrasted to the world of struggle and suffering in terms of the family and the community of the ghetto. Throughout the text, suffering is depicted as the inability to fulfil desires and the frustration inherent in the knowledge of that lack. Suffering is due to lack of pure consciousness, a lack of vision either profane or spiritual. The desire to reach this more powerful world is merely on the level of manipulative ritual, especially by Azaro's parents; and although these rituals do seem to have some limited results, nothing alleviates their misery and the desperation of poverty.

The enigmatic figure of Madame Koto is the one figure who merges temporal and spiritual power; she is an opportunist in times of social change, who exploits all avenues, calling in prostitutes, political bullies and hostile non-human beings as pawns in her bizarre power games. She exemplifies all the corruption of the "mimic men"; with social change literally at her backdoor as the destruction of the forest and the white man come ever nearer, she embraces and manipulates new technology to ingratiate herself with newness while still on the path of her "traditional" goals. Like the road of the book's title, she is hungry for transformation. This recurring symbol takes on mythical dimensions: the road is also history, a path that leads to heaven or hell (375), the road is changing, but has no end. Like the road being forged through the forest (the symbol of the new destroying the old), a road represents the people's soul: "an infinity of hope and an eternity of struggles" (379).

Yet the ultimate tone of the novel is one of hope for possible transformation. The father's vision that " 'nothing evil will enter our lives'" and so the door to life must be kept open (571) endorses a brave defiance of tragedy and an affirmation of life over suffering. His vision is one of redemption: that the apparent lacks and losses of life contain the infinity of spiritual possibilities. Although Azaro is the "spirit" child, it is his father who speaks the spiritual message of the novel:

> "There is no rest for the soul. God is hungry for us to grow. When you look around and see empty spaces, beware. In those spaces are cities, invisible civilisations, future histories, everything is HERE. We must look at the world with new eyes. We must look at ourselves differently. We are freer than we think. We haven't begun to live yet. [...] We can redream this world and make the dream real. Human beings are gods hidden from themselves. [. . .]The world that we see and the world that is there are two different things.[...] There is a stillness which makes you travel faster. There is a silence which makes you fly. If your heart is a friend of Time nothing can destroy you". (571-2)

Thus, ultimately, the true border crossings from ignorance to enlightened understanding are made by Azaro's father; it is he who reconciles the spiritual and quotidian worlds, it is he who defeats the demons of both tradition and modernity.

5. *Heart of Darkness* and *Season of Migration to the North*

Edward Said has pointed out how Tayeb Salih's famous novel *Season of Migration to the North* stands as reversal of *Heart of Darkness*, where the journey is now to the north into Europe. He sees Mustafa Sa'eed as "a mirror image of Kurtz", whose violence destroys both himself and "the narrator's understanding" (1994: 255). This argument can be elaborated further than Said takes it, especially since the narrator is frequently referred to by his friend Mahjoub as "mad" and that he soon finds himself in a similar predicament to Marlow as narrator, in having to bear witness to the other man's story and eventually endorse its terrifying contradictions. The passage to knowledge and its inherent responsibility is an ethical challenge to both the narrators, one that endorses the dilemma in T.S.Eliot's poem "Gerontian": "After such knowledge, what forgiveness?" The knowledge that both narrators gain is so powerfully corrosive that both men fall into a state of willed annihilation, a willing lapse into a death-like state of illness (in the case of Marlow) or near-suicide (for Salih's narrator). These men lack a stable notion of the self as an expression of non-changing consciousness. They lack the knowledge of immortal never-changing reality of the self that Lord Krishna gives to Arjuna as described in the Bhagavad-Gita: "Weapons cannot cleave it, nor fire burn it; water cannot wet it, nor wind dry him away. [. . .] It is eternal, all pervading, stable, immovable, ever the same"(2, 23-24).

The powerful negative entropy that both Kurtz and Sa'eed display apparently obliterates the maintenance of ego in the men who act as their confessors, their witnesses. Like Coleridge's wedding guest, they are unwilling victims of apparently life-negating narration. Just as Marlow recounts his story to the four friends collected on deck one evening at a time and place far removed from the original events, so *Season*'s narrator is telling his story to the undisclosed "gentlemen" addressed in the opening sentence. Who are these mysterious "gentlemen": the jury in a court of law, perhaps, or us as readers? Are we in fact unwittingly being put into the same position as these narrators, or the fated Wedding Guest himself, by being told the story?

Yet for these witnesses to narrative, it is a process of discovery of both the other and the self: the reader/listener is also taken on the path of growth of personal wisdom. This journey reaches its crisis in a similar manner in both novels, at the moment of the opening of a "secret" room and unknown text. The narrator's eventual unlocking of Sa'eed's secret room mirrors Marlow's discovery of Kurtz's hut, which he can barely bring himself to glance inside. Sa'eed has his trophies of the women he has both loved and eliminated. Like Kurtz, Sa'eed bequeaths his writing, his book collection, to the narrator. Kurtz had written "exterminate all the brutes": Sa'eed has metaphorically taken his revenge by murdering the white women with whom he has had sexual relations. In Conrad's novel the position of the European woman, Kurtz's Intended, is fraught with the problem of her positioning: she is both "innocent" and "guilty", pristine and yet condemned as part of the imperial civilisation and its materialist and emotional demands that pollute the hearts of both Kurtz and Marlow. The complicity is also alluded to in the characters of Isabelle Seymour and Jean Morris, the English women in Sa'eed's life, who seem self-aware of their volatile cultural position while being with the self-confessed "Othello", a man who will both love and murder them.

To take Said's comparison to *Heart of Darkness* one step further, one can also argue that Mustafa Sa'eed's journey taken into the heart of colonial darkness—in other words, London—is on a metaphorical level an inner journey. If the heart of darkness is located in the Congo, it is clearly London that is the omphalos of darkness, the origin and centre. It is the seat of the government that for centuries has maintained a foreign policy of global destruction, through its main maxim of Divide and Conquer, and through the arms trade. London is, as Marlow comments as he sits in meditative pose, one of "the dark places on earth" (Conrad 1995: 18).

The interconnections between metropolis and colony in Conrad's novel, the interplay of and contrasts between metropolitan leisure and imperial "reality", are signified through commodity fetishism (ivory) and the body of the colonial African (Chrisman 2003: 28-29). The various instances of dichotomisation in how the symbolic and the representational co-exist in the novel, described at length by Chrisman, can also be used to chart how Marlow's narrative is torn between periphery and centre, a feature that is again comparable to Heidegger's concept of *das Riss*, the violent striation in space-time that forges a new artistic state of understanding. Gayatri Spivak extends Heidegger's concept to discuss the violence inherent within the colonial project, the rending apart of a landscape to create a "recovered and interpreted" space of colonial power (Spivak 1999:114). Marlow can be seen as a part (if unwilling) of the colonial project of reinscribing the blank spaces of Africa. Similarly, the distancing narrative techniques provide such a time-space rift, and one that Conrad exploits for its full effect, swinging the reader's awareness between polarities of veracity.

While *Heart of Darkness* is a tale told on the banks of the Thames, in Salih's novel the setting of confrontation of interpreted narrative and truth, between Empire and Africa, is a village on the banks of the river Nile in Sudan. It is here that Sa'eed reveals his life story and having told his story, mysteriously disappears. The symbolism of the river in *Heart of Darkness* has been much commented on; the river for Marlow is a place where "the surface, the reality [. . .] fades. The inner truth is hidden—luckily, luckily" (60). A spiritual questor, such as Marlow, who has spent over six years in the East and sits to tell his story in "the pose of a Buddha preaching in European clothes and without a lotus flower" would be aware of the river traditionally as a place of spiritual transformation, a place where enlightenment, Moksha, is gained through meditation on non-change within change. For the Marlow of "Youth", the sea stands as the symbolic background to knowledge and experience, the sea that the test of physical strength; it is the river that is the test of spiritual and moral strength.

Yet speaking of the time back in the Congo, in *The Heart of Darkness* Marlow describes the snake-like river is a place of mysterious intensity and supernatural dangers: "Going back up that river was like travelling back to the earliest beginnings of the world [. . .] An empty stream, a great silence, an impenetrable forest" (959). The river of terror that runs though the Congo is one that the older and wiser Marlow cannot escape, since for him it is an extension of the same river on which he sits to tell his story—the Thames.

In *Season of Migration*, the confrontation of self (or lack of self) and other is more acute since it is also one of culture, a juxtaposition of the Islamic and western worldviews. Amin Malek, however, has discussed how the novel was written to redress previous romanticisation and to spearhead the idea of cultural tolerance (2005). Mustafa Sa'eed travels to England in a reversal of the colonial desire to travel east and plunder the new country for its inherent wealth both physical and intellectual. He goes beyond being a mimic man, wreaking his own sense of revenge on the culture, chiefly through its women. In *Orientalism* Edward Said writes that for the western man, the Orient suggests "not only fecundity but sexual promise (and threat), untiring sensuality, unlimited desire" (1979: 146). Salih's protagonist directly reverses this view, seeing Europe as the location to unleash his desires for satisfaction and revenge. This is problematic in itself, since it seems to endorse the white myths and fears described by Sara Suleri's "The Unspeakable Limits of Rape" and by Said who cites the Eurocentric trope of India as a female body to be raped, a metaphor similarly used by Fanon earlier in the context of Algeria.

Sa'eed's story is narrated much as Marlow narrates the events in "Youth" and *Heart of Darkness*, as all part of a distant past, and it is recalled in the hindsight of greater knowledge. Indeed, the courteous and neighbourly older Mustafa Sa'eed seems to bear little or no resemblance to the man he claims to have been. His young wife obviously adores him and he is the kind father of two young sons. Can we therefore assume that he is the same man? The narrator is convinced that Sa'eed "is a lie" (49). He defines his own reality by the fact he is from "here" rather than "there": he throws into juxtaposition the reality of Africa and the unreality of London. The problem stems from the fact that the lies the narrator is confronted with, personified by Sa'eed, are the creation of the colonial encounter:

> The fact that they came to our land, I know not why, does that mean that we should poison our present and our future? Sooner or later they will leave our country just as many people throughout history left many countries. [. . .] Once again we shall be as we were—ordinary people—and if we are lies we shall be lies of our own making. (50)

For the narrator, Sa'eed is a fabrication of the colonial power, and therefore lacks reality. Once the narrator has exposed the core of Sa'eed's life and library (there is significantly nothing Arab among the books), he has freed himself from being the custodian of his life and his family. The narrator finds himself to be the mirror image of Sa'eed and fears the consequences: if Sa'eed's life is a lie then the narrator's must be also. Salih's narrator sinks almost literally to the same level as Sa'eed in that he takes the life of another, or appears to (the reader is left to assume the man dies), yet he finds redemption through the ritual and metaphorical death by drowning. His near drowning in the river is symbolically the start of a new life, and the deliberate choosing of life over death—and indeed the same symbolic rebirth takes place for Kipling's Kim and Ondaatje's Kip. All three of these characters have been torn between loyalties and identities of nation and *culture,* and it is at this climactic moment where they actively choose to which culture they belong—they make a conscious reformulation of self after which their lives will be transformed.

Sa'eed is a man who is full of hatred and full of anger against the civilisation that has nurtured and educated him. Yet from anger comes delusion and disillusionment, and also the failing of the rational intellect. The mythos of the new life, of strength out of weakness and knowledge coming out of ignorance incorporates a transformation of consciousness. This aspect of the novel can be explored through the mysterious and seemingly indefinable character of Mustafa Sa'eed. The moment of illumination is a short conversation between the narrator and his friend, when both are drunk—a moment when the intellect can be suspended and the intuitive truth realised—but, like in a dream, probably forgotten. Indeed, next morning "each of us woke up in his own house not knowing how he'd got there" (108), and the narrator does not refer to the idea again. This is the idea that "Mustafa Sa'eed is in fact the Prophet El-Khidr, suddenly making his appearance and as suddenly vanishing" (107).

According to Barbara Annan, El-Khidr comes to raise consciousness and to lift the veil of maya, illusion. Khidr, the Islamic messenger of God, represents "the stranger, who shakes our subjectivity and alters our consciousness" (2002: 101). Moreover, an encounter with Khidr is "a mythic meeting with the archetypal Other" (ibid) that causes a permanent shift in perception, to "break down old ways of being and knowing" (107). These new ways of gaining knowledge go beyond and undermine the intellect; they "bestow a *khirqua*, a mantel of spiritual responsibility and non-judgemental acceptance" (ibid: 109). This perhaps is the key to the role of Marlow and Salih's narrator: they are ultimately non-judgemental; they pass on their stories without condemning their protagonists. Here, then, we have another similarity; they are both presented as figures on the mystical journey from spiritual ignorance to knowledge. Annan concludes that:

> Out of this experience of disorientation the intellect must alter its horizon, admit to unknowing in the face of the Other, and accept what could not have been tolerated previously. [. . .] it is a liminal passage of re-birth, for the new consciousness is more inclusive and tolerant of that which was previously rejected. Ethical horizons are broadened as the experience of the Other creates an influx of previously inaccessible wisdom, and perhaps a form of grace (113).

One predominant form of Islam in some parts of Africa is Sufi, and it is in the Sufi poem *The Conference of the Birds* that a story "The fool of God and Khidr" indicates that man and Khidr are not compatible since "the trickster" has "drunk long draughts from the water of immortality so that you will always exist. [. . .] Whilst you are busy preserving your life, I sacrifice mine every day. It is better I leave you, as birds leave the snare" (Attar tr. Nott 1974: 17). The meeting of mortal man and the immortal El-Khidr seems threatening to man and yet, viewed from another perspective, or level of consciousness, it must be transformative in positive ways. Encounter with these narratives is also life transforming, as we have seen. "What is established when the human 'I' the subject, the doer, expresses its object in accordance with reality, is a new personality" (Massingnon 1982: 293). If this is the case, then the reading of *Season of Migration to the North* must change to become one of an encounter with the sacred as life affirming. Tayeb Salih's novel can thus be read as being about both a colonial and a spiritual encounter. The moment of illumination is the realisation that all is Maya, illusion. This can result in a destablising of self, leading to a *via negativa* of doubt and suffering, or a moment of bliss, such as that experienced by David Lurie in *Disgrace*—where the eternal moment negates the doubts of temporality. This is one meaning of the "migration", of the diaspora experience of relocation—a repositioning of self within one's perception of the cosmos.

El-Khidr is traditionally the eternal wanderer, the green man, the trickster, and teacher of Moses, whose appearances and disappearances are associated with water. Most importantly, he moves between the temporal-material and spiritual worlds; he is "the spiritual teacher within us, the spark in the heart, our inborn secret. [On the mystical journey] Khidr is always present, is always our invisible companion" (Vaughan-Lee 2000: 163). Here, the introduction of El-Khidr, the figure who gives access to the inner reality (ibid) also provides a figure of Islam to counter and provide an antidote, and alternative spirituality, to Christian English colonialism "from within the heritage of the society"—as Soyinka discusses is evident in other African novels (1976: 78). Sa'eed/El Khadr is a deconstructive figure, the voice of anti-British culture–although he is uncritical of previous Arab invasions and colonisation. Soyinka perhaps answers this seemingly problematic omission by citing how:

> In colonial societies which constantly seek a world-view to challenge the inherent iniquities of any philosophy which can be associated with the colonial intrusion, we naturally encounter works which make a point of claiming that Islam—a very effective organised challenge to Christian cultural authority—is

one religion whose ethics, philosophy and form of worship reconciles races and encourages universal fraternalism. (ibid: 77)

Significantly, the narrator and his friend realise the truth about Sa'eed when they are drunk, a condition that has long been a metaphor of spirituality in Sufi, a trope of *insight*. (The poems of Rumi, for example, frequently use the trope of drunkenness to indicate the bliss of the Absolute, or of union with "the Beloved".) Madness and drunkenness are both metaphors for the pure joy of transcendence. As Hazrat Inayat Khan explains, Devotion, one of the paths to God-realisation, "is the heavenly wine, which intoxicates the devotee until his heart becomes purified from all infirmities and there remains the happy vision of the Beloved, which lasts to the end of the journey" (2006). The same experience is described in Sanskrit poetics by the oxymoron "wild tranquillity" and "passionless passion" (Krishnamoorty 1968: 26), an ecstasy that transcends ordinary emotion. The goal of the journey for the Sufi is ideal perfection, which is:

called Baqa by Sufis, is termed "Najat" in Islam, "Nirvana" in Buddhism, "Salvation" in Christianity, and "Mukhti" in Hinduism. This is the highest condition attainable, and all the ancient prophets and sages experienced it, and taught it to the world. (Khan : ibid)

Similarly, from the Vedic perspective:

The goal is no longer elevation in life (*abhyudaya*) but liberation from all the limitations of life (*moksha*). The bonds of life are caused by ignorance (*ajnana*). That which alone can remove ignorance is knowledge (*jnana*). (Ramachadran 1980: 37)

For the fragmented and unenlightened, and significantly name-less narrator of *Season of Migration*, the encounter with El Khadr negates his other possible identities we may have toyed with as readers: Was the Sa'eed episode a figment of the narrator's imagination, of his playing out some desired "Mr Hyde" persona? Or did Sa'eed represent an embodiment of his repressed desires, the life he did not live during his seven years in England, and his own anger towards colonialisation? He comes face to face with himself in the mirror—an instant where self becomes indistinguishable from Other. Viewing his character from the perspective of the spiritual traveller, however, the narrator undergoes "traditional" trials by fire and by water. His illumination comes in an "instant":

> I know not how long or short it was—the reverberation of the river turned into a piercingly loud roar and at the very same instant there was a vivid brightness like a flash of lightening. [. . .] Then my mind cleared and my relationship to the river was determined. Though floating on the water, I was not part of it. (168)

He "dies" to self and emerges as a seeker of truth: "Now I am making a decision. I choose life" (ibid), where he must surrender all and cry for help, just as he does in the last word of the book. From whom does he cry for help—from man or from God?

The narrator is then propelled on the inner path to purification, a path that entails both the mental purification of knowledge and the transformation of action from being driven by desire and goal-orientated, to being performed without the desire for objective results. The narrator chooses life because "I have duties to discharge. It is not my concern whether or not life has meaning" (168). His detachment is such that he compares himself to " a common actor shouting on the stage" (169): he is able to witness himself as performer of action. His experience can be likened to that described by Krishna in the Bhagavad-Gita:

> "Truly there is in this world nothing so purifying as knowledge;
> he who is perfected in Yoga,
> of himself in time finds this within himself". (3, 48)

According to Vedic texts, in the state of Enlightenment, the individual awareness wakes up to reality: The Self becomes aware of its own fluctuations, the fluctuations that eternally exist within the eternity of its own silence. Every experience of transcending (the experience of Pure or transcendental consciousness) is a step of further awakening, in which the Self becomes progressively awake to itself. Vedic Science describes how first the Self knows itself; it is awake to itself as the field of infinite silence. As the Self wakes up more and more to its infinite status, it cognises and re-cognises within itself the totality of intelligence. Infinite dynamism is located in the field of infinite silence. For the narrator of *Season of Migration*, the moment of consciousness in-between life and death, in-between sleep and waking awareness, is an extended moment of silence. It is also a location significantly "between north and south", neither this place nor another, neither one culture nor another, in which he "was unable to continue, unable to return" (167).

This gap is significant in terms of the growth of consciousness. In all the higher states of consciousness preceding Unity Consciousness in the growth of individual enlightenment there is an apparent dichotomy between the infinity of the Self, which is wide awake, and the finiteness of the world. This gap or dichotomy provides an opportunity of relocating consciousness from ignorance to knowledge. In the Vedas, the "mistake of the intellect" is known as *Pragya Apharadha* and it exists when the knower does not find the process of knowing (Devata) and the object of knowledge (Chhandas) within itself, and none of the three finds its full value as Samhita (togetherness). There is thus a gap between relative and Absolute, and a gap in the structure of knowledge. As individual awareness awakens to its infinite value, the specific impulses of consciousness are all absorbed in the infinity of the Self, and *Pragya Apharadha* is transcended. The awakening of individual consciousness means that the mistake of the intellect *Pragya Apharadha* is dissolved. Here, the narrator suddenly finds that "my mind cleared and my relationship to the river was determined. Though floating on the water I was not part of it" (168). The final stage of awakening of human consciousness reveals that this dichotomy is an illusion; it is a product of maya. The sense of separation is an experience of partial enlightenment, where the world perceived is still distinct from the inner experience of pure consciousness. When the experience of transcendental consciousness becomes a living reality sustained throughout the states of waking, sleep and dream, then the experience dawns that "I *am* self-referral consciousness. The world is as I am: I am infinite and so is the world".

6. A revolution of relationships: *Admiring Silence*

A novel that in many ways can be seen as a rewriting of *Season of Migration to the North* is Abdulrazak Gurnah's *Admiring Silence*. In both novels, the intellectual prowess of the protagonist takes him to London, and the hostile world of English culture and women. Both novels involve a return to the homeland of East Africa, and the social and political ("postcolonial") ramifications of returning as an "alien" in one's own home. Where, in *Season of Migration*, relationships with women become an individual's form of exacting a brutal cultural revenge, in *Admiring Silence*, a relationship with an Englishwoman is depicted as the sole means of reconciling cultural differences and overcoming alienation. In this novel, the protagonist-narrator relocates as a student from the East coast of Africa to London, a city that he finds alien and inhospitable until he begins a long-term love affair with Emma, with whom he eventually has a daughter. His happiness is unalloyed, and even the hostility of Emma's parents can be overcome through the construction of narratives of "enlightened Empire" with which to indulge all their preconceived notions of the savagery and squalor from which he apparently comes, and through which to confirm their own superiority as white and English.

The narratives are told with bitter irony, totally lost on a willingly-beguiled Mr Willoughby (Emma's father). The stories through which the narrator constructs his own identity and family background for Emma, however, are more subtly destructive: for they fabricate a more plausible personal and national history, one so close to the "real" one that it is alluring for the reader, as well as Emma, to believe that this narrative is the true account of events that brought him to England. However, the narrator reveals early on (the start of chapter two) that the main players in his family history, his father and his Uncle Hashim, are "created . . . more or less" (35), as are all the stories of family and national history –and these involving the struggles for and aftermath of independence.

When the narrator has the opportunity to travel back to his home on Zanzibar, the main journey is to rediscover his family roots, and above all the identity of his father, who abandoned his mother before his birth. The "father" he invented for Emma is non-existent, a figment constructed out of a void of wishes and projections. The truth he eventually learns from long conversations with his mother in fact reveals nothing more than the fact his father had left mysteriously; no one knew exactly where or why, only that he had gone. One void being replaced by another, the narrator falls back on his love for Emma for his sense of belonging. He rejects his family's attempt to marry him to a local girl and re-establish his life with them. Like his father, he must leave, this time under a cloud of disapproval and his mother's disownment. Frustrated in his attempt to create a "true life narrative" in Africa, he returns to his fictionalised world; his stepfather is once again referred to as the character "Uncle Hashim" and as an exoticised "grandee in his threadbare emporium" (185). Once he dares to at last tell the one *true* event of his life, that he has an English wife and daughter, he is, according to his step-father and the community, lost: " 'You've lost yourself, and you've lost your people. A man is nothing without his people'" (193).

Returning to England, he discovers that he has also lost Emma, who leaves him for another relationship, away from "the fanged love that made her want to diminish and silence me" (210). Finally free from being silenced, from twisting narrative into being what he thinks other people want to hear, and from honouring silence in all its forms as a valid modus operandi, he is able to speak from the heart, and speak with the violence of own voice at last: "May God block her anus with clotted blood" (211).

From having admired silence, the narrator is ultimately silenced by the vast hostility of both society and family. In an ironic reversal, his desire to reveal and narrate both roots and routes ends in his being silenced *by* them. By the end of the novel, he is intent on becoming a breaker rather than a maintainer of silences—now that silences are not indicative of a refined or ironic private knowledge, nor do they represent any spiritual transcendency. Rather, the silence indicated by the novel's central theme is revealed to be that of the silent complicity with evil. This is in juxtaposition to those who do not nod their heads in silent acquiescence, to the Salman Rushdie's of the world who speak out their versions of truth, even if it is misunderstood. "He was another admirer of silence, the Imam [Khomeini]" (209).

Throughout the novel, the narrator's reconstruction, or rather invention, of the past goes beyond a mere Fanonian desire to reclaim historical validity in the wake of colonial palimpsests, however. It also undermines the validity of the Fanonian rewriting project, since it poses the question, whose "native voice" is the authentic one anyway, and how do we know that this account is not one of partial or traumatised, inaccurate memory. In *Admiring Silence*, the past that is reconstructed is constantly shifting, as much a product of the perceived desire of the audience or listener as it is the intent of the narrator to recite a catalogue of "truth". For that truth is internal, not external, it is constructed in consciousness, relating to the need of the present moment rather than faith to any past continuum. The unnamed narrator is not beholden to his absent family to tell the truth about them, and his omissions in his life story as he has failed to recount to them leads to his eventual abandonment and disownment. His family reject him, leaving him to his only other option which is to re-enter the foreign incomprehensible narrative of life in England. His family and his father are a heritage to be played with, manipulated, turned upside-down, more in the spirit of carnivalesque than postcolonial. Even though the colonial and postcolonial play a large part in constructing the uncertainties and problems of the narrator's fractured and "alien" life (for, like most exiles, he can identify "home" with neither England nor his homeland), his return to his native Zanzibar is doomed through his own inability to adapt his own invented story to their reality, with all its quotidian trials of food shortages, electricity cuts, blocked toilets, and corrupt politicians—just the sort of squalid "African-ness" he had exploited in his stories to Emma.

The reader is beguiled by the stories, just as are Emma and her father. In the layers of twisted truth, the narrator acts like the Trickster, arriving from outside to upset society, expose truth, and having left havoc behind, disappear again. The layers of narrative, the "inventions" of personal and national history, co-exist however for the reader; they become equally valid versions of the past. The "true/false" versions co-exist, just as do the characters of the father, the stepfather, and Uncle Hashim. This is the "truth" of the narrative: that opposites co-exist in our consciousness. Like the narrator, as readers we are searching for the untold truth of the past and piece together the "whole" out of the information revealed. The search for his absent father is also a search for the "truth" as the infinitely deferred transcendent. His unknown father—the seed of identity and self-awareness—can only be known through knowledge of the self.

The sacred surrender of Islam and the enlightenment of Sufism are projected as a "solution" to the colonial situation in *Season of Migration to the North*; Islam also holds a place of significance in *Admiring Silence*. The narrator finds "a home" he can relate to and find peace in the village mosque, a fact that surprises him. Only there is he accepted for himself, free from narration. Like the female sanctuary of the *hammam*,[ix] (and involving similar rituals of preparation and cleansing) at the mosque one leaves one's pretences of class, wealth and education at the door with one's shoes. In the mosque he overcomes his feelings of inadequacy, fear, and rampant sardonicism, and at last he finds a place where, "They did not think me alien" (137).

The absent father can be seen as representing a longing for transcendence, and the novel suggests Islam as a possible mode and system of transcendences. The silence of the mosque is a void in thought that represents escape, the sacred space that does not require (or permit) narration. The narrator's story-telling and fabricated "truth" do not extend to his hours spent in prayer; the mosque remains a place represented by the aporias, by the gaps in his text. He mentions his daily attendance at the calls to prayer, he mentions his returning home: but the experience inside is a time/space that transcends the need for oral or textual documentation.

In other texts, however, religion in all its forms is divorced from experience of growth of conscious awareness. For writers such as Chinua Achebe and Naguib Mahfouz, viewing the postcolonial condition from a historical perspective, religion is the catalyst of political turmoil and social unrest.

7. Sacred struggle: *Things Fall Apart* and *The Arrow of God.*

In Achebe's trilogy of the colonial project in Nigeria (of which I discuss here the first two novels *Things Fall Apart* and *The Arrow of God*), it is Christianity that is implicated in the destruction of traditional society, or more ironically in "The Pacification of the Primitive Tribes of the Lower Niger" (the title of the book planned by the District Commissioner in *Things Fall Apart*). Both novels deal with the personalisation of social tragedies, the downfall of clan leaders, inherent when indigenous beliefs and the new religion clash. The epitome of African "otherness" is ironically transposed; the belief in the protection and vengeance of the gods of the Africans becomes tragically transmuted into ignorance and gullibility. The religiosity of the Christians merely, of course, covers their real political and commercial intentions, yet the efficacy of the traditional gods is erased through their *social* failure to protect the interests of the villagers. The power of the gods (and the ancestors) depends on their masked representations; in the *egwugwu* ceremony the masks that permit people to represent the spirits come to life, yet they are unable to prevent the downfall of the society. The "mask" of easy compromise worn by the missionary Mr Brown is ripped off to expose the heart of the new religion in the form of the wrathful Rev Smith, who "saw the world as a battlefield in which the children of light were locked in mortal conflict with the sons of darkness" (151). In both cases the sacred is perceived by the characters as a source of power, of influence and of manipulation: the sacred is not entered into as an experience through which to gain "higher" (by which I intend to mean altruistic) wisdom, and therefore the result is inevitably a continuation of suffering. For "darkness" to be removed, a third element of the light must be introduced; without that principle of the third element, the "sacred" remains a secular domain.

In *The Arrow of God*, the "native" rites of the people take on a Conradian heart-beat of darkness, while the new religion offered by the established colonials is toyed with by the Igbo as a useful means of gaining "whiteman's knowledge". The village people, particularly the ambitious chief priest Ezeula, tolerate and assimilate the new religion in their desire to gain acceptance. The attempt to juggle maintaining power over his own people, retaining contact with his god and performing all the necessary rituals of appeasement, meanwhile currying favour with the white administration, creates a seemingly unworkable dichotomy of loyalties. Although an ordinary man, for the villagers he is the direct connection between god and the elders, and the only source of maintenance of a harmonious society. Outside this framework, the existence of Winterbottom and his colonial administration removes any real agency from these traditional Igbo institutions.

The narrative highlights the importance of ritual in maintaining the social order, yet neither religion has ethical ascendancy, nor efficacy, over the other. Belief in the protection of the sacred python is challenged through Ezeulu's son Oduche (whom the priest has sent to learn the ways of the new religion) when he tries to suffocate a living representative of the belief. Rather than eliminating the source of external threat to the community, Ezuelu unwittingly is the source of the collapse of the old ways. The trapped python comes to represent a clash of civilisations and world-views, the perspectives of individuals and society, when individual ambition causes the collapse of social cohesion—ultimately, a selling out of the old indigenous to the foreign and new. Through his personal ambition, Ezuelu steps outside being the core of cohesion for his society, yet he still represents the entrapment of his people, as Ezuelu literally walks into the trap of being imprisoned by the colonial foreigners (whom he had been so eager to impress) with all the symbolic loss of dignity and power that this involves. Trapped also between his religious and political roles, he is caught between his god and his community, and he ultimately destroys himself through a decision instrumental in making his people suffer. Unwittingly, he creates the necessary gap in power and control of the god he represents to allow the Christian God and the white man to come in and "save" the harvest and the people. Here, the balanced coexistence between nature, man, and the sacred is destroyed, and the future of the society is left in a fragile and volatile impasse. Like his earlier novel *Things Fall Apart*, this novel reveals all the tragedies of loss of cultural integrity—a result of the inability to maintain stability, integrity, and yet adaptability in collective consciousness —in the midst of the "preventable historical tragedy" (Newell 2006: 87) of cultural contact with Europe.

For much of the globe, Christianity and Islam are (apparently) irreconcilable) religions spread through invading cultures. Yet both religions represent a diverse and multicultural panorama of customs and beliefs, and engender a corresponding diversity of literature. Due to its long history, the "alien" nature of Islam and Arabic is contested by most African Muslims, who are able to identify with a more global Islamic identity (Newell 2006: 45-46), although writers such as Nawal El Saadawi and others cite the patriarchal and masculinist nature of the language as being more problematical than its origins outside Africa. Wole Soyinka sees Islam as being as external to African culture as Christianity (although historically, the first mosque outside Arabia was set up in El Quarouran, Tunisia). Both religions have influenced African literature and the interplay of literature, language and culture, while both Christian and Islamic schools vie for political and religious control via language and education across Africa. While these two great religions scramble for dominance, the origins of the sacred are obscured, and it could be argued that oral literature accesses more intrinsic realities of the expressions of consciousness and its manifestations without mediation. African literatures that attempt to access tropes of oral tradition often do so with all the unexpurgated "rawness" of those modalities where the sacred meets the chthonic, before cultures separated the raw from the cooked.

8. Social struggle: novels of Egypt

Travelling in literary terms to North Africa and Egypt, in Ahdaf Soueif's *Aisha*, the context of devotional and mystic Islam becomes a threatening backdrop to gendered violence, and presents a void of conceptual meaning or social stability. Implicating Said's formulations of the historical invention of a Western discourse that persistently misrepresents Islam, especially within the Arab world, the novel addresses orientalist issues of feminism and agency within contemporary Egyptian society. Yet traditional religious structures are characterised within class dichotomies (attendance at a Sufi *Zar* is depicted as lower-class and beneath Aisha's social and educational status) that further problematize their efficacy and continuing contemporary relevance. Through the societal intermediary of her nurse, Aisha is able to pass between social strata, however, with her nurse acting as guide, manoeuvring her through the unknown cultural and religious terrain. Colliding with forces of inescapable masculinist power structures inherent within religion and society, Aisha, while consciously attempting to free herself from these hegemonies, unconsciously plays into the power fantasies of a young man, who enforces through rape the power society traditionally bestows him. Aisha's search for alternative "spiritual" experience and female empowerment thus has disastrous, and ultimately fatal, consequences.

In Mahfouz's allegorical novel *Children of the Alley*, religious "myth" is recast within the mould of social reality; the mystical or sacred is translated into the machinations of power and inter-clan violence. Written in the oeuvre of Mahfouz's concern with diagnosing and documenting the human predicament and suggesting remedial cures in socialism and science, the novel displays a panorama of characters, who lead the reader through the stories of Adam and Eve's expulsion from Paradise, Moses, Jesus and Mohammed. The narratives are structured both to reveal the original religious bases and simultaneously deny their sacred foundations; the "myths" are in fact "demythologised" (El-Enany 1998: 76). Even "God" is killed. Yet this is not a simple oppositional structure, the binaries of sacred/profane are endorsed through the very nature of the intertextuality and the hint of utopianism in the novel's ending. The series of political rebels and despots becomes a catalogue of human suffering and exploitation, each one ultimately failing the "people of the alley" who represent humanity. Apparently championing "modern science" as a saviour of mankind, despite its obvious dangers if it is used for the wrong purposes, Mahfouz spells out "what he had only half said before [...] the irrelevance of religion to the social predicament of modern man" (ibid: 77). Denying the possibility or reality of mystical transcendencies also implicates a collapse of ethical bases to behaviour: the novel reads as a tedious catalogue of amoral villains and tyrants. In *Children of the Alley*, this void in belief simultaneously exposes the need for one; the flagrant denial of the sacred exposes in Miltonian style how perilous and hollow life is on the edge of the abyss.

In terms of postcolonialism, Edward Said's arguments explicate how literature must be read in a way to foreground unethical issues and illuminate cultural injustices. This can be achieved by close reading through political awareness and making critical connections between apparently disparate phenomena. The ability to hold contradictions within a single thought, to achieve contrapuntal readings of texts is a characteristic of consciousness itself: the ability to perceive a unity beneath apparent appearances. Said's work strove to overcome contradictions and urged for the need for reconciliation in political life by embracing that which appears irreconcilable. The next chapter analyses texts that access the territory of direct experience of the sacred, through the quotidian encounter with the undivided though apparently opposing space of the physical and spiritual. Texts again explore and differentiate between the religious, the sacred and the experience of higher states of consciousness. A formulation of higher states of consciousness, both individual and collective, is suggested as valuable in breaking down the self-Other dichotomy. A new paradigm of sacred space transcends boundaries and goes beyond a Bhabhian hybridity to a more profound formulation that offers the possibility of co-existence and reconciliation, expanding current understanding of the concepts of self/other, and local/global. As Vaughan-Lee (2000: 167) emphasises, the "way of Khidr is both an inner mystery and a practical reality".

[i] I am aware of the position of Fanon and Ngugi that can be summed up in the argument that African writers using languages other than their indigenous mother-tongue are "vehicles of a foreign culture whose continuing imitation or acceptance in the literature of post-colonial society is indicative of persisting subjugation" (Asante-Darko 2005).

[ii] The need to shift mode of awareness is comparable from the shift in physics from the classical to the quantum mechanical: a shift that the general public has never made in its world view. This is one reason why the development of quantum mechanics was so problematic. The physicists of that era attempted to understand quantum mechanical phenomena in terms of the principles of classical physics. They failed miserably, for two main reasons: Firstly, the axioms of the theories necessary to understand quantum mechanics are different from those of classical physics, and secondly, quantum mechanics is at a deeper, more profound level of Nature. Thus, in the opposite direction, it *is* possible to understand classical phenomena in terms of the principles of quantum mechanics – they are expressions of the quantum mechanical. The quantum mechanical is *not* an expression of the classical, and cannot be explained in those terms.

[iii] The sacred and profane, even within European cultures is a dichotomy often expressed linguistically, the Italian *destra/ sinistra* being an obvious example.

[iv] I am in agreement here with Malekin and Yarrow who delineate, "The sacred is not, in the ordinary sense of the word, religious, especially in the way the term has developed within the context of the monotheisms" (Malekin and Yarrow 2001:59)

[v] See John Hagelin (2006) inter alia.

[vi] See also the discussion on *The Mistress of Spices*, where magic is seen as both terrible and wonderful.

[vii] To corroborate this claim, extensive scientific research has shown that when a group of people practice techniques of meditation (the TM and TM-Sidhi programme) in which they regularly reach this level of experience, trends in the society are influenced in a positive direction.

[viii] The depiction of the "jungle"/ bush as an experience of otherness is comparable to Hawthorn's short story "Young Goodman Brown", where the forest of the unknown is the source of fear for the community.

[ix] For writers including Assia Djebar and Fatima Mernissi, the *hammam* is a female space of cleansing and purification, both a place of escape from the outside world and a space of agency. It is only in this space that the voice "speaks true", for it speaks the "heart's truth" (Djebar 1985: 149).

Chapter Seven
The Literature of Human Survival:
Envisaging Alternatives

The nightmare is over; we are free at last. But the thing that is making me tremble, that I do not want to say out loud—and I'll say it once only and its done.
Was it for this, the sacrifice. . . ?

(Julia Alvarez, *In the Time of the Butterflies*, 1995: 318.)

1. The Diaspora of the Caribbean

In 2005, Oxfam reported: "Each year, more than 30 million people flee their homes as a result of war, riots, political unrest, floods, earthquakes, typhoons, and other forms of conflict and natural disaster".[i] Moreover, the report highlights that every year about half a million people are killed by armed violence ("that's one person every minute"). Conflict often occurs in areas of vast deprivation—"indeed, such deprivation is often one of the chief causes of conflict" (Oxfam 2005.) Themes of the diaspora, as we have seen, are often explored in terms of a loss and return to "home" and the actual or intrinsic sense of scarcity of empowerment that this entails. On losing the sense of home by displacement or by migration, the individual can categorise their experience as "exile" or as opportunity for a new life, particularly in terms of economic prosperity or political freedom. While for most migrants, the journey is a physical and social migration, it cannot be denied that for some it is a spiritual journey—a voyage that enforces a renegotiation of "I-ness" both outer and inner. The relocation of home is a metaphorical and metaphysical opportunity to locate the source of all knowledge within the Self. The problem has been also put in terms of perennial exploration in the field of knowledge, which has been marked by questions that have recurred in every culture and in every age. How does the human mind discover or construct the principles through which we can understand the universe? How does it create the laws through which we govern our own affairs and interact with our environment? What is the source of intelligence in the universe and how can we use that intelligence to bring progress to society? (Clements 1998: 1)

These questions are significant in today's world and particularly so in countries still challenged by historical roots in slavery and the mass transplantations of peoples in and from the African diaspora.[ii] The ongoing crisis in Haiti, for example, has been cited as one that challenges its democratic neighbours, including the Bahamas, where the islands' 360,000 citizens now include 60,000 Haitians, and where the Prime Minister Perry Christie recently argued that "with 200 years of independence, Haiti is still struggling to come to terms with its existence and how it should operate. But in the meantime, we carry the brunt of it. [...] Haiti is more than just a pastime. It has to be dealt with" (Smith 2005).[iii] Countries such as the Bahamas receive countless illegal immigrants from Haiti and Cuba annually: many are turned away and repatriated, many remain and integrate into the existing social system despite language differences.[iv]

This chapter analyses some of the novels originating or relating to the island nations that, to adapt a phrase used by Brown and Wickham (2001: xiii), could be described as the "non-cricket playing" Caribbean: Haiti, the Dominican Republic and The Bahamas, looking at the colonial legacy and how post-independence has been characterised by violence, tyrannical dictatorships, and other problems relating to governance, education, and the ongoing situation of "illegal" immigration. (Cuba, physically located within this area, could also be included in this domain, although obviously the past forty years has seen a divergent history.) The repetitive trends of history and scenarios of domination echo from Frantz Fanon in his 1959 speech at the Congress of Black African Writers:

Colonial domination, because it is total and tends to over-simplify, very soon manages to disrupt in spectacular fashion the cultural life of a conquered people. This cultural obliteration is made possible by the negation of national reality, by new legal relations introduced by the occupying power, by the banishment of the natives and their customs to outlying districts by colonial society, by expropriation, and by the systematic enslaving of men and women. (179)

Moreover, in terms of literature, the effects of this colonial obliteration of both life and cultural expression lead to an "orientalist" positioning, one where resident and foreign voices vie for positions of authenticity and power. Clashes of culture are translated into wars of words, the battle of domination of hegemonies, simplified into terms of coloniser and colonised:

> Where the colonizer celebrated his literature, his written records, as a mark of superior and developing civilization, the colonized intellectual emphasises oral traditions, which were claimed to *preserve* the past, and celebrated the language and voice of the non-literate "folk". (Innes in King 2000: 127)

Innes continues to argue that even while indigenous writers define their culture in these terms, they are still "almost inevitably to some degree shaped by European culture" (ibid). Within a Caribbean setting, this argument elucidates the tendency of inclusion and exclusion prevalent in the Caribbean, manifested in a conflict of the authenticity of Creole and oral versus Euro-American and written. Ramifications of this rift are expressed in terms of traditional versus modern, civilised versus dehumanising savage. Furthermore, if orality is a feature of Caribbean literature, it is also defined within colonialist discourse in terms of the "feminisation" of "the native" and his writing, part of the othering of the native as "the negation of the world of the settler" (ibid: 126), as discussed originally by Fanon.

By extension, notions of gendered access to narrative are also implicated, together with questions of how different cultures and islands may overcome this dichotomisation that extends to a gendered privileging of the ownership of speech as male.[v] If text is gendered, what strategies, subversive or otherwise, have women been able to adopt? It is both relevant and ironic here that the female ability to enunciate her voice has been effectively silenced since, and repeatedly reinforced by, the Genesis myth of temptation and expulsion.

Within this framework of gendered inscriptions of historical record-keeping and cultural memory, the novels Edwidge Dandicat create a powerful record and preservation of not only the culture of Haiti. They provide a sense of nostalgia of the dream of paradise that was Haiti: the first black republic and model of inspiration for writers from the Romantic poets to diverse literatures of slavery since the 1790's. The formation of the independent black republic of Haiti in 1804 after the Haitian Revolution played a critical role for black liberation struggles across the Atlantic diaspora, and created its own literary mythology for blacks as well as whites. Dandicat, a writer of the Haitian diaspora, uses memory as the stepping stone across time and between cultures, as she explores diasporic experiences of exile and freedom juxtaposed with life in the terror of remaining in the homeland. Her works validate a female historiography, emphasising the matriarchal tradition of Haitian storytellers to produce a heightened awareness of women's entanglement with history, nation, and narrative, as I discuss later in this chapter.

Contact with social change may provide an alternative world-view, and accommodated into the pre-existent or "traditional" perspective. The west Africans brought to the Caribbean islands as slaves, for example, effortlessly incorporated their beliefs in magic into their new Christian faith; an amalgamation that is still in evidence today where a subculture of the "old" religion sits not far beneath the surface of the "new". The African legacy in The Bahamas, for example, incorporates music and cultural festivals based on spirit possession rituals (the celebrated Junkanoo New Year procession is based on masked slave dances), and obeah (magic or sorcery) is still widely practised (Cash et al 1991: 231). Overtly the Bahamas is a proudly self-proclaimed "Christian nation", yet Christianity here still combines elements of obeah and aspects of spirit possession; just as secular and profane combine in areas of Goombay music (Bantu for 'rhythm') and story-telling (Saunders 1990: 165-68).

2. Novels of the Bahamas: Keith Russell

Of the various Caribbean nations, the culture of the Bahamas is perhaps the most influenced by the United States, and concern is evident over the loss of "African heritage" in the onslaught of rampant Americanisation. An ex-British colony and part of the British Commonwealth, the Bahamas does not share in traditions of writing to the extent of the other Caribbean islands, relying instead on alternatives of orality and apathy. In the context of Caribbean writing, therefore, the nation is underrepresented in terms of novelists, although a handful of dynamic playwrights and poets (such as Ian G. Strachan, Marion Bethel and Michael Pintard) are gaining international recognition. The novels of Keith A. Russell also provide a significant departure from the silence: his topics are the local culture of Grand Bahama and the urban conglomeration of Nassau.[vi] His works echo many of the colonial deprivations of the local population, a nation where, for example, under British rule education was segregated and higher education unavailable to Bahamians until after independence. Russell examines and exposes the restrictive education and governmental system and illustrates postcolonial responses to the aftermath of ignorance and hardship.

Written with a characteristic brutality and linguistic rawness, the novels find a voice that reflects the anger of that legacy, while also exposing sympathy to the plight of its victims. Russell's novels *The Disappearance of J.D. Sinclair* and *When Doves Cry* explore the inability of men to exist and remain whole within a system that both creates and denies freedom. The young Bahamian man, J.D. Sinclair is raised in the island of Abaco and leaves to New Providence when he passes the Common Entrance examination and wins a scholarship to the exclusive high school: an experience of English-centric education he ultimately realises is a process irrelevant and damaging to Bahamian culture and traditions. J.D. refuses to act in the mold of mimicking the behaviours and culture of the colonial masters, and openly challenges the repudiation of the traditional past, where, just as V.S. Naipaul's narrator in *A Bend in the River* complains, "our history ... [we] have got from books written by Europeans" (1979: 11). J.D. learns to speak patois so that he can move with ease between English and Caribbean cultures, the new and the old ways of life. In response to the alienation he feels from the colonial present, J.D. attempts to make his own stand by renarrating the content of his school classes, to correct the revision of both past and present in terms of "Englishness". As Walter Rodney states in his analysis of African colonial education:

> The main purpose of colonial school system was to train Africans to participate in the domination and exploitation of the continent as a whole . . . Colonial education was education for subordination, exploitation, the creation of mental confusion and the development of underdevelopment. (1981: 263)

Set firmly in a postcolonial tradition, Russell's novel centres on the clash between traditionalism and Westernism, and the irrelevance of the latter to the Bahamian culture. The final disappearance of the educated and street-wise J.D. Sinclair (his name a significant play upon concepts of culpability and innocence) in Nassau leaves a void that indicates the disappearance, or rather eradication of Bahamian culture by the British, as well as providing an example of the Fanonian desire to drop the "white mask" that a "black skin" is forced to wear. His character in fact demonstrates the kind of psychological damage discussed by Fanon in his analysis (1967) of the colonised African. Similarly, he fights against the fate decreed to those who succumb to the imposed education system, those who like the educated Africans described by Rodney "were the most alienated Africans on the continent. At each further stage of education, they were battered and succumbed to the white capitalist system [...] that further transformed their mentality" (ibid: 275). In *Decolonizing the Mind,* Ngugi also observes the lack of relevancy between local culture and colonial education, and the destructive effects result in the native people quickly losing their identity and hence their sense of reality. In the case of the ex-slave islands of the Bahamas, culture has long been dead and the African heritage already long been lost. Moreover, as Rodney (1981) observes, this educational process of transforming the colonised peoples into a new class of European-educated clone-slaves, is how, by enforcing their dependence on the imperial power and alienating the people from their needs and their environment, neo-colonial society is founded.

Russell's novel clearly illustrates all these processes and their cost. J.D.—his names (Jeremiah David) indicative of both strength and weakness—is ultimately lost to himself, his family, and his society. Triggered by his witnessing the brutal murder of his best friend Val, any sense of purpose or reason disappears from J.D.'s mind, and the loss of innocence he undergoes indicates that the original sin is not the human desire for greater knowledge but the violation of man's inner and outer freedoms. Opting out of reality, he first relinquishes his sexual innocence in a deliberate act of both initiation and sacrifice, before symbolically walking naked and willingly out of the "garden of Eden" into a self-inflicted exile, naked into a New World free from the impossible constraints of being the black over-intelligent underdog in the brutal and ignorant white colonial presence, which is also in the throws of a near-death. As the 1960's passed, "Colored people were being upgraded to Black. Colonialism was dying—everywhere—from overindulgence"(70).

J.D.'s "disappearance" is indicative of the systematic fading away of the Bahamian culture and patois in this century through the imposition of an alien education and legal system, just as much as the forced eradication of the original African languages and religions brought over three hundred years by the slaves. Yet if there is in this world no sinner for whom redemption is not possible, then the system has indeed failed, failed both J.D. and the British alike. He drops the mask of his Anglicised sanity, in a world that from him already seems insane. In this novel, as in Russell's second novel *When Doves Cry*, the protagonist becomes the victim of society, yet it is a morally ambivalent victimhood, which in both novels occurs through choice. In each, the character decides the only path possible: violence begets violence. In both novels the loss of the self is indicated through loss of memory of one's true nature.

In *When Doves Cry*, lives are lost as a consequence of a necessary and sacrificial murder. In *J.D. Sinclair*, a life is lost through "insanity", the loss of knowledge of the meaning of "home" so that every street is an alien experience. At the end of the novel, in a moment of "eternal silence" J.D. refrains from committing suicide on the bridge leading from Nassau over to Paradise Island, and instead "turned his back on Paradise, and went strolling awkwardly, towards New Providence, singing joyfully as he went" (144). Expelled from Eden, like Geoffrey Firmin, he embraces the disorientation of his new mental/spiritual locale, his new rootless identity. The theme of psychological disintegration found in Naipaul and Harris, where "psychic wholeness is presented as a continually retreating vision, always just out of reach" (Gilkes, xv) are similarly explored in Russell's work. Colonial violence has apparently deprived the Bahamians of the knowledge of what constitutes "home": there is no homeland. Through potent exploration of Bahamian culture, history and characters, Russell's novels frame the postcolonial question: who owns the keys to the garden of Eden, and who has the right to dictate or to judge who comes and goes?

3. Novels of Haiti: Edwidge Dandicat

Linked historically and geographically with the Bahamas, since every year thousands of refugees cross the waters in the attempt of finding new lives in the Bahamas or the United States, Haiti and its literature provides further testimony of the uses and abuses of postcolonial power. Following in the footsteps of giants such as Jamaica Kincaid, the Haitian-American writer Edwidge Dandicat also promotes a new voice of diasporic identity in the Caribbean. With the ongoing suffering in Haiti, the novels of Edwidge Dandicat create a powerful record and preservation of not only the culture of Haiti but also the lost lives of thousands of its inhabitants. Dandicat, an exile from Haiti herself, has lived since her teens in New York. In her book of short stories *The Dew Breaker* (2004) the loss of the earthly paradise in terms of geographical location is mirrored in the shock of having to revise memory. The characters not only have to revisit trauma but to live with the consequences of their albeit unwilling participation in the violence of historical process. The stories in this volume confront and problematise Rushdie's claim that "To be a migrant is, perhaps, to be the only species of human being free from the shackles of nationalism (to say nothing of its ugly sister, patriotism)" (1991: 124).

The various characters—all ultimately linked with one horrific incident in Haiti—must come to terms with meeting their "deepest selves", necessitated through the extremes of colliding circumstance and actuality, in a new terrain in which "the migrant suspects reality: having experienced several ways of being, he understands their illusory nature" (Rushdie 1991: 125). Forced back onto the self in a response to this realisation, the characters pick their way through the shards of memory in attempts to construct new selves and then struggle to live with the new self-identities they have created. The tragedy is exacerbated when the new location of exile is also found to be inadequate and cannot fulfil the dreams it promised. Exile may mean freedom, but at the cost of a life of perpetual alienation, fragmentation and loneliness. In these stories, a traumatic event involving rape rendered "unspeakable" through post-traumatic stress disorder, and a migrant nurse's consequent inability to phone and speak to her parents in Haiti becomes mirrored in the hospitalised woman who is rendered forever speechless through a laryngectomy. A young male political exile is reunited with a wife he has not seen for seven years, when she is at last able to join him the United States. Her sense of alienation in that bewildering culture is indicative of their emotions paralysed in a past they cannot escape, and their words silenced by their inability to move forwards. A group of Haitian women in New York struggle to learn the new language, but ultimately one of them can only justify her life by returning to Haiti to join a militia and fight—but only after she has sung her own funeral song and thereby undergone a symbolic ritual release from existence.

In the first and pivotal story, "The Book of the Dead", the loss of innocence involves the loss of moral certainty as honourable victims, and the nostalgia for an oppressed past: the shattering of belief in (postcolonial) victim-hood, and the justified pride in the state of worthy exile. Denial here has been honed to a long-term survival strategy. The realisation of what the narrator's father actually was— not a prisoner in jail but a state torturer ("your father was the hunter, he was not the prey" [20])—leads to the traumatic loss of innocence and of belief in the Father-figure, the representative of the lost homeland. The culpability or involvement in the horror of past-present regimes is brought home by the father's insipid disclaimer, "I did not want to hurt anyone" (20), only moments after wringing his daughter's wrist in the same painful manner he had to his prisoners.

The characters are paralysed in a precarious and painful vacuum, a state of hybridity that does not offer the opportunity for new "border-crossings" that Homi Bhabha (1994) suggested. All traumatised by past events, the characters seek a new form of awareness with which they can face the reality of their experience, protecting themselves from the past world of horror, loss and death. While new identities are formulated and lived out, the memories of the past disallow any mental movement or resolution of past conflict.

In the final story, the diverse characters are given a more substantial meaning through the narration of the "original" event that propelled their exiles. The father of the initial story "The Book of the Dead" is the protagonist: a state torturer whose role it is to capture, imprison and eventually murder an outspoken priest. Issues of culpability are also complicated by the presence of the priest's sister, Anne, a woman prone to epileptic fits, "mysterious spells" (242), and a religious zeal that link her to an invocation of the female perceived as witch or woman of indigenous knowledge, the healer. In a state of confusion following a fit, Anne encounters a fleeing man, apparently just escaped from the notorious jail, whom she "rescues" and spends the night with to watch over him and tend his wounded face. He is the torturer, who has just murdered her brother, and, despite guessing the truth, Anne stays with the man, travelling with him to exile in the United States—where they become the parents of Ka (the narrator of the first story). Despite spending the majority of her time every day in church to atone for her husband's sins, Anne's endorsement of his silence perpetuates the myth of his past, and she is deeply implicated in his crimes and culpability. Yet she is left in a state of suspension, where memory and knowledge are equally bereft of a capacity to heal, hoping that:

> [. . .] atonement, reparation, was possible and available for everyone. [. . .] There was no way to escape this dread any more, this pendulum between regret and forgiveness, this fright that the most important relationships of her life were always on the verge of being severed or lost, that the people closest to her were always disappearing. (242)

Just as her husband had violently inflicted obliteration upon others, her identity along with that of her brother, her husband and her daughter have all disappeared, are expunged, devoid of authenticity; they are merely "masks" against their own faces (34).

Dandicat's earlier novel *Breath, Eyes, Memory* (1994) in contrast offers the possibility of revisiting the past to reconstruct psychic wholeness. Again, the underlying theme is the concern with loss and regaining of the self. The self can be equally lost staying at home as in exile, as the characters of the narrator Sophie and her peasant aunt demonstrate (103-4). Since being fully "conscious" relates to our ability to be in the present time, a continual inability to escape the past will fragment or shatter the ability to enjoy "present-time awareness". The harrowing past (such as the damage done by trauma such as slavery, or later postcolonial dictatorships and despotic regimes) renders present time inaccessible since the past has become unlocatable and unreconstructable. Without a past, the present is without foundations, and the future inconceivable. Frantz Fanon speaks of a similar process in the development of colonial literature as a literature of combat, where the sense of struggle is necessary to overcome and re-adjust, so to speak, the time values of the nation:

> Literary creation addresses and clarifies typically nationalist themes. This is combat literature in the true sense of the word, in the sense that it calls upon a whole people to join in the struggle for the existence of the nation. Combat literature, because it informs the national consciousness, gives it shape and contours, and opens up new, unlimited horizons. Combat literature, because it takes charge, because it is resolve situated in historical time.

At another level, oral literature, tales, epics, and popular songs, previously classified and frozen in time, begin to change. The storytellers who recited inert episodes revive them and introduce increasingly fundamental changes. [...] The method of allusion is frequently used. Instead of "a long time ago," they substitute the more ambiguous expression "What I am going to tell you happened somewhere else, but it could happen here today or perhaps tomorrow." In this respect the case of Algeria is significant. From 1952-53 on, its storytellers grown state and dull, radically changed both their methods of narration and the content of their stories. Once scarce, the public returned in droves. The epic, with its standardized forms, reemerged. It has become an authentic form of entertainment that once again has taken on a cultural value. Colonialism knew full well what it was doing when it began systematically arresting these storytellers after 1955. (1963: 173-174)

The role of the storyteller, and particularly of the oral storyteller is of significance throughout the Caribbean and has considerable social importance in the Haiti described by Edwidge Dandicat. In *Breath, Eyes, Memory*, it is the oral story telling tradition that rescues three generations of women, who have been either physically or psychologically abused, and links them in a healing quasi-exorcism through the sharing of knowledge. The women realise the oral narratives traditionally have "mother-and-daughter motifs to all the stories they told and all the songs they sang. It was something that was essentially Haitian. Somehow, early on, our song makers and tale weavers had decided we were all daughters of this land" (Dandicat, 1994: 230). With the background of escalating national violence, however, the narrator's aunt, Tante Atie, who is the novel's central figure in the preservation of oral narrative, not only learns to read but also begins to record her words and "poems". Her personal transition from oral to written story-telling mirrors the country's changing political perspective: the rapid departure from traditional values, the senseless brutalising of innocent citizens, the unrecorded deaths and disappearances. Another young woman, Louise, goes to town to get her name registered so that:

"Her name can be on some piece of paper for future generations," said Tante Atie. "If people come and they want to know, they will know that she lived here."
"People don't need their names on a piece of paper for that", said my grandmother.
"I will list my name too," said Tante Atie.
"If a woman is worth remembering," said my grandmother, "there is no need to have her name carved in letters."

Louise hollered Tante Atie's name from the road. [. . .]
"If a person is worth remembering," mumbled my grandmother, "people will remember. It need not be cast in stone". (128-9)

The oral recitation of names is significant; just as Louise hollers her friend's name from the road, so Tante Atie validates the dead in the cemetery by calling out their names, both to remember them and to signify their continued existence in society: a testimony to collective group consciousness. The resting place of the dead also denotes a meeting-point of indigenous and modern belief systems, a place that is sacred since it bears witness to an overlapping and interlocking narrative of women's lives:

Tante Atie walked between the wooden crosses, collecting the bamboo skeletons of fallen kites. She stepped around the plots where empty jars, conch shells, and marbles served as grave markers.
    "Walk straight," said Tante Atie, "you are in the presence of family." She walked around to each plot, and called out the names of all those who had been buried there. There was my great-grandmother, Beloved Martinelle Brigitte. Her sister, My First Joy Sophilus Gentille. My grandfather's sister, My Hope Atinia Ifé [. . .] Tantie Atie named them all on sight. (150)

The importance of oral speech is detailed in Indian language theory. As Coward explains, the principle form of language is "not written but oral . . . In the Indian tradition, language is considered to be fully alive only when it is spoken"; moreover, "Thinking is seen as an internal speaking to which not enough prana or energy is given to make it overt. Writing is merely a coded recording which can never perfectly represent all the nuances of the spoken word, and is therefore always secondary" (1980: 8).

Oral record keeping is, therefore, contrary to European traditions, deemed to be more accurate and reliable than written. Knowledge is kept lively in the consciousness of the knower, rather than entombed in an unopened volume of script. *Vac*, or speech, is taken to be "a manifestation of the all-pervading Brahman", a truth that is handed down from generation to generation (Coward ibid: 11). Again, the importance of memory is central, since each word contains a unity of the "sound-bearing" and "meaning-bearing" or revelatory aspects of language—which, according to the Indian linguist Bhartrhari, are eternal and manifest in consciousness (ibid: 12).

Here in Dandicat's novel, the ancestors "live" in significance through being remembered in the present, through the recitation of their names. The oral recitation of the past becomes a textual enunciation through the female body, albeit those of the dead. Similarly, although on a darker note, the past narratives are indefinitely reproduced as the recurring nightmares of the mother and daughter, who seem to inherit the same dream of rape from her mother. "Some nights I woke up in cold sweat wondering if my mother's anxiety was somehow hereditary or if it were something I had 'caught' from living with her. Her nightmares had somehow become my own" (193). The historical process of past living in the present is also confirmed since Sophie, the daughter, also represents the mother's trauma visually: she is a child born as a consequence of the rape and "A child out of wedlock always looks like its father" (169).

According to Bhartrhari's theory of language, cognition of the two-sided unitary aspect of sound/meaning (the aspect of *sphota*) involves "special perception" or intuitive abilities. At underlying levels of language, the sound and meaning (the signifier and signified) aspects of a word converge. It is only through an ability of the mind to reach these "deeper" levels of language experience that this reality can be cognised. The narrator, Sophie, inherits her mother's and grandmother's heightened uses of consciousness, especially the ability to hear and comprehend events while the mind itself is functioning from a state of silence, "beyond" speech. This ability provides an alternate means of agency within a national situation of the silencing of women within the violent patriarchy; it also is a remedy to a common response to trauma, in which normal speech is inadequate, or even impossible to produce. In situations where events must be formally documented, for example, as testimony, women's speech is often distorted, elliptical, or inadequate, since there generally exists "a punishing standard of purity imposed upon women as cultural biases converge around gender, race, ethnicity, male honor, female worth, and truth-telling" (Campbell in Gilmore 2005:102). Furthermore, even outside these rigid demands, trauma has to be "narrativized in ways that complicate the sentence of 'unspeakability'"(Gilmore ibid: 102).

Hence, as in Dandicat's text, the importance of the women finding their source of knowledge and the means to express it in means outside the standard hegemonies of society. The alternate modes of consciousness here include the ability to hear and cognise unseen and distant events, "Remember, all of us have the gift of the unseen" (229). This perception is beyond the range of normal sensory impressions of hearing or sight, as the grandmother explains:

> "There is a girl going home [. . .] You cannot see her. She is far away. Quite far. It is not the distance that is important. If you hear a girl from far away, there is an emotion, something that calls to my soul" [. . .]
> "There is no way to know anything unless you apply your ears. When you listen , its *kòm si* you had deafness before and you can hear now. Sometimes you can't fall asleep because the sound of someone crying keeps you awake. A whisper sounds like a roar to your ears. Your ears are witness to matters that do not concern you. And what is worse, you cannot forget". (Dandicat 1994: 152-53)

The tapestry of small historical events, never forgotten, is used by the grandmother to re-member (as in Toni Morrison's *Beloved*) to weave a pattern of narrative, of past and present, in order to pass this legacy to future generations. Sophie is also able to achieve what she terms the *marassa* or "doubling", the ability to divorce the mental from the bodily, to separate what she is experiencing subjectively from the physical reality. According to Shea, it is a process whereby "people make separations within themselves to allow for very painful experiences" (1996: 385). Thus, when Sophie's husband is with her at night, she is able to distance herself, "really I was somewhere else" (Dandicat 200); she witnesses her body rather than being part of it in a denial of self that excludes self-knowledge.[vii] Her repulsion of the physical is also expressed in her bouts of bulimia: like rejected memory, a further attempt to rid the body of unwanted material. The mother-daughter bonding throughout the generations is both traumatic (depicted in the continuation of the practice of digital "testing" for their daughters' virginity) and wholesome, something that preserves culture and meaning. At her mother's funeral, as the women sing the traditional songs of ritual passing over, Sophie's perception is able to encompass this larger cultural paradigm and thus to reach a state of understanding and forgiveness. Individual consciousness expands to embrace a more holistic collective consciousness:

> Listening to the song, I realized that it was neither my mother not my Tante Atie who had given all the mother-and-daughter motifs to all the stories they told and all the songs they sang. It was something that was essentially Haitian. Somehow, early on, our song makers and tale weavers had decided that we were all daughters of this land. (230)

By implication, Dandicat also sees herself as part of this female tradition of Haitian storytellers, stories being passed on from mother to child in the same DNA that houses "alternative" encoding of wisdom such as second sight, and encourages a reading of heightened female awareness. In *Breath, Eyes, Memory,* Dandicat fractures the masculinist notion of patriarchal based narrative and the consequent political and religious hegemonies. The rupture in social and metaphysical narrative also occurs since the women worship the female deity, Erzulie, a pagan goddess and counter-part of the Virgin Mother, who becomes both a substitute mother for Sophie and a source of *vaudou* power, "the healer of all women [. . .] who was always with me. I can always count on her, like one counts on the sun coming out at dawn" (59). When her mother dies, she buries her in crimson clothes to resemble "hot-blooded Erzulie who feared no men, but rather made them her slaves, raped *them*, and killed *them*" (227, emphasis in original). This rejection of male power is further endorsed by the marginalisation of masculine figures in the novel: the feeble and ineffectual Marc, the mother's lover, and Dessalines, the coal man murdered by the Tontons Macoutes are the only male characters in the novel—both too weak to impinge much at all on the women's lives. Assimilation into the harsh and masculine world of New York is never achieved; Haiti remains the psychic and spiritual home for all the women, as it no doubt will also be for the infant daughter Brigitte when she grows up.

Yet within the subject matter of her novels, the notions of male versus female power are problematic. In *The Dew Breaker*, agency through recourse to the figure of the indigenous goddess as a totem of female power—as in *Breath Eyes Memory*—is replaced in first story by the father figure's obsession with the Egyptian gods, especially the god of death, the "jackal-headed ruler of the underworld (13). The narrator herself has been given the Egyptian name Ka, from the *Book of the Dead,* referring to the "double" of the body that guides it through life to death. Thus she both signifies and is defined by a cult of death—Haitian and Egyptian—(and we became aware of the ritual importance of naming and names in Haitian culture in *Breath Eyes Memory*, as discussed above, with the incident of the recitation of the ancestors' names.) The "feminist" religion of life and healing in Dandicat's earlier novel, and the alternative hegemony of female oral narrative are replaced by the masculinist texts and religion of death. The certainties of a healed future through matriarchy and matrilocal land ownership are replaced by the disassociation of daughter and mother from their emotional integrity because of the terrible legacy of guilt and silence bequeathed to them by the father, the torturer.

Furthermore, in *Breath, Eyes, Memory*, Sophie, the daughter feels "raped" and shamed by her mother's probing fingers during "testing" to such an extent that it is her mother's name that she cites in her therapy session as her abuser (202). Through the procedure of "testing", the patriarchal notion of honour being bound up with female virginity is also corroborated and perpetuated, rather than being destabilised. It is only because of the perpetuation of such myths that rape becomes a political and social means of control and punishment (here used by the Tontons Macoutes[viii]—one of whom was probably the narrator's father) as well as physical weapon. Yet by challenging the authority of narrative by reallocating/relocating it to a female domain, she also obliquely challenges the basis of male power gained through, for example, the paradigm of dishonour through rape.[ix] Although confirming the traumatic and lasting repercussions of rape through the seriousness of the damage it does to both victim and offspring of a rape incident, the fact that the women *survive* that trauma through a series of stratagems of consciousness validates female subjectivity. These strategies include the worship of the indigenous female deity, Erzulie, as mentioned above, and various means of healing through ritual naming and the literal inscriptions of self-hood. The tangible and metaphorical links between female generations is pivotal in accessing healing, redeeming the past, and in giving a narrative voice to loss, trauma, and alienation. At the end of the novel, through the repeated question *"Ou libéré?"* Are you free? , spoken at the end of every story, Sophie realises the power of the female narrative tradition to convey memory and to restore wholeness.

The alternative mechanisms of women's narrative are endorsed through the characters' emancipatory survival strategies and alternative modes of consciousness. These alternatives are depicted as modes of heightened awareness through which the women characters gain knowledge of both self and environment: they are part of Dandicat's exploration of female subjectivity and the way that the power of the feminine can be wielded to overcome political and physical disadvantage. The ability to "double", for example, accesses a technique to avoid conscious participation in an unpleasant life experience, usually sexual, one interpreted as violation of the physical or psychic self. The female body throughout the novel is seen as the locus of memory, both individual and collective. It is through the female body that women are controlled both by society's expectations and by other women playing out the roles of patriarchal socialisation. It is through the violation of the body that social stress and national memory is articulated: the mother's rape is replayed, for example, by her suicide in which she stabs herself repeatedly in the stomach, as well as by the daughter's "self rape" whereby she tears herself open to destroy her hymen and negate the hold of traditional "testing" of virginity.

The account of Sophie's "alternative" modes of consciousness is introduced through her ability to dream of her absent and unknown mother (symbolic of the lost motherland), dreams that will prove to be prophetic when she is sent to meet her sick and psychologically shattered mother in America. Both women live in a bleak space of disassociation from each other and from their own inner needs, unable to access or articulate their feelings. Part of their sense of alienation is their identity as Haitian migrants; they live within an omnipresent atmosphere of discrimination where Haitians are despised "boat people" infected with HBO "Haitian Body Odor" (51). To overcome these debilitating factors, the ability to "double" is a way to avoid becoming traumatised and succumbing to the post-traumatic stress disorder suffered by the mother, Martine. This willed "separation" from self, however, is a split from reality, a survival mechanism beset with problems, since it implies a denial of self, a type of self-erasure rather than self-fulfilment. It becomes for Sophie a type of self-punishment, linked to her bulimia, self-mutilation and self-hatred. These problems are eventually healed through reconciliation with her home, when she revisits Haiti and re-integrates with her culture, an experience that coincides with the acceptance of her mother. The healing takes place through a process of reintegration with the female traditions of knowledge—personal, religious and judicial—within her country and an acceptance of memory: that the past provides not only accounts of trauma but also the wisdom through which the power to survive is passed on from generation to generation. The fragmented self is made whole. From the self being erased through trauma and the dislocation of female agency (mirrored in the phenomenon of the "disappeared" in Haiti, as depicted in Dandicat's *The Dew Breaker*), the growth towards a subjective and emotional "completeness" in the novel shows how narrative is reflective of the power of human consciousness in its desire for unity and liberation.

This theme is also at the core of Julia Alvarez's story of struggle against tyrannical dictatorship, *In the Time of Butterflies*, set in the Dominican Republic of President Trujillo. The four women in this novel—historical individuals who have become celebrated national figures of resistance—are both the protagonists and the narrators of history. Through the text of journals the pieces of the political nightmare are forged into a documentation of human strength in the face of psychotic national leadership. In a society where the women are circumscribed within patriarchal dictates of behaviour, the bravery of the women is demonstrated both through their altruism and through the "blanks" in the narrative, when events are too personally abusive to render them expressible. Their punishment and tortures are also based on sexual violation—yet their narratives express the power of the human spirit to combat oppression and to seek justice. It is due to the fact that they determinedly continue campaigning for the release of their husbands that three of the sisters are eventually murdered.

4. Conclusion

The intellect plays a crucial role in the first stages of awakening of the individual awareness to its full unbounded status. In the Bhagavad-Gita this is described as, "A lamp which does not flicker in a windless place, to such is compared the Yogi of subdued thought practising Union with the Self"(6, 19). The next verse describes the process by which thought, or the relative impulses of the mind, wake up to their infinite source in the Self: "That state in which thought settled through the practice of Yoga retires, in which seeing the Self by the Self alone, he finds contentment in the Self." In Maharishi Mahesh Yogi's commentary on this verse, he explains:

> The process of retiring begins with the expansion of individuality, and when this happens the intellect, losing its individuality, begins to gain universality, begins to gain the unbounded status of Being. While merging into Being, it cognizes Being as its own Self and gains bliss consciousness [. . .] The intellect has to surrender its existence in order to find its place in the eternal Being of the Self. (1969: 423-424)

Here, Maharishi describes the awakening of the intellect. The intellect is transformed in its mode of functioning, from the "horizontal" capacity of discriminating between objects or concepts in the relative, to a "vertical" function in which there is the absolute value of discrimination between Absolute and relative. Moreover, with this transformation of the mode of mental functioning comes a sense of "being deep in peace, freed from fear" (Bhagavad-Gita 6,14); this is the "Yoga which destroys sorrow" (6, 17.) Maharishi describes this experience of the intellect ultimately surrendering its own existence as infinite joy, the glory of the Self, and employs a significant metaphor: "Having come back home, the traveller finds peace" (1969: 424).

"Knowledge is structured in consciousness" is a universal principle of every level of consciousness and every aspect of knowledge. Bankruptcy of knowledge is responsible for all problems encountered in society, which stem from the basic inability to use the human mind competently. "Knowledge leads to action, action to achievement, and achievement to fulfilment" is an equally general principle of life. This is the underlying driving force behind the unquenchable thirst for knowledge in every generation. The misguided search for power through terror or creating fear demonstrates not real empowerment but a selfish seeking of a limited sense of self. It is action based on undeveloped consciousness, a lack of valid education. In terms of the development of consciousness, the more a technique of meditation is practised, the more one has direct contact with the Self, and the more this silent stable aspect begins to become a permanent feature of life. Moreover, since this is also the most basic level of nature's functioning, comparable to the Unified Field, thought projected from this silent level could be described as being "in tune" with the natural laws that govern the quantum universe. Thinking and acting from this level should therefore endorse qualities that uphold, rather than negate life-enhancing tendencies. The profitless seeking of power through fear-based action is contrasted to the purpose of development of consciousness as I see it: the betterment of society and the use of consciousness as the source of creative/artistic expression means that the source of art and literature is tapped at the source—at the deepest levels of human creativity and inspiration—a topic I explore in the next chapter.

---

[i] Flight, as Dudley Young (1991: 284) elaborates, is "our oldest answer" to violence of all forms.

[ii] The cultural and literary impact of migrants from the Caribbean islands into Great Britain is dealt with in James Procter's comprehensive works *Dwelling Places: Post-war Black British Writing* and *Writing black Britain 1948-1998: An interdisciplinary anthology* (both Manchester University Press).

[iii] Racial discrimination towards Haitians in the Bahamas is ongoing. The undertones of violence and prejudice are dealt with particularly in Keith Russell's *When Doves Cry* (2000) in which a Bahamian-Haitian is the protagonist.

[iv] In the Bahamas, Haitian Creole is fast becoming a second national language.

[v] I discuss this topic at greater length with particular reference to Arab women writers in *The Woman in the Muslin Mask: Veiling and Identity in Postcolonial Literature* (Pluto: 2004).

[vi] Ian Strachan's novel *God's Angry Babies* (1998), possibly the first major novel published by a Bahamian author, deals with social issues from a largely party-political framework, which arguably restricts its readership to a more local audience.

[vii] The character of the little girl, Bethany, in Fred D'Aguiar's novel *Bethany Bettany* also possesses a similar defence mechanism to avoid pain and the obliteration of self that the frequent beatings at the hands of her uncle and family are aimed to produce. She is able to transport herself in her imagination through doors and into spaces where she can witness her oppressors in order better to understand them. She explains this ability: "I think *door,* not the word but a picture of it" then finds herself relocated "with the speed of that thought" (2004: 38). Again, the quality of witnessing divorces the mind from the pain being inflicted on the body, or the attempt to comprehend such violence. The use of consciousness to manifest desire is one that sets her apart from, and raises her above, the other—mainly ignorant and abusive—characters and ensures her survival. D'Aguiar also uses the image as indicative of the colonial condition of the Caribbean island where the novel is set, a culture abused, confused and breaking up.

[viii] A member of the infamous militia, the Volunteers for National Security, created by the dictator Francois (Papa Doc) Duvalier.

[ix] Graham Greene's 1966 novel *The Comedians,* also set in Haiti, hints at the gendered violence perpetrated by the Tontons Macoutes but cannot engage with it directly. In one episode, the wife of an Englishman is brutally pushed by one of the Tontons, a violence that shocks and terrifies her (apparently) ineffectual husband.

Chapter Eight
Encounters in the Earthly Paradise:
Relocating the Self

"Often, the true glory of existence is confined to individual consciousness. That's okay. Let us live for the beauty of our own reality".
(Tom Robbins, *Only Cowgirls get the Blues*, 407.)

"This journey into the depths is not specifically national."
(Frantz Fanon, *Speech at the Congress of Black African Writers*, 1959.)

1. Patria and paradise

Edward Said speaks of the diasporic experience as being "the voyage in" (1994), and colonial writing is frequently dominated by the motif of encounter and discovery (Singh 1996: 8). In this chapter I examine a seemingly diverse range of Caribbean literature that reflects the fragmented and diverse nature of the islands—shards of land scattered across the ocean searching, as it were, for a unifying factor outside colonialisation and a shared trauma of slave history. The postcolonial process of remodelling the past to regain a definition of self-hood involves the reassertion and imaginative restructuring of myth-history. As Benedict Anderson (1983) and others have stressed, nations are imagined communities, structured from bonds of fraternity and necessity, blends of fact and fantasy, unities forged from diversity, created from "conscious and unconscious selves" (Singh ibid: 154). Taking a broad sweep of countries into consideration, my argument here takes examples of literature to illustrate a theme of the search for the lost self, lost either through historical event or national catastrophe, played out through the imagery of the myth of the expulsion from the Garden of Eden, the lost earthly paradise.

In terms of the postcolonial world view, Salman Rushdie argues, "To be a migrant is, perhaps, to be the only species of human being free from the shackles of nationalism (to say nothing of its ugly sister, patriotism)" (1991: 124). Patriotism, like nationalism, is a concept fraught with problems and lethal paradoxes. This is, it can be argued, due to the meaning of *patria*, defined as one's native country, or homeland, but which in its original—now archaic—sense also meant 'heaven, regarded as the true home from which the soul is exiled while on earth' (*Oxford American Dictionary*).

Thus, the concept of patriotism also contains the now-subliminal association of homeland with a prelapsarian reality, of the desirable return from the wasteland of a universal diaspora to the Garden of Eden, of the elusive and ineluctable search for paradise. Nowhere is this more true than in the Caribbean, which has long been imagined in the colonial psyche as the location of the Earthly paradise, whether defined as an elusive location of wholeness and fulfilment of the human spirit; a land of colonial plunder for fabulous riches, or a haven of political safety. The Caribbean has long been associated with the lost Garden of Eden, ever since Christopher Columbus's declaration, "For I believe that the Earthly Paradise lies here, which no one can enter except by God's leave" (qt Strachan 2005). As Ian Strachan points out in his book *Paradise and Plantation:*

> At various times in the past five hundred years, paradise has been associated with notions of the primitive, innocence, savagery, and a lack of civilisation, as well as of ignorance and nakedness, health and happiness, isolation from the rest of the world and humanity, timelessness, nature's beauty and abundance, life without labor, human beings' absolute freedom and domination over nature as God's stewards on earth, and connections of paradise with concepts of wild pleasure, perpetual sunshine, and leisure. (2005 : 5)

Within this framework, the Caribbean was a pre-civilised world, a locus that could feed both the imagination and the interests of commercial gain. Yet for the indigenous peoples, paradise was more literally and quickly located, and their demise ensured a void that was filled by the enslaved Africans who were to work the plantations for the next four centuries. For these Africans, disassociated from their roots, heaven lost its connection to "patria" and became instead firmly entrenched as the religious "kingdom" promised by the Christian missionaries. As the old slave Whitechapel explains in Fred D'Aguiar's novel *The Longest Memory:*

> Where do runaways go when they don't get caught? I always pose this question to the young because I can see their dreams as plain as their colour and youth on their faces. Paradise is the answer I get from them. Damn right, I shout. When they are captured by the trackers they are consigned to paradise, sent there forthwith. Free at last . . . (1995: 12)

The human desire to find an "earthly paradise", whether geographically or internally located is a theme already located within Chitra Banerjee Divakaruni's *The Mistress of Spices*, and can equally be argued of the nostalgic conceptualisation of Haiti in Dandicat's novels. (To some extent, this chapter continues the discussion begun in the previous chapter on The Bahamas and Haiti.) Interestingly, a number of novels refer to this symbolism of the search for the lost paradise to articulate the postcolonial condition, while here I shall also relate it to a fundamental search for a seemingly unattainable experience of higher consciousness. The writers and works I address here are Malcolm Lowry's *Under the Volcano*, Mario Vargas Llosa's *The Way to Paradise,* and Wilson Harris's *Palace of the Peacock*. I include the first two novels here, although in one case, the author comes from England, and in the other, the setting of the novel is not the western Atlantic but the islands of the South Sea—and is moreover by a South American author. This blurring of island identities is deliberately realised with an ironic glance towards the colonial "Romanticisation" of tropical islands, in which escap(ad)es to erotic/exotic otherness were imagined and pursued in both Caribbean and South Sea locations. Likewise, a nostalgia for a lost paradise, a geographically unlocated and irretrievable island domain, simultaneously characterised by simplicity and savagery, promise and perdition, has formed the basis of narratives from Daniel Defoe (via William Golding) onwards to fantasy fictions and beyond.

A cursory overview of the production and dissemination of literature within the context of the Caribbean locates a plethora of expressions enabling a trend of redefining the importance of self-and nation-hood. Within the sprawling spine of islands reaching down to span the waters between the southern United States and the northern shores of South America, the peoples share a common heritage of colonial plunder, forced migration from Africa and eventual emancipation from slavery. While the indigenous tribes of Arawaks, Caribs, Tainos, and Lucayans have long-since disappeared, they are nevertheless remembered as emblems of centuries-old ethnic cleansing even by the Africans who were brought in to replace them. Racial memory and a sense of belongingness in these nations is relatively short-term; and unlike an African retracing the cultural and literary heritage of his own national locale, the inhabitants of the Caribbean are rooted by their namelessness, identity obliterated through their forced indoctrination into other civilisations' cultural history. On to this foundation came the other relocations, from India, from the Middle East, peoples coming to fill the void of a middle class entrepreneurship, the middle men negotiating the fraught path of mimicry and colonial mismanagement.

As we saw in the previous chapter in the case of *Season of Migration to the North*, the location of self often involves the archetypal quest story, the voyage into the unknown (Said 1994: 34). In Salih's novel, the journey is both an exterior and interior journey, one that involves becoming a "mimic man", the hero who learns and incorporates the language and culture of the other (here, that of Europe) but eventually subverts that knowledge to undermine and expose its underbelly. Yet the same experience can be found within the homeland: the Trinidad-set novels of V.S. Naipaul, such as *The Mystic Masseur* and *A House for Mr Biswas*, for example, exemplify how this process also forms the core of colonial juxtapostionings before independence.

The journey to locate the true nature of the self need not involve the shock of cultural encounter of a *Heart of Darkness* to awaken the protagonist to the "reality" of the illusory nature of man's social constructs, but nevertheless it involves an epic journey of danger and loss, a passage through the *via negativa* in order to gain a larger understanding. This journey must involve the loss of the personal sense of ego—of the "me, my and mine"—the curtain that covers the true experience of Self. This journey is hazardous and can also end in failure; the willingness to give up the self can be undertaken initially through insight and wisdom but result in a path to self- annihilation rather than revelation. A classic example of this misguided giving up of self is Geoffrey Firmin in Malcolm Lowry's *Under the Volcano*, where the hero's disgust and disenchantment of the colonial situation leads to his self-loathing and path to self-abuse through drink—a wish to destroy himself as the symbol of all he detests in his imperialist culture of moral impoverishment and senseless relationships.

2. *Under the Volcano*

Although written by an English author, Malcolm Lowry, who lived most of his life as a recluse in Canada, *Under the Volcano* reveals much of the diasporic dilemma with which this book is concerned. Lowry's novel is described as being interested in "matters of flight and deterritorialization" that presents a picture of the displaced nomadic self, a "self to which all boundaries appear both permeable and contingent" (Miller 2004: 1-2). The Mexican setting is the location for a struggle of oppositions, the rise and fall of "human-ness", the inner dissolution of character versus the outward composure, that lies at the heart of man's quest for survival, of finding an identity as "real" and honest to one's sense of self. The postcolonial locale of the novel is also evidenced by the background of the British in India and the overall demise of the Empire in the days leading up to World War II. Miller argues for the novel's positioning as "postnational" since the social dysfunction of the central character mirrors a historical and political engagement with the "growing irrelevance of national citizenship as a source of identity and solidarity" (2004: 1).

The novel resonates to themes within Fanon's psychological analysis of the colonial situation, one where the colonial intellectual is "fated to journey deep into the very bowels of his people" (2004: 149) in the face of the palimpsestic landscape rewritten by the colonisers as a "den of savages, infested with superstitions and fanaticism, destined to be despised, cursed by God", a belief based on "Colonialism's claim that the precolonial period was akin to darkness of the human soul" (ibid: 150). Irrespective of continent—Fanon here refers to Africa—coloniser and the colonised are both caught in the intransigent web of this bipolar hegemony. As Caryl Phillips emphasises, Fanon understood that the revolution was not merely confined to issues of race but was primarily for the upliftment of *people* regardless of racial origins, a fight for human dignity (2001: 133).

Responses to cultural alienation form part of the landscape of inner void through which the characters of the novel, most especially that of the British Consul, Geoffrey Firmin, move in their bleak search for meaning and self-location. His respected position in society, albeit mainly constituting a social round of diplomacy negotiated in a Prufrock-like miasma of "insidious intent", etherised through alcohol, is the mask behind which he negotiates a symbolic terrain of despair. Rejecting the outward "reality" for the illusion of power and failed personal relationships that it embodies, Firmin creates for himself a via negativa, a quasi-spiritual path to locate an alternative, personal, "truth". Again, this positioning of "stigmatized homelessness" in the novel "depicts the expatriate experience not as a marginal aberration but, rather, as a paradigmatic instance of what is means to be modern" (Miller: 4).

As Lowry writes in his poem, "For *Under the Volcano*", "There will be no morrow, tomorrow is over" (xvi), the action of the novel takes place in a single day, the last day of Firmin's life. Through a rapacious desire for alcohol and mescal, Firmin's reality is firmly in the present, but it is a present at odds with that of the other characters, especially that of his ex-wife, Yvonne, who has returned that morning hoping for a reconciliation. Firmin is directly compared to Marlowe's Dr Faustus, one who is a seeker of a "new life" and yet who knows he must ultimately pay for his crime or sin. His crime is that of putting men to death in the war, as a result of which "it was easy to think of the Consul as a kind of lachrymose pseudo 'Lord Jim' living in self-imposed exile" (39). Within this exile, made the more unbearable since the departure of his wife, Firmin works on his book "still trying to answer such questions as: Is there any ultimate reality, external, conscious, and ever-present etc. etc." (44). Firmin's Faustian search for Secret Knowledge is also set within the parameters of the fact that whatever occurred externally, "one's own battle would go on" (15). When this battle relocates from the fields of France to Mexico, from the onset the setting becomes compared to "the beauty of the Earthly Paradise itself" (16). Paradoxically, Firmin knows he is in hell, and the vision he holds out—for a new life of peace and love—is potentially real since, like Blake, he realises, "right through hell there is a path" (42). Like Milton's Satan in *Paradise Lost*, his ideal "Hell" is a viable place of agency and an alternative to the futility of Heaven.

The reiterated theme of the lost Garden of Eden is played out in the character's full knowledge that he has willingly relinquished his "innocence" for an alternative reality. The "unity" of his abandoned marriage to Yvonne (should we read a pun on the name of the original Eve?) is the only symbol of a happy alternative to his present condition in which he fights to be able to distinguish illusion from reality, the truth from a lie. In his mental state of fluidity, his constant drinks substitute for the eternal fixity of the holy sacraments (45); yet neither is able to prevent him moving inevitably into the darkness. This is the void of misconception that the Upanishads speak of as *pragyaparadha*, the initial error of the intellect: that individual consciousness is separate from universal consciousness, or also defined as "the mistake of the intellect in which differences are not appreciated in terms of the integrated wholeness of pure existence" (Clements 1996: 11).

The paradox—and tragedy—of Fermin's coexisting and conflicting realities becomes more apparent as his ideal hell becomes a preferred alternative to the unbearable pain of heaven. Returning after a year away, Yvonne is shocked to see the neglected garden of their once-shared house: "'My God, this used to be a beautiful garden. It was like Paradise.' 'Let's get the hell out of it then'" (102) replies the Consul. Continuing in this vein, the garden then becomes the scene for a brilliantly comical encounter between Fermin and his neighbour, Mr Quincey, again a clash between drunkenness and sobriety (albeit with its suggestion of opiates), in which Fermin plays with the comparison of the savage and the civilised, the God who created the garden and the delights it hides within it (that bottle of tequila!). "'I'm afraid it really is a jungle too,' pursued the Consul, 'in fact I expect Rousseau to come riding out of it at any moment on a tiger'" (136). Fermin uses this brilliant and farcical encounter to reveal his devastating conclusion:

> "Do you know, Quincey, I've often wondered whether there isn't more in the old legend of the Garden of Eden, and so on, than meets the eye. What if Adam wasn't really banished from the place at all. [. . .] What if his punishment really consisted", the Consul continued with warmth, "in his having to *go on living there*, alone, of course—suffering, unseen, cut off from God . . . [. . .] And of course the real *reason* for that punishment—his being forced to go on living in the garden, I mean, might well have been that the poor fellow, who knows, secretly loathed the place! Simply hated it, and had done so all along. *And that the Old Man found this out*—." (137-8, italics in original)

This reversal and subversion of the Biblical myth obviously describes Fermin's own inner state, yet it is an appealing concept, a negative transcendence. Confronted with ignorance and derision, the Consul knows the "burlesque" of their civilities over a garden wall give but a hollow sense of satisfaction. The garden has been spoilt, and just as Geoffrey's hero figure William Blackstone realised that he preferred life with the native American Indians rather than the Puritan settlers, now the Consul realises that the real realm of the Indians/Paradise is "'in *here*. . . the final frontier of consciousness, that's all'" (139).

The constant theme of lost paradise is ultimately summed up in a sign at the bottom of the garden written in Spanish, which occurs in the text (132) as well as forming the epitaph to the novel:

> "¿Le Gusta este Jardin? ¿Que es Suyo? ¡Evite que sus Hijos lo Destruyan!". . .
> You like this garden? Why is it yours? We evict those who destroy!

Fermin sees these words and regards them as "simple and terrible words, words which took one to the bottom of one's very being" (132), and they are at the core of the theme of the human expulsion from Paradise. Yet it is a sign that is as readily deconstructed as believed:

> Not that he had any intention of "verifying" the words on the sign, which certainly seemed to have more question marks than it should have; no, what he wanted, he now saw very clearly, was to talk to someone . . . .(133)

Whilst Geoffrey Firmin's path leads him further towards hell, Hugh, his (half-caste) half-brother's revolutionary thoughts agonize over Dante's *Paradiso* and *Inferno* (*"Nel mezzo del* bloody *cammin di nostra vita. . ."* [154]), while attempting to assess his own location of "home" as an Anglo-Indian. Yet unlike Geoffrey, who is firmly rooted in a national culture and civilisation, Hugh wonders, "how on earth can I be escaping from myself when I am without a place on earth? No home" (157). The Garden of Eden cannot be destroyed by the children who do not belong there. Later in the novel, Hugh also indicts Sir Walter Raleigh as the instigator of the "lie" that is the colonial (ad)venture. As Hugh searches for his identity, the Consul's fate is sealed when he lies about his name to the police. Choosing to relocate his identity in space and time, he calls himself instead William Blackstone, he opts out of confirming the authorities' reality (preferring the Indians to the Puritans), a choice that is his final undoing, as he is accused of being both the antichrist and a spy (or more ludicrously, " 'de espider, and we shoota de espiders in Mejico [. . .] You are a spider'" (371).

The tragic comedy of his death is heightened by the fact the events of his final hour also implicate his wife and half-brother Hugh. His search for a justifiable true path through life, or at least one day of it, is a negative transcendence, a search for transcendental consciousness, which he approaches though the otherworldliness of obliterating his waking consciousness through alcohol. Michael Schmidt, in the novel's introduction, likens Fermin to Conrad's Mr Kurtz, in that: "with all his resources of learning, linguistic genius and wit, he surrenders. He is conscious of surrendering" (x). Yet the elimination of the self is not the subject of the novel, it is a meditation on the nature of the self, for as Lowry explained he intended the four main characters to be aspects of the same man (xxi)—an exploration in human consciousness, a navigation of both hell and heaven, of the extrapolations of ignorance and knowledge. The affirmative significance of the text (and it is certainly with a feeling of upliftment that the reader is left at the end of the novel) is revealed in the Sophocles quotation with which Lowry prefaces his novel: "Wonders are many, and none is more wonderful than man" (7).

3. *The Way to Paradise*

Mario Vargas Llosa approaches the question, explored in literature and philosophy at least since Rousseau, of what constitutes the "savage" versus the "civilised" man. In a theme explored by writers as diverse as Aldous Huxley (*Brave New World*) and D.H. Lawrence (*Lady Chatterley's Lover*) as well as Malcolm Lowry in *Under the Volcano*, the truly "savage" man becomes imagined as a sought-after identity, bestowed with either or both sexual prowess and intellectual enlightenment. Whereas in *Brave New World*, the savage is ultimately destroyed though mind-numbing social control in conjunction with the soma drug enforced as panacea, in *Lady Chatterley's Lover*, sexual experience is both socially liberating and defiant of social norms. While neither text is truly within a genre critiquing the colonial experience, both can be extrapolated from class war to national struggle. Whereas the gamekeeper Mellors, for example, is depicted as being close to and in tune with nature—and hence his unaffected sexuality—yet at odds with society (with Lawrence's aim being to expose the malfunction of the latter), so "the colonizer has contemptuously dismissed the native as belonging to the natural rather than the human world" (Innes in King: 127).

In Vargas Llosa's depiction of the life of Paul Gauguin, it is again the colonizer who regards the natives of French Polynesia as being "closer to nature" than the European, child-like and innocent, and therefore both exploitable and "othered" even while being envied. While condemning the situation of the French colonisation of the south sea islands, seeing the French as bringing unwanted "civilisation" to the primitive world, he himself takes full advantage of his position *as* alien and empowered coloniser in his plunder of the Tahitian society for both material for his art and women for his bed. According to Llosa, it is the colonial reality that is stifling to creativity, and thus to the development of human consciousness, yet it is a seemingly ubiquitous experience.

Llosa's novel plays upon the concept "Didn't everyone dream of reaching Paradise?" (2003: 11) and is concerned with the search for "paradise", spiritual, geographical and political. *The Way to Paradise* derives its title from the children's game called Paradise, where the children alternate asking "Is this the way to Paradise", with the answer, "No, try the next corner"; as the child runs from corner to corner "seeking the elusive Paradise, the others amused themselves by changing places behind her back" (ibid).[i] Two story-lines run through the novel: that of the artist Paul Gauguin in his quest for creative and social expression in Tahiti, and that of his grandmother Flora Tristan, a French-Peruvian social reformer. Both follow their individual path of conscience and creativity to reach an elusive sense of purpose and fulfilment. For Gauguin, this is a path of seeking pleasure and making art, while trying to express his inner vision despite the disapproving and judgemental French colonial regime. Paul Gauguin retreats, or rather escapes, from French society and the "control" of laws, both matrimonial and financial, to find a "savage" paradise where he can be himself freely, sexually and artistically. The apparent freedom of the remote islands allows him to be "freed of scruples, respectability, taboos and conventions, proud of your impulses and passions" (74). The "freedom" of his sexual activity, is however enacted against the growing symptoms of the "unspeakable disease" (syphilis) swiftly corrupting his body. Freedom for him is—outside the text—to penetrate to the heart of both young flesh and the culture it represents, even though, in doing so, he also condemns them to share his malaise. For Paul—called Koké by the Tahitians in the closest pronunciation they could render of his name—the sexual enjoyment of the forbidden makes him feel like the "noble savage". Once he takes the step "from life as a bohemian and artist to life as a primitive, pagan, savage", in this new world "living was a perpetual process of creation" (70).

Dudley Young suggests that the association of sex with a loss of innocence—inextricably connected as it is in the Judeo-Christian tradition with the expulsion from the Garden of Eden—is because "we moderns have wandered so far into history's oblivion" (325). It is man's appetite for more, of wanting to "unite ourselves to too much" that is the cause of "all our acts of appropriation and communion becoming problematic" (ibid). Gauguin longs to go beyond the restrictions of logic and reason (represented by French culture) to experience the human imagination in its rawness or primitiveness. He is able at some moments to reach an ecstatic state where mind and body are unified and from which his creativity flows and art becomes meaningful. Like the poet Rainer Maria Rilke, he realises that what is important to art is not the necessity of finding answers, but it is "to live everything. Live the questions now" (1903, 1986: 32). For Young, as for Milton, it is this overreaching desire for knowledge that is the cause of man's exile—and the human desire in the face of finding "our newly found freedoms in a context of distressing alienation" (1991: 324)—to "embrace and commingle, eliminate the space that separates us one from another" (Young: 325). Gauguin's inability to function without a native woman acting as both servant and mistress—and the fact that he is aroused spiritually and artistically by them—can be explained in terms of Young's argument of how:

> Waking to find ourselves alienated from nature, we instinctively hold hands with the one who might symbolically restore us to unity. The sexual act is now asked to bear and redeem the loneliness of creatures who not only live increasingly within the symbolic structures they build to replace an instinctual repose [but also discover] a distance between us that we would for the most purposes prefer to erase or deny. (325)

Having lost contact with the gods, our "lost repose" as Young terms it, man seeks recompense in carnal as well as in scientific knowledge (ibid), a return to the sexual to try to recapture the paradise of enlightenment, a symbolic restoration of unity, no matter how fleeting that may be.

Whereas his grandmother Flora tries to change the fundamentals of society, Gauguin recognises that the Paradise can only be sought outside society. It is to be accessed in rare cognitive events at once animal and divine: and it is at these moments that sexuality, spirituality and creativity converge. While materialism usually masks the spiritual, Paul is concerned with how the artist is able to locate the sacred in the quotidian, and thus has travelled to the place least touched by the modern world. As he explains to his artist friends in France:

> "To truly paint we must shake off our civilized selves and call forth the savage inside." [. . .] In him, as in the savage mind, the everyday and the fantastic were united in a single reality, sombre, forbidding, infused with religiosity and desire, life and death. (26)

Rather than being a juxtaposition of opposites, nature (as symbolised by the unspoilt "primitive" world) and culture (the expression of human creativity in art) unite at moments of heightened significance in a frictionless flow within his consciousness. (His fascination with the androgynous men-women of Tahiti also implies his desire to reconcile opposites—but this can only be achieved through using logic outside the realm of European rationality. Enlightenment is, after all, defined as a state of non-duality, beyond opposites.)

The moment of expanded consciousness occurs without warning; it comes for Paul Gauguin not out of craft or talent but out of "circumstance", not of skill but of "fantasy and utter devotion" (28). Placed by Llosa within religious terminology, since Paul argues that art must feel like the renunciation of living for God alone, this moment transcends the normal range of human cognition, it is an encounter with the Self and the unity of self with other. Social space and spiritual space merge to create an encounter with the sacred; his awareness reaches for the intangible, the sacred beneath the material. This epiphanic revelation becomes immortalised in his painting "Manao Tupapau", "the Spirit of the Dead Watches." The encounter with the sacred is the source of artistic creation. The "primitive world" (20), which he longs to find, becomes embodied in his young mistress, Teha'amana. Arriving unexpectedly at their hut one evening:

> he saw a sight he would never forget, and would try to rescue over the next days and weeks, painting in the feverish, trancelike state in which he had always done his best work. As time passed, the sight would persist in his memory as one of those privileged, visionary moments of his life in Tahiti, when he seemed to touch and live, though only for a few instants, what he had come in search of in the South Seas, the thing he would never find in Europe, where it had been extinguished by civilisation. (23)

The vision in the darkness of her naked and terrified posture is a moment of revelation and of communion with a primitive naturalness that was "Something of the lovely past that still beat beneath the Christian trappings the missionaries and pastors had forced on the islanders" (24). This moment is his first direct contact with the sacred beliefs of the people—the eternal presence of the dead, the feared spirits, the interrelationship of the realities visible and invisible, known and unknown. The connection of his premonitions and forebodings, his attempts to recreate the hidden through the visible, are based in his desire to resuscitate and partake in the secret beliefs of the people through his painting (152-3). For Paul, the sight of her body rigid with fear is an encounter with the mythical past, one that stimulates him both sexually and artistically. Shaking off his "civilised self" he gains access to the savage freedom he so desires, and the moment becomes one of the "timeless present" for Gauguin: the epiphany he has so long desired. In this time of heightened awareness of mind and senses, he gains access momentarily to his "real" inner self. In the gap of suspended time, the sacred offers a self-initiation into the savage. Through the primitive world, he seeks to access a kind of spirituality, and then attempts to repeat this contact with the mythical through his art, to recreate this moment in his painting. As with consciousness, that which cannot be proved can be experienced. The gap is both a moment of suspension of thought and a bridge between realities. In this moment of suspension, through the flash of inspiration where art meets the sacred—a dislocation of self, intellect and ego, space and time—he cognises his masterpiece.

The experience tears through normal perception: just as in Vedic Science it is described that Chhandas (the "cover" that hides the reality beneath) becomes "transparent", and in it is located the wholeness of intelligence, the Samhita. The creation of a work of art involves the flow of awareness from the subtlest to the most manifest levels of awareness, comparable here to Martin Heidegger's notion of the act of creating a rift, a rending apart in space-time that forges a new state of understanding, a new work of art. Heidegger posits a seemingly-paradoxical self-referral process of creation that is also applicable here, that of the interdependence between consciousness and expression: "The artist is the origin of the work. The work is the origin of the artist" (1977: 149). His phenomenological approach creates a circular argument, in which "being emerges into the unconcealedness of its Being" (ibid: 164).

Paul's experience is similar:

> The night of Teha'amana's fright, you told yourself, the veil of the everyday was
> torn and a deeper reality emerged, in which you were able to transport yourself to
> the dawn of humanity and mingle with the ancestors who were taking their first
> steps in history, in a world that was still magical, where gods and demons walked
> alongside human beings (28).

In consciousness studies, this encounter with the sacred as source of artistic creation can be explained through the formulation of dynamics of artistic creativity and the concept of self-referral. The aesthetic response of Gauguin to the sight of the naked girl creates a suspension of breath, a moment of aporia (a gap between two states), where his awareness draws back on its own status as the source of thought and creativity. The gap in space also renders a gap in time: a merging of present and mythical time. Creative expression is the result of this alternation of silence and activity, infinite silence to infinite dynamism, the alternation of finite expressions and the infinity of silence, of sound and gap. The repeated sequence of sound to gap displays the mechanics through which the Samhita, the Self, sequentially awakens to itself.

Moreover, the subjective experience of this encounter ensured that "In the weeks after [. . .] Paul enjoyed a peace of mind he hadn't known for a long time" (28). The masterpiece was painted at this time "in a trance-like state" (23), in a state "of incandescence" (407). Moreover, "As time passed, the sight would persist in his memory as one of those privileged, visionary moments of his life" (23).

This is explained in Indian literary theory in terms of *rasa*:

> *Rasa* is defined as a dynamic process of aesthetic response through which an
> individual perceives both the inner meaning of an art object or performance, and
> an appreciation of the particular *rasa* (emotion) it evokes. This leads to an
> ultimate transformation in awareness towards emotional, intellectual and
> intuitive integration: an experience traditionally associated with higher
> consciousness. (Dehejia 33)

This theory of *rasa-dhvani* focuses on the dynamic interplay between concealment-suggestion-revelation-meaning, a theoretical process that parallels Paul's experience in this moment. The "suggested content" of rasa is necessary to "incite subtle modes of approaching art and performative experience" (ibid). Haney compares the theory of rasa to defamiliarisation, which "prevents the audience from identifying with a conventional referent or expression [. . .] thereby heightening the sense of aesthetic delight" (1993: 49). This same process in which "*rasa* strips the veil of familiarity from our perceptions" (ibid: 47) results ultimately in an experience of expanded consciousness, where sound and meaning, or self and other, are united. This manifests in the awareness as the "intrinsic bliss of the self" (Ramachandran 1980: 101).

Moreover, only if consciousness is truly self-referral, when consciousness is aware of itself and it is both subject and object, can the experience then be transmuted into a source of further creativity. Self-referral in consciousness occurs during the experience of the fourth state of human consciousness, Transcendental Consciousness, which is the direct experience of the integrated wholeness of pure intelligence. This is why it is described as "Pure" Consciousness. It is the fourth state of consciousness, which can be known only through becoming it. It is the self-referral state of consciousness. In Transcendental Consciousness, the three ingredients of experience—knower, knowing, and known—are completely integrated. This is the *samhita* (togetherness) of pure knowledge. This integrated totality of intelligence is absent in the changing states of waking, dreaming, and sleeping. This is why Transcendental Consciousness is the first stage in the growth of higher states of consciousness. It contains the totality of intelligence, just as the gap contains the full potential of possibilities.[ii]

The character of Paul Gauguin in this novel has bursts or moments of clarity—similar to Heidegger's lightening "happening" of truth, when the concealed ("sheltered") is revealed (1977: 170)—when the self becomes self-aware. Triggered through aesthetic visual events, these are moments of "sacred" encounter, where the experience of pure consciousness is not an experience of emptiness but of completeness, the moment of revelation of creativity when an artist feels "divinely" inspired. It is when that which is *shruti* (that which is heard or cognised in self referral consciousness) comes to be manifest in human awareness and can be accessed and manifested by the intelligent mind. As Clements explains: "The fundamental status of Transcendental Consciousness is expressed in an aphorism from the Upanishads—'know that by which everything else is known'. Through the experience of Transcendental Consciousness every other experience gains its full significance" (1996). This spontaneous moment is beyond language, and can only be described when the moment has passed.

The infinite intelligence and organizing power of nature are eternally available in the unmanifest field of Transcendental Consciousness: "When the mind is established in Transcendental Consciousness, then whatever you desire, those desires are fulfilled" (ibid).

From the Vedic perspective, consciousness, since formless, is sometimes expressed negatively. Similarly, within Homi Bhabha's formulation of locating culture and consciousness, "Identity is only ever possible in the negation [...] that always renders it a liminal reality (1994: 33). Gauguin moves beyond perceiving a mere reconciliation of opposites, which could be expressed as the classic *neti neti*, 'not this not that' of the Upanishads (Desphande 1996: 136), to an affirmative, *iti iti*: 'it is here, it is here'. As an artist, Gauguin tries repeatedly to recapture the moment of heightened consciousness in his painting, but it is only retained perfectly in his memory, it cannot be recreated. He is not able to sustain the experience nor function from the level of transcendence, only to access it in rare glimpses. Once the state of pure consciousness is lost, the blissfulness inherent within that experience cannot be sustained. [iii] The non-sustainability of experience however, relates to the fundamental tenet of Vedanta that knowledge cannot be separated from practice: knowledge without practice is as useless as practice without knowledge—thus philosophers link inner knowledge to outward social behaviour (Deshpande ibid: 144).

Through this event, however temporary, Gauguin locates the source of his creativity—and the way in which the infinitely dynamic intelligence of nature functions. In the Bhagavad-Gita, this is explained by the verse:

Prakritim svam avastabhya
Visrijami punah punah
Curving back on my own nature, I create again and again. (9,8)

Here, the principle of the infinite dynamism, or self-referral, is explained to be constantly "curving back" on to its own nature, which is within transcendental, pure consciousness. Expressing from the absolute is found to be the source of creativity and the source of art. Creations is not just that which occurs at "the beginning of time", it is occurring at every instant and at every point in space. Paul's aim could be summed up by Joseph Campbell's classic description of the quest (here he refers to Odysseus's journey) led on by the:

allure of the beatitude of paradise, or, as the Indian mystics say "the tasting of the juice" accepting paradisiacal bliss as the end (the soul enjoying its object) [...] a non-dual, transcendent illumination [. . .] the ultimate threshold of unitive mystical experience leading past the pairs-of-opposites.... beyond all forms of perception, to a consciousness participation in the consciousness inherent in all things. (Campbell 1964: 172-3)

This special quality of perception is not available to everyone, but is dependent on the development of consciousness, and this can usually only be gained from the experience of a systematic teaching.[iv]

In Llosa's novel the search for an earthy paradise is taken from both political and aesthetic dimensions. Gauguin's life is dedicated to art and beauty (224), while that of his grandmother Flora is dedicated to redefining society and civilization, to find ways of freedom from servitude and oppression. While Paul seeks heaven on earth through highs of creative ecstasy and artistic inspiration (and physical abuses), Flora tries to establish it through politics; she seeks Eden through political space—and rejects the barbarism of slave-based material capitalism, as well as the utopian ideals of Charles Fourier (together with the hedonism of the sexual freedom it endorses.) Both seek escape from the stifling effects of society.

As Mario Vargas Llosa explains in an interview, the two protagonists, grandmother and grandson:

"[. . .] had very similar personalities: stubborn, a propensity towards idealism, utopian constructions, very courageous in trying to materialise their utopias, even though they were very different ones. Flora was collectivistic in her ideas, a society without exploitation, with equality for women, while Gauguin's utopia was very individualistic, a world in which beauty would be a common patrimony of everyone and in which sensual pleasure would be recognized as a value, something that was desirable and necessary to keep creativity flowing". (2006)

Both their lives, as depicted by Llosa's novel ask the question, what must one endure or sacrifice to achieve the earthly paradise? Their diverse paths are linked through the motif of the children's game—paradise as it is sought by human players is always located elsewhere. The novel's counterpoint structure conveys the complexity of their struggles, together with hinting at the interplay of past and future generations, of how the present resonates with structures from the past, and consciousness is structured in DNA's memory.

Like Paul searching for a native Eden, so Paradise is always ultimately deferred, defamiliarised, and non-locatable. At the end of the novel, Paul realises that Paradise is not available on earth –even the remotest parts have been spoiled by the colonial presence.[v] Originally, Gauguin's romanticisation of island life enables him to erase the contradictions of colonialism—it is, after all, only since these islands are a French colony that he is able to gain easy access to his new life. Gauguin rails against the strictures of French imperialism, yet also exploits the benefits of the new horizons it provides. Ultimately, whilst Flora "compared her travels in the south of France to Virgil and Dante's descent into hell" (365), Paul realises that: "'Tahiti, it was clear, wasn't an earthly paradise after all. There were men in uniforms there who prevented human beings from living a life of freedom'" (356). As a French citizen struggling against his identity as foreign bourgeois and preferring to "go native", Gauguin represents both oppressor and oppressed. The suggestion that the colonial encounter stifles creativity endorses Fanon's arguments that after some years of colonization, "there is no real creativity and no overflowing life. The poverty of the people, national oppression and the inhibition of culture are one and the same thing" (1959: 3) so that, by extension, consciousness is also repressed. Since "the world is as you are", the implications of colonialisation (and neocolonization) are the creation of a society where collective consciousness is unfulfilled at best and brutalised at worst.

In terms of consciousness, the character of Gauguin in this novel glimpses but is not able to live a complete life based on the experience of transcendental consciousness. The state of yoga or fully awake consciousness is vibrant in the totality of intelligence of Nature and has the ability to accomplish anything. The fully enlightened person is established in wholeness of life. When this quality of consciousness is lived—or even glimpsed in life—then consciousness becomes the source of dynamic creativity. The knowledge of the transcendent can be related to the fathoming of deeper levels of awareness that are necessary for the creation of a work of art. This is a process of self-referral functioning, of pure consciousness being aware of the fullness of its own dynamic potential, the fullness inherent within apparent void (in mathematical terminology: the empty set that contains within it all possible sets). In the Bhagavad-Gita, Krishna advises Arjuna: "...Be without the three gunas, O Arjuna, freed from duality, ever firm in purity, independent of possessions, possessed of the Self" (2, 45), he is telling him to perform action established in the field of Transcendental Consciousness—a state beyond time-bound waking awareness. The three gunas, the material qualities of existence, could also be compared to being attached to the past, present and future. Krishna instructs Arjuna to "go beyond the three gunas", the field of eternal change and difference, to the eternally unchanging field of Pure Consciousness. Living in this state, man becomes free from suffering. Moreover as stated in the Chandogya Upanishad:

> Where there is creation there is progress. Where there is no creation there is no progress: know the nature of creation.
> Where there is joy there is creation. Where there is no joy there is no creation: know the nature of joy.
> Where there is the Infinite there is joy. There is no joy in the finite. Only in the Infinite is that joy: know the nature of the Infinite. (Trans. Mascaro: 111, 119)

The Mexican Nobel Prize winning poet and author Octavio Paz writes of the role of the writer and artist in society:

> The Hindu ascetic aspires to liberation: ending the cycle of death and birth, destroying the self, dissolving himself in the unlimited and unconditioned [...] The artist seeks to realise himself or realise a work, rescue beauty or change the language, dynamite men's consciousness or free their passions, do battle with death, communicate with men if only the better to spit on them. (1973)

In diverse ways, the "lost" characters in the novels I have discussed here also reorder the past and control the present through narrative: Firmin through his long (undelivered) confessional letter to his wife, and his general ability to access classical texts to ironically reflect and subvert the present, and Russell's J.D. Sinclair (discussed in the previous chapter) in his reading and analysis of the newspapers as if to locate a sense of relevance in the colonial regime's hegemonic definition of "current events". Faced with extremities of survival within alien frameworks of nation and time, and both seeking a sense of renewal in universality and constancy, Geoffrey Firmin and J.D. Sinclair both realise the futility of attempting to lead invalid lives where the past (either personal or postcolonial) dictates the present, together with the lack of reliability inherent in that fracture of not living in the present moment. If everything is always changing, there is paradoxically a sense of the permanence implicit in the "always".

Delving into the colonial history of the Caribbean for some writers also involves taking on the mythical past and the lost legacy of indigenous peoples, places and beliefs. The novel *Palace of the Peacock* is one of Wilson Harris' early novels (1960) in which he explores notions of identity of both individual and society—the coming to terms of a nation with the imperial yoke, with the need for both individual and nation to find true expression of freedom. My next, and concluding chapter, deals with this novel as it expresses a dream of a kingdom of freedom, with the mythical past garden paradise and the present earthly hell created by men juxtaposing as alternative and co-existing realities.

Indeed, this interrelation is recognised in Sufi texts:

> Thus, if you truly look and seek the reality, you will see that everything is interconnected and really one. The celestial tree called Tûbâ growing in Paradise is connected by its roots to the poisonous tree of Zaqqûm growing in hell. (Ibn 'Arabi, tr. Bayrak and al-Halveti, 2005: 106)

The Sufi scholar Llewellyn Vaughan-Lee explains how Ibn 'Arabi locates the importance of the imagination, regarding it as a bridge, as we see in the quote here, a faculty that links the visible world with the world of mystery (2002: 113). Through the imagination, human beings have access to "an intermediary, symbolic world" one that links inner and outer, the material and the spiritual (ibid), which Vaughan-Lee compares to Jung's proposal of a collective understanding, where reality is not defined in terms of separateness but an inner sense of oneness (ibid: 114).

I conclude with Wilson Harris's first and latest novels, as, more than any other novelist I have located, he deals with an expanded vision of reality as just this: the alternative choices and views of what constitutes social and political "reality" depending on individual consciousness. Where there is difference, there can also be sameness:

> "Look at the whole creation under one single light, so that you will see the truth. There is only one light, but under that light different things are seen. The light unites all. This is the meaning of the unity of being" (Bayrak and al-Halveti ibid: 59).

ⁱ Interestingly the same game is also featured in the cultural context of Naguib Mahfouz's Cairo in his novel *Sugar Street* (Gordimer 1995: 108). One could conjecture that the game of "paradise" was part of the French colonial legacy, a cross-cultural phenomenon, perhaps introduced at the time of Napoleon's invasion of Egypt.
ⁱⁱ Transcendental Consciousness is equivalent to the modern definition in physics of the unified field of all the laws of nature: it is the integrated, unified totality of nature's intelligence.
ⁱⁱⁱ Since every state of the physiology has its own corresponding state of consciousness, the key is to be able to know how to use the knowledge of higher consciousness to structure progress in life. In the first awakening of the awareness, the boundaries of the waking state of consciousness are transcended. In time, through further experience of pure consciousness as a transitory state (as experienced in "moments" of illumination) and through the stabilisation of this in every moment, the dynamism of the field of pure silence is experienced: the infinity of finite expressions of intelligence is located in the infinity of unbounded consciousness.
^{iv} One of the proven ways in which the human mind can identify itself with the infinite creativity of nature is through Transcendental Meditation and the TM-Sidhi programme, techniques through which the mind experiences a lively self-interacting dynamism within the silence of the self and learns by "curving back on itself" how to "create again and again".
^v What is lacking for the character, however, is a profound understanding of consciousness—and it is the experience of consciousness that lies at the basis of the understanding of the expressions of consciousness. When a writer of poetry or prose formulates a creative expression, (or an artist creates a piece of art) what distinguishes this from gibberish, what makes it comprehensible, what inspires the reader? This occurs when the work of art enlivens certain basic principles, patterns, in the functioning of consciousness, that it evokes a response and also can be comprehended. Paul Gauguin's ability (as portrayed in this novel) to access this knowledge is at best random and out of his conscious comprehension and control.

Chapter Nine
Cosmopolitanism, Political Conscience and Higher Consciousness

A human being is a part of a whole—called by us "Universe"—a part limited in time and space. He experiences himself, his thoughts and feelings as something separated from the rest ... a kind of optical delusion of his consciousness. This delusion is a kind of prison for us, restricting us to our personal desires and to affection for a few persons nearest to us. Our task must be to free ourselves from this prison by widening our circle of compassion to embrace all living creatures and the whole of nature in its beauty.

(Albert Einstein, *New York Post*: 1972.)

The world is slowly waking up to the proposition that, as Kwame Anthony Appiah argues in "Liberalism, Individuality and Identity": "A free self is a human self" (2001: 326). Yet the concept of exactly what constitutes freedom is contingent and variable, as are the means of how to attain it; it can be based upon religious zeal and fought for by hunger strikers or suicide bombers, by the saint and the fanatic. This is nothing new, yet the extent to which so-called "religious" extremists or neo-fundamentalists (who in fact follow a political jihad) claim their status of freedom implicates increasing violence to populations around the globe. A recent novel such as V.S. Naipaul's *Magic Seeds* dramatises the historical uncertainties of winners and losers, oppressed and oppressors, and problematises concepts behind notions of revolution and violence against imperialism. By avoiding questioning realities and choices, the protagonist is trapped within his jaded ethical stance and ambivalent involvement with freedom fighters/terrorists, until he realises: "'one man's quest or self-fulfilment, can be noble. But what I am seeing is awful'" (2004: 200).

Postcolonialism revolves around the concept and positioning of the "other", yet now the "other" is increasingly non-locatable within geographical space. The postcolonial has negotiated and expressed the voice of the oppressed, problematising agency and freedom, but the current status of neo-colonialism demands a new level and mode of understanding issues of self and other. The world is in need of a cross-cultural vision, one that offers alternatives to conflict and violence based on racial and national identities, the small "i" of identity.

1. Cosmopolitan concepts

In this global era, cultures can no longer be defined as separate entities; the world is being re-mapped and re-visioned, necessitating a holistic understanding based on a more profound level than mere concern or intellectual reasoning. Women and men of goodwill have, after all, since the dawn of civilisation struggled to ameliorate the suffering of their fellow humans on this planet. More recently, some academics have striven to keep up with the fast moving trends in world events and the world's mood, the international moves for peace, for example, represented and endorsed by Nelson Mandela, who was able to move beyond concepts of retribution and reparation.[i]

In a review of V.S. Naipaul, Salman Rushdie eloquently explores how the notion of migration can also contain within it that of rebirth. He locates the urgency and sentiment inherent within the

> sense of a writer feeling obliged to bring his new world into being by an act of pure will, the sense that if the world is not described into existence in the most minute detail, then it won't be there. The migrant must invent the earth beneath his feet. (1991: 149)

In another essay, Rushdie has claimed that the effect of mass migration "has been the creation of radically new types of human being: people who root themselves in ideas rather than places [...] people in whose deepest selves strange fusions occur" (1981: 124). If, as we have seen, we are all to certain degrees definable as migrants, so hopefully such strange fusions of imagination, memory, and being-ness are possible on ever-widening spheres of "imaginative relationship with the world" (ibid: 125).

The growing interest in concepts such as cosmopolitanism confirm the awareness amongst academics and writers that alternative realities can and must be envisioned. The notion of cosmopolitanism is one that has long been projected as an alternative to the nation-state and as a basis for a boundary-free ethic of life, with the aim of creating the redefinition of social hierarchies and an alternative approach to existence to one based on wars and conflict. It also now presents an important method of analysing literature and film, as well as a mode of cultural production based on new interactions and alliances. (New areas in art and performance, such as international and transnational cinema and theatre, reflect this trend.)

As such theories break down boundaries and definitions of what seems all too often to be a rigid hypothesis of human interaction, Harold Pinter warns that distinctions must often be made between the academic, the literary, and the artistic and the real social responsibility of writers. Citing the co-existence of opposites as equally valid, he explains his personal conviction in his recent article "Art, Truth, and Politics":

> "There are no hard distinctions between what is real and what is unreal, nor between what is true and what is false. A thing is not necessarily either true or false; it can be both true and false."
> I believe that these assertions still make sense and still do apply to the exploration of reality through art. So as a writer I stand by them but as a citizen I cannot. As a citizen I must ask: What is true? What is false? (in Eno, Pinter et al 2006: 14)

Paul Gilroy has argued recently that gestures of solidarity and the utopian political model that "another world is possible" could be viewed as today's version of the witnesses to the nationalist struggles of previous years' conflicts, as commented on by Fanon and Orwell, both of whom took their part in the commitment to arms to overcome colonialist terror (Gilroy 2005). Umberto Eco has also addressed the world of the new millennium in terms of the global situation of migration, with all its inherent problems of what he terms "tolerance and the intolerable", which cites forms of fundamentalism as the historical source of "intolerant rejection" (1997: 89-111). Everyday we are exposed to "the trauma of difference", he argues, and although academics often concern themselves with the doctrines of difference, they "devote insufficient attention to uncontrolled intolerance, because it eludes all definition and critical consideration" (100).

Recent discussions of global citizenship emphasise obligations across borders, tolerance of other cultures, truly international communities that imply the ideal of a world community.[ii] Feminism has also engaged with the ideal of global citizenship, often emphasising the "feminist ethic" of care and compassion.[iii] Others have expressed the concept of global responsibility in terms of citizenship of planet earth, stressing our shared dependence on nature (Carter 2001: 4-5). Cosmopolitanism is also associated with the quest to end war between nation states and establish an international ethic of human rights transcending borders.

Overall, the definition of the global citizen denotes:

a coherent understanding of a relationship between human rights and human duties and cosmopolitan beliefs, including a commitment to prevent increasing world poverty, and the destruction of ancient cultures and the natural environment. (Carter ibid: 10)

It is encouraging, therefore, to see that the field of postcolonial literatures now embraces areas under such rubrics as "literature as a world language", the "literature of human rights" and the "literature of healing and reconciliation".[iv] Cultures, as Terry Eagleton discusses, make sense of the world in different ways and although concepts of truth are relative, this is no reason why there should be conflict between cultures based on what is "truth-for-us" and "truth-for-them" (2003: 107). Tolerance or intolerance precedes either doctrines or relative concepts of truth, for "truth", like knowledge, is structured in the level of consciousness—and the majority of the human population have scant knowledge of knowingness, the field of intelligence, the field from where all action originates. To be able spontaneously to utilize this potential of unlimited intelligence and the organising power inherent within it, is one formula for maintaining progress and evolution, regardless of culture or location.

Discussing the implications of postcolonial literature in the academy, Cameron McCarthy writes:

In its most compelling forms, postcolonial literature struggles to embrace the old and the new, multiple worlds, divided loyalties, and the passionate desires of the Other [. . .] These literary works document the other side of the postmodern—cultural worlds from which there are no longer exits for retreat. (1998: 2)

While postcolonial migration and exile entail movement, this comment suggests the obliteration of private spaces of safety. The postcolonial still needs to reconfigure many cultural concerns in face of the new forms of conquest and slavery within the ever-increasing inter-relatedness of the world community. One of the new forms of slavery is that perpetrated under the name of "global progress" and "new technology" by the genetically modified food companies, where farmers who previously owned both land and crops are bought out, disenfranchised, and impoverished. (In India this has resulted in a broad wave of suicides amongst desperate farmers, amounting to genocide, according to Vandana Shiva [2006].) The mentality behind these recent ventures is not divorced from that behind slavery or other forms of dehumanisation. Vandana Shiva argues that GM companies are today the "highest form of dictatorship" and the loss of freedoms through their power-driven campaign to "own" the patents on life forms and traditional agricultural knowledge, she terms "biopiracy" (2006). Fighting for a democracy of the earth, she locates that among the giant multinational biotech food corporations:

> [. . .] the imperative to stamp out the smallest insect, the smallest plant, the smallest peasant comes from a deep fear—the fear of everything that is alive and free. And this deep insecurity and fear is unleashing the violence against all people and against all species. (2000)

She also persuasively argues how the impact of globalisation is removing traditional areas of agency from women. Women are the custodians of local knowledge of bio-diversity and are the primary food producers of the Global South. As economic globalisation spreads, agricultural women themselves are devalued, removed from their traditional role as expert food producers who work in harmony with nature's processes. Thus, the traditional role of food provider becomes disassociated from women and is dependent on global agribusiness and biotechnology companies:

> This deliberate blindness to diversity, the blindness to nature's production, production by women [. . .] allows destruction and appropriation to be projected as creation. [. . .] Global law has created new property rights to life forms just as colonialism used the myth of discovery to take over the land of others as colonies. (2000)[v]

Issues such as these are imperative and must be addressed by postcolonial theory and literature, either in terms of concerns with neo-colonial land ownership, or the removal of agency from women. Such practical and theoretical issues are crucial for the future of the planet, along with other related changes in climate and ecology—all of them man-made.[vi]

An author who has long been concerned with the interrelationships of the ecology, conquest and decolonisation, cross-culturalism, articulations of colonial identity, and concerns with what constitutes "human-ness"—all inextricably linked to a vision of human consciousness—is the Guyanese novelist Wilson Harris. His extensive output of novels ranges from topics such as the pre-Columbian past of the Caribs, to a confrontation between the last of the Incas and Pizarro, the conquistador, to the apocalyptic events of Jim Jones's sect in Jonestown, but, as Stuart Murray argues, the transcendental quality of "the un-graspable" that is a feature of much of his writing, puts him outside the mainstream trend of postcolonial, deconstructive practices (1997: 54). Rather than juxtaposing opposites inherent in the postcolonial situation, the boundaries are blurred, individualities annihilated, identity becomes a continuum of unbounded awareness, a collective consciousness that surpasses time and place.[vii]

2. Wilson Harris's visionary perspective: *The Palace of the Peacock*

Born in what was then British Guiana, South America, Wilson Harris is well-aware of the problems of growing up under colonial rule; it is perhaps due to this experience he was "haunted since childhood [. . .] by vanished cultures and places and kingdoms" (1960: 9). He cites the failure of Sir Walter Raleigh in finding the lost kingdom of El Dorado as one of the defining moments of history that provides an echo and "re-visionary cross-cultural medium between the Americas and Europe" (ibid: 10). *The Palace of the Peacock* is the first of Harris's novels that have become known as The Guyana Quartet. The novel plays with concepts of the unreliability of history, the non-linear nature of time, and the fractured self as multiple, shifting and contingent. In his introduction to the novel, Harris discusses "the regenerative womb of time" and "the skeletal fabric and artifice of history's masquerade"; time and place are made visible as "terror-making faculties" that "acquire luminous density in the music of living landscapes" (11). The main character, a man whose name puns upon his exploits and forebears, Donne, is an explorer and man of Empire who has gone "bad" and like Kurtz before him, is both a child of and an exploiter of colonial oppression. Yet his name also plays upon Harris's concern that "No man is an island". Harris describes Donne as the embodiment of "a plurality of voyagers, a plurality of living deaths" (11). Similarly, his abused mistress Mariella, who will ultimately murder him, "embodies a plurality of women", all that is sensual and wild, passionate and powerful. Like Mr Kurtz, Donne is demonic and damned, a caricature of the oppressive colonial and, not unlike Lowry's Geoffrey Firmin, a representative of the ineluctable allure of the *via negativa*.[viii] Yet it is these characters who are the "heroes", for they are the men who have seen beyond the *maya* (illusion) of material existence and are seeking some alternative path to self-knowledge, albeit through the path of not knowing.

In this novel, the journey upriver is the search for the state of knowingness, in its fundamental state, the place where knowledge in its pure form knows itself: pure consciousness. The novel is one hailed by critics as being beyond the capacity of modern theories to deal with the "creative disruption of Harris's configuration of the imagination, the drama of consciousness" (Murray 97: 53). With problems such as a disappearing narrator, the constant reappearance of characters already apparently dead, the juxtaposition of the living and the dead, the narrative is fraught with apparent uncertainties, fractures, and aporias. As Murray puts it: "The inevitability of the unknowable, the untranslatable, the un-graspable, underpins much of Harris's fiction" (ibid 54). Yet these are beyond simple binaries or even co-existing opposites, so much so that: "Harris positions himself against the arguments within postcolonial theory that function through binary oppositions" but rather "reconfigures them as a flexible continuum" (Murray ibid). Avoiding the simplicity of linear thought or logical oppositions is a challenge to the reader, and yet these facets of text must be overthrown it seems, for the reader's awareness to go beyond the bounds of normal ratiocination. The search for El Dorado, or pure knowledge —like that of the earthly paradise—is one where delusion of the "covering" of so-called "reality" must be recognised and challenged. The reader's journey must also follow this pathless path.

The "bewildering" obscurities of the texts have been compared to writers such as Blake, Yeats, Christian mystics and with the world of surrealist painting (Gilkes 1975: 47). Yet the *Palace of the Peacock* is concerned with "the journey inwards", the exploration of a unified consciousness (ibid). Kathleen Raine, however, is able to locate within Harris's work experiences that are closer to postcolonial reality, since: "In reality that 'norm' is fragmented and incoherent" (1997: 42). This, then, is in many ways closer to a postmodern perspective than attempts to apply rational approaches to historical arbitrariness. For Raine, however, this fragmentary norm is dependent on the level of one's consciousness:

> We live, for example, as if our waking and our sleeping selves were different persons; our past and our present were separate worlds, as if our dead are no longer with us then they no longer share our present. More and more we have come to live in the immediately sensibly perceptible space circumscribed by our bodily senses at a given moment. Wilson Harris, by contrast, sees clearly that there are really no such boundaries and frontiers to the universe we inhabit. He gives us access to ourselves in a way that does not destroy but restores an original simplicity, the simplicity of our original Edenic state, which we have lost and to which we are ever seeking to return—and which in reality we have never left. (ibid)

Harris, according to Raine's insights, writes of the quantum mechanical world, one where particles of so-called matter are also waves, without contradiction simultaneously located and unlocated, a space-time universe that is measurable only by quanta on their "invisible trajectories to which we are continually but for the most part unconsciously exposed—if indeed these quanta are not ourselves" (43). Harris continues his exploration of modes of awareness in terms of the language of dream, the unconscious, and the quantum creation in his latest novel *The Ghost of Memory*. Here, he elaborates on the colliding energies that create works of art, dynamic impulses of ancient and modern traditions that are ultimately based upon silence. Creativity from silence continues his theme of time as cyclical, for in the end is the beginning: "By such stillness Art perpetuates a continuity that no one understands" (2006: 13). Harris's protagonist searches through the wreckage of memory, a quantum trail of incompletion and indeterminacy, for the "Nature of natures" (92), an underlying field of consciousness that will make sense of physical and spiritual evolution, myth and history, art and truth.

Yet the material world we have chosen to call "reality" is no more than a misperception. In Sanskrit, this is called the mistake of the intellect, *pragya aparadha,* which can only be dispelled or dissolved once the individual awareness awakens. The real world, according to Kathleen Raine, is the world of consciousness in its triple aspect of *sat-chit-ananda* (eternal-bliss-consciousness) (ibid: 43) and it is this dimension of understanding the universe that is the subject and setting of *Palace of the Peacock*. The concept of *pragya aparadha* is mentioned in the Kaushitaki Upanishad: "If, however he makes in this unity even the smallest gap, fear is born", and its eradication is described in the Isa Upanishad:

He who sees everything as the Self, and the Self in everything he sees [. . .]
So how could any suffering exist, for one who knows this unity?

As we have seen, according to Vedic philosophy, reality, defined as a state of pure knowledge, is divided into the three levels of *rishi* (the knower) and *chhandas* (the known), which are linked by *devata*, the process of knowing. The word *chhandas* literally means 'that which covers'. Its purpose is similar to that of *maya;* it hides the real (*rishi*, the 'knower') through a process of covering—identification with the material, physical world. The inner silence and intelligence on which the world is based are ever-present but always hidden from view. Thus, in the usual human condition where perception is unenlightened, what is taken for reality is merely the cover of *chhandas*. The unified, balanced state of these three constituents is *samhita* (togetherness), an integrated state where the unity of diversified values is revealed. Once an individual consciousness has reached this level of balance, it can be said that that person lives in accord with natural laws. Moreover, this has a practical application for both individual and society, since according to Maharishi Mahesh Yogi, "Natural Law is for security–prevention of problems; security is for peace, happiness, progress, and fulfilment in life" (1994: 110). In terms of the expansion or awakening of consciousness, all levels of the expressed, manifest world are inter-related to such an extent that both are the extension of the awakening of the Self. In the state of full enlightenment, the awakening of every level of the manifest creation is found to be nothing other than the awakened Self. This is when the individual realises that "the infinity of myself is eternally identical to the infinity of the Self of the whole Universe" (Clements 1996: 17).

Although Harris's first novel has been compared, with obvious points of reference and similarity, to Conrad's *Heart of Darkness*, it is with two other works that I find the most relevant parallels here. The first is with another of Conrad's short stories, "The Secret Sharer", which, while set within contexts of colony and empire, also involves a more multi-layered concern with the nature of self and other that are comparable with the fractured sense of self found in Harris. Ford Maddox Ford, the great friend of Conrad (and according to some critics, the "secret sharer" of the story) saw the story as one of the most important in the twentieth century, yet it has received little attention compared to his other stories and novels. In postcolonial terms, the story recounts the moment when the self meets the other, and recognises it as oneself. It implicates notions of the uncanny, with all its connotations of "silence, solitude and darkness", and which "is a feeling that happens only to oneself, within oneself, its meaning or significance has to do [...] with what one is not oneself" (Royle 2003: 2). The other self arises from the dark sea—the unconscious—like the hidden self/ other, and Conrad's story both poses and destructs a construct of real self with all its implications of the growth and expansion of awareness, the struggle to live with compassion and altruism.

While Harris's characters struggle to find their way up the river to find the mission of Mariella, echoes of both *Heart of Darkness* and *Paradise Lost* exist amidst broader cross-cultural references, above all to the twelfth century Sufi poem *The Conference of the Birds*. The concept of the journey of Harris's characters to the palace of the Peacock, the realm of heavenly joy or El Dorado (the city of gold) is directly comparable to the visionary pilgrimage to the City of God in *The Conference of Birds* (Attar, tr Nott: 1971). For the characters in Harris's novel, the journey is one fraught with both real and imagined hazards, with both physical and metaphysical trials. Most importantly, the journey is one that is both external and internal, as much *within* the consciousness of the traveller as without. It could be argued to be as much representational as mimetic. Harris, in fact dispenses with concerns of realism and traditional narrative in order to draw the reader into the process of creation, so that the reader also becomes a co-creator of meaning, thus becoming another traveller on the path to the dream-city: the ultimate meaning of the text. Just as one of each type of bird makes to journey to the Simurgh, so the boat in Harris's *Palace of the Peacock* symbolically contains representatives of every nation (D'Aguiar 2007) endorsing a multiculturalism that sustains truths as plural and cultures as fluid.

As Kenneth Ramchand points out in his essay "Pursuing the Palace of the Peacock", at the end of the novel, "the reader realises that he is the Dreamer [narrator], and the novel he has just read is an exploration of his own journey towards resurrection" (138). Avoiding the religious connotations of "resurrection", one could argue that the reader is led on an exploration of his or her own growth of consciousness. Ramchand's argument, however, that the crew of travellers represent the various facets of the humanity of the Dreamer, is valid if we think of the Dreamer as the leader, the voice that has lead both the characters and the reader through the experience of fragments to the realisation of wholeness at the end of the novel. The realisation that "The Palace of the Peacock, El Dorado, call it what you will, is inside us" (ibid) is in essence the same message as that given in *The Conference of the Birds*.

In the Persian poet Farid ud-Din Attar's allegorical poem, the story follows the journey of a group of birds that set out on a pilgrimage to find the Simurgh—the city of God—and to gain union with Him. Sharing enlightening stories as they go, the Hoopoe and his followers undergo trials of the elements of earth, fire, and water to reach the Simurgh. Although a thousand birds start the epic journey, only thirty eventually reach their destination. There, "the Chamberlain, having tested them, opened the door; and as he drew aside a hundred curtains, one after the other, a new world beyond the veil was revealed." As a new life begins for them, they realise that

> They were the Simurgh and the Simurgh was the thirty birds. [. . .] And perceiving both at once, themselves and Him, they realised that they and the Simurgh were one and the same being. (Attar, trans Nott: 132)

According to Sufi thought:

> The only way to know your Lord is by knowing your non-existence. Man is nothing but a mirror where God's attributes are reflected. He is the one who sees Himself in that mirror. [. . .] The unity of essence is the concept that there is only one existence, one cause—inconceivable, unknowable, yet responsible for the existence of all and everything. (Ibn 'Arabi 2005: 58)

Contemporary writers in grappling with their task sometimes engage similar imagery in powerfully challenging ways:

> When we look into a mirror we think the image that confronts us is accurate. But move a millimetre and the image changes. We are actually looking at a never-ending range of reflections. But sometimes a writer has to smash the mirror—for it is on the other side of the mirror that the truth stares at us. (Pinter 2006: 32)

Yet the Sufi tradition *is* to confront illusions: the purpose of life's path is for inner development; its aim is the union of the soul with God (Nott: 139). On the way, there may be foretastes of the bliss of the final goal: moments of revelation and ecstasy. Nott emphasises that "religions in themselves are not important, though they may serve to lead men to reality" (139), and although union is gained through renunciation, attachment to a path of self-development can be just as hindering as a life of worldly enjoyment. According to Sufism, all human life is a journey and everyone is capable of becoming a traveller on the path of inner development. As in the Vedantic tradition, various techniques and exercises exist for the expansion of consciousness. On the path of developing human consciousness, when the silent state of pure consciousness is permanently established and coexists along with the changing states of waking, dreaming and deep sleep, the fifth state of consciousness, cosmic consciousness, is reached. This is the first stage of enlightenment. The journey towards awakening is described in the expression "*Swarupe Avasthanam*" from Patanjali's Yoga Sutras, which explains that the Self, which is the field of infinite intelligence, is known to itself, and thus awakes to itself. As the Self wakes up more and more to its infinite status, it cognises and re-cognises within itself the totality of intelligence, just as the birds in Attar's poem recognise themselves in the mirror of consciousness to be nothing other than expressions of consciousness.

The Conference of the Birds has remained a popular and influential poem over the centuries, and has recently gained contemporary relevance and prominence again in an adapted production by Iranian artist Sherin Neshat (2002) and by the Moroccan sociologist and feminist Fatima Mernissi, who cites the *Conference of the Birds* as a spiritual and social model from within Islam for a realisation of the importance of the world living in harmony. Mernissi hopes that with present-day communications and technology, we should be able to "create that global mirror in which all cultures can shine in their uniqueness"(1993: 174). She shares the poet's dream for a world where every individual recognises themselves for what they truly are: just as the birds see themselves in the Simurgh's mirror, which reflects not only themselves but the whole planet. Shirin Neshat in the multi-media event *Logic of the Birds,* which explores through film, music and performance "the consciousness of illusion and reality and individual and collective", takes the fundamental theme of Persian and Islamic mysticism in order to make sense of "our confused identity, to go back to our roots and translate them into a universal language" (Neshat 2002). The poem, and this contemporary adaptation, produce "an epic affirmation that true enlightenment comes from within" (ibid).

The mystical leader of the birds, the Hoopoe, is an enigmatic figure whose nature encompasses opposites of human and divine, compassionate and fearless. In comparison, the leader of the travellers in *The Palace of the Peacock* is ostensibly the violent and abusive character, Donne. It is the narrator, however, who is the leader of both the characters and the reader towards the ultimate destination of the text, and could better be compared with the Hoopoe figure. In Harris's novel, when the narrator/ the Dreamer reaches the end of the journey—seven days out of Mariella (both an outpost of the colony and the name of Donne's mistress)—he realises, "This was the palace of the universe and the windows of the soul looked in and out" (112). Like the mirror of the birds, he sees himself for the first time in completeness. Standing looking out of his window, he sees both his own face and those of the other crew members who have died many times and yet been repeatedly resurrected. He sees Carroll, who is dead but whistling music that is:

> tremulous, forlorn, distant, triumphant, the echo of a sound so pure . . . It was the cry of the peacock and yet I reflected far different. I stared at the whistling lips and wondered if the change was in me or in them. (113)

Seeing the men, each standing at his own window and looking out at each other, the narrator realises they are united in their "wish and need in the world to provide a material nexus to bind the spirit of the universe" (114). It seems difficult to imagine that the similarities to the *Conference of the Birds* are coincidental. Harris has rewritten the voyage of the birds within the framework of the postcolonial condition, where both social and spiritual boundaries must be transcended or overcome—the human spirit must strive to be liberating itself from both social and spiritual boundaries. The ending of the novel involves the death and reappearance of the novel's characters, in a seemingly dream-like and otherworldly narrative. If, however, this text reflects the experience of a higher state of consciousness, it makes perfect sense, for what is reality in waking state consciousness appears to be a dream once one has gained enlightenment.

In fact, enlightenment has been described as similar to waking up after a long dream. It is also a state of invincibility: Krishna describes to Arjuna the qualities of the quality-less field of Pure Consciousness, the Self. He says: "Weapons cannot cleave him, nor fire burn him;

water cannot wet him, nor wind dry him away" (Bhagavad-Gita: 2, 23). This state is one of freedom from attachment to any future results of action: "Established in Yoga, O winner of wealth, perform actions having abandoned attachment and having become balanced in success and failure, for balance of mind is called Yoga" (2, 48). Later in the Bhagavad-Gita, the process of gaining enlightened perception is described in terms that echo the end of Harris's novel:

> The moment man perceives the diversified existence of beings as rooted in the one supreme Self, and the spreading forth of all beings from the same, that very moment he attains to Brahman. (13, 30)

Knowing that, reality is "infinite joy" (ibid: 6, 21). Moreover, once the experience is gained, enlightenment is an irreversible reality; once gained, it is not lost. When this final stroke of awakening is gained, the individual awareness realises that this is the only reality that has ever existed or that will ever exist; all previous states of experience were clouded by the illusion of *maya*, even when one's Self is experienced internally as infinite. In Harris's novel, Carroll's experience as he climbs the waterfall is comparable to the symbolic ascent to higher states of consciousness. In the eternity of time, the loss of his restricted "small" self to gain the "Self" is described as "the mystical conceit" for Carroll to see himself as "he had once lived and pretended he was and at the same time to grasp himself as he now was and had always been—truly nothing in himself"(114). His whistling came from "a far source within—deeper than every singer knew", and the sound was filled with memory, "It was the inseparable moment within ourselves of all fulfilment and understanding" (116).

The Indian teacher and mystic Paramhansa Yogananda advocates a path of knowledge and experience, described in terms of a search within the soul, for that is the location of:

> true happiness and lasting peace, or bliss [...] The soul's nature is bliss—a lasting, inner state of ever-new, ever-changing joy which eternally entertains, even when one passes through trials of physical suffering or death. (2006: 138-9)

This bliss can be attained through practice of meditation, the insights gained through intuitive introspection, and the realisation that the quest for happiness—one's life path—lies not without, but within. Harris's narrator (who oscillates in and out of the text, as if bi-located in dualistic actualities) also describes an experience so sublime it illustrates how from a perspective of enlightened, unity consciousness, normal waking consciousness no longer appears to be reality at all; it was:

> Idle now to dwell upon and recall anything that one had ever responded to with the sense and sensibility that were our outward manner and vanity and conceit. One was what I am in the music—buoyed and supported above dreams by the undivided soul and anima in the universe from whom the world of dance and creation first came. [. . .] It was the dance of all fulfilment I now held and knew deeply, cancelling my forgotten fear of strangeness and catastrophe in a destitute world. (116)

Again, without knowledge of a paradigm of higher states of consciousness, this final chapter might be too obscure to understand: with it, the poetic passages make perfect—and thrilling—sense. The creation is the dance, the *lila* of the universe as described as the Veda Lila—the self-referral play of the universe within itself, unfolding all the diverse manifestations of the cosmos. That the human mind can fathom this self-referral *lila* is demonstrated by the narrator of *Palace* who can hear the "inner music and voice of the peacock" within himself, and he joins in the singing, "and sang as I had never heard myself sing before" (116). The boundaries between self and other dissolve, the "distance from each other was the distance of a sacrament" and finally, "Each of us now held at last in his arms what he had been for ever seeking and what he had eternally possessed" (117).

Harris's most recent novel, *The Ghost of Memory*, also accesses the trope of the play of the quantum universe in terms of the interactive dynamics of creating art:

> "How do the paintings on the wall live?" I insisted . . .
> "They live," Christopher said, "because you make a play with them and people act various roles."
> "Precisely," I said. "A play brings a group of figures in a painting into a measure of new life which is still unfinished. A play is also a work of art. This is the new mystery of universal Art which acts through new energies from one medium to another." (2006: 92)

The mythical conceit of the Garden of Eden is generally called the "prelapsarian" reality. In terms of consciousness, the lapse is one of memory. For the narrator and Carroll and the other characters, merged into a single identity at the end of the novel, the sound of the celestial music was the trigger to dissolve memory, as fulfilment came to unite the past and present and obliterate the "chains of illusion" that memory has held locked in a lower state of understanding. Memory is of the totality, of himself, his "true alien spiritual love" (116). As Arjuna in the Bhagavad-Gita comes to realise the truth of his existence, he uses the words *smritir labdha*: "I have regained my memory". This memory of the source and reality of the Self resides in consciousness, the integrated wholeness or totality of intelligence. In itself, it is eternally undivided and indivisible, nothing can touch its unbounded status. This realisation comes in Unity Consciousness, a state of awareness described in the Upanishads as one that eliminates the source of all mistakes, problems and suffering: "Having realized the Self, the wise find fulfilment. The path of evolution is complete and at peace, and free from unfulfilled desire, they experience oneness with everything" (Mundaka Upanishad).

This is the zenith of the process whereby the Self realises the eternal reality:

> Awakening begins at the level of the unmanifest, absolute Self, Pure Consciousness. When Pure Consciousness awakens to itself, the entire intelligence of nature begins to flow within it. Thus, the awakening of the Self, Atma, is the awakening of knowledge. In the state of full enlightenment, the awakening of every level of the manifest creation is found to be nothing other than the Awakening of the Self. (Clements 1996)

This awakening of knowledge within the Self is also manifested in the creative process in writers and artists. In terms that reveal an intuitive grasp of this dynamism, Wilson Harris has recently illuminated his own creative process: "All my novels are instalments in one work. I have a sense that the work writes itself with another self beneath myself, that can rise up suddenly and push me into a new novel"(qt Jaggi 2006).

His latest novel *The Ghost of Memory* was written, "by a voice in myself", he explains, one that links imagination, language, culture, and what it means to be part of humanity. He continues his interview to warn that "the pressures of the unconscious [make] it clear that Man is a broken animal; he thinks he knows himself, but he doesn't. [...] That's the incompleteness in Man—he's not striving to know himself deeply (ibid).

It is reassuring, at least, to know from Vedic wisdom that the Self of everyone is the integrated wholeness or totality of intelligence, which in itself is eternally undivided and indivisible. With unbounded status, its own internal composition is the structure of infinite completeness.

It is a state in which:

> The wise, their intellect truly united with the Self, having renounced the fruits born of their actions and being liberated from the bonds of birth, arrive at a state devoid of suffering (Bhagavad-Gita: 2, 51).

3. Conclusion

The *Palace of the Peacock* argues that we are all journeying— either into a void of misconceptions or into knowledge of ourselves. While we are always aware of boundaries and separateness, in reality nothing is static, fixed or separate—this is only the view from the waking state of consciousness. Ignorance of the true nature of human consciousness and human dignity, in other words what the mind is capable of in terms of creativity and intelligence, are implications of the development, or lack of development of consciousness. From the explication of the nature of human consciousness we learn that: for full knowledge unfold full consciousness. Without this evolutionary development of the human mind, in which the unused ninety percent of the brain is "woken up" so to speak, and its ramifications of social improvement—decreasing crime, freedom from discrimination and wars, even world peace—what we do have is ignorance, misuse of resources, inequality of access to the planet's wealth, the creation and fear of the Other. It is not terror or its "ism" that is killing the world but ignorance. The fundamental quantum mechanical reality has never been accepted by the world, by the man and woman on the street. Neither, therefore, has the change in perspective nor shift in awareness been made to incorporate the thinking of the implications of the quantum mechanical, that is to say, the non-linear self-reflexive, self-creating nature of consciousness within each person and at the basis of the creation.

Discussions in terms of unified field theories, in particular superstring theory, although controversial, have within the past two decades located a single, universal unified field of intelligence at the basis of all forms and phenomena. The unified field is a dimension millions of times more fundamental and powerful than the nuclear force, and as physicist John Hagelin argues, is the source of order and intelligence in the universe. Qualities of the unified field are those of intelligence, dynamism and self-referral, which are also qualities describing pure consciousness. Scientists such as Hagelin have equated the experience of pure consciousness, the fourth and most expanded state of consciousness, with "experience" of the unified field. By experiencing—having one's consciousness based on and functioning from this level—one is thinking and acting from the source of thought in the brain, a level of interconnectedness with all phenomena in the universe. The resulting changes for the individual brain are well documented (increases in global EEG coherence, increased alpha power indicating utilisation of the total brain, for example), while the benefits for society are those of decreased social stress and of a peaceful and more cooperative global environment (Hagelin 2006)—and as Edward Said (1994: 25) stressed and as we know all too well today, global cooperation is imperative.

When one is living one hundred per cent value of national law in daily life, the conduct of the person will also reflect this –because they are living in the most "natural state of life". As we have seen, this is a state where one is in present-time consciousness, where both mind and body function perfectly all the time. When everyone in society functions in this mode of conscious being, in the total potential of life, then this is a time described by the Vedas as Sat-Yuga. In traditional Indian philosophy, time is described in terms of four cycles or yugas: in Sat-Yuga consciousness on both individual and collective levels is fully awake and in tune with the laws of nature, so that every aspect of life is evolutionary and "the family of nations enjoys perfect health in every way" (Maharishi 1993: 217-18). As, due to the passage of time, this state of being is gradually lost, the world passes into the other yugas, characterised by less and less of the qualities of enlightenment and harmony, or rising and falling values of natural laws. The state of least liveliness in human awareness is Kali-Yuga (the present state of the world).

If the world, where local grievance and suffering are played out on a global stage,[ix] is to be transformed into something "better", then consciousness must be enlivened at the source of "world" thought in all its myriad of expressions. Like actors on the stage, human beings often pretend to be other than we are, and our lives can be a performance that mimics, rather than validates, life. The desire to know the self, however, creates a path, albeit often obscure and unstructured, to finding an authentic core to what it means to be alive with a human body and brain. Consciousness studies provides an approach to and means of understanding alternative modes of experience, as expressed through levels of language and subjective awareness, providing a possible avenue for the self-understanding and "affirmation" that LaCapra (2001: 194) endorses as a means of constructing lost wholeness. Peace cannot be founded at the most manifest expression of life (activity), until it is located at the source of the problem: the lack of developed consciousness. Yet for religious, intellectual or other cultural reasons, the development of consciousness is invalidated, at worst viewed as a threat, or at best forgotten. It is undermined either through prejudices (underdeveloped intellect), or hubris (over-zealous intellect) both of which, through ignorance, bring about the negation or refutation of consciousness and thus the catastrophes of the world. If knowledge is based in developing consciousness, only then will the thoughts, words, and actions change.

While I do not go so far as Adorno, who claims that "Art may be the only remaining medium of truth in an age of incomprehensible terror and suffering" (qtd. Schweizer 1997: 3), it is through art and literature that the human mind can best appreciate the importance of consciousness as the foundation upon which knowledge and thus behaviour, understanding and ethics are based. Literature, in all its various forms and genres, will always be part of the articulation of human truth. This aim is best served when an author's awareness is sufficiently developed to be able to appreciate the more subtle levels of consciousness. Similarly, as the level of language that is accessible to the mind is parallel to the state of consciousness, the richness of expression and how near that utterance is to the level of "pure" language will determine both its potential power and its enduring validity. Harris's novels, for example, demonstrate through his unique poeticism how the shift can be made from isolation and separateness to a perception and experience of oneness. Moreover, his texts (from *Palace of the Peacock* to *The Ghost of Memory*) indicate that our cultures *must* step into this quantum mechanical paradigm: the alternatives to developed consciousness in terms of suffering and annihilation are, as Ahdaf Soueif has expressed, "too horrible to contemplate" (Grace 1999b).

One of the central thematic concerns of Harris's oeuvre is that of "cross-culturality", and it is this that he believes is "a threshold into wholeness. It means one faction of humanity discovers itself in another; not losing its culture, but deepening itself. One culture gains from another; both sides benefit from opening themselves to a new universe." By endorsing and creating new world-views that challenge habitual reality or accepted normality, means, as Harris argues, "you can advance, see things you never saw before, move out of the boundaries that have been a prison"(qt Jaggi 2006).

Yet writers such as Harris and Vargas Llosa are aware that in creating fiction dealing with both historical realities and projected futures there must also be a sense of caution, as Vargas Llosa comments:

> In fiction, which is my field, it is always possible to pretend that certain historical events did not take place, to project our fantasies into the past, to imagine utopias. But it is not possible or desirable to do that when coping with social and economic problems that are all too real. [. . .] As Karl Popper noted, people have an easier time identifying human misery than agreeing on the nature of ideas in societies that would make everyone happy. (1995: 30)

Similarly, the author and playwright Harold Pinter voices the cautions necessary in relating language, art, and life, but emphasises the urgency of the matter:

> Language in art remains a highly ambiguous transaction, a quicksand, a trampoline, a frozen pool which might give way under you, the author, at any time. But as I have said, the search for the truth can never stop. It cannot be adjourned, it cannot be postponed. It has to be faced, right there, on the spot. (Pinter, in Eno et al 2006: 17)

While acknowledging the intricate links between social experience, language, and literature, it is worth noting in conclusion that the literary world is lacking in literature that expresses higher states of consciousness, or explores the avenues available for nurturing consciousness. Thus, a work such as this must ultimately acknowledge the dearth of novels that deal with any sort of expansion of human awareness, or the task of rescuing the distopian future from repeating the past by projecting alternative paradigms of exactly *how* to live to be absolutely human. In terms of pedagogy, this study on literature and consciousness emphasises the benefits of going beyond the logical and the linear, allowing for the play of all possibilities in life and in expression. The genre of historiography has been seen also to be a form of writing that allows for reinvention, renegotiation and relocation of memory and self in terms of breaking down boundaries of fact and fiction, true or false, accurate or inaccurate. Thus, history of the past, like memory, is not rigid or frozen, it can be fluid and changeable—which gives us hope that there can also be alternatively structured futures. Ultimately, the determination of so-called truth depends upon the limitations of an individual's consciousness, or their development to higher consciousness, which provides a broader cognitive capacity, an ability to be fully present. Knowledge here is expressed as truth in terms of ethics, and agency in terms of the power of compassion. Knowledge provides the only bridge between self and other, between states of fear and empathy: a harmonious state of infinite correlation across spaces and times.

Knowledge and experience are the two steps of evolution. Knowledge reinforces the experience and provides the ground for deeper experience, which in turn is the platform for deeper understanding on the intellectual level. The source of real knowledge is simply the Self, and is thus accessible by everyone, regardless of intellectual attributes, culture, race, gender or creed. It is in this way that consciousness is universal: it is universally accessible, but not necessarily universally accessed. The heart of darkness—where consciousness remains overshadowed—still exists wherever expressions of ignorance and stress dominate over those of enlightenment. Achieving a transformation to the heart of light-ness is only a matter of education and intention.

---

[i] I have discussed the implications of postcolonial academics within today's climate of terrorism and violence elsewhere. See: "21st Century Approaches to Postcolonial Studies: Incorporating Consciousness", in *Consciousness, Theatre, Literature and the Arts*. (Newcastle: Cambridge Scholars Press, 2006).

[ii] See April Carter, *The Political Theory of Global Citizenship* (2001: introduction).

[iii] See for example Charlotte Bunch and others in *Explorations in Feminist Ethics* (eds Eve Browning Cole and Susan Coultrap-McQuin) Bloomington: Indiana University, 1992) and Uma Narayan, "Colonialism and its Others: Considerations on Rights and Care Discourses" in *Hypatia* 10: 2 (Spring) 1995.

[iv] All these topics are included in the theme of the USACLALS conference, Vancouver, Canada: August 2007.

[v] See Vandana Shiva, "Poverty and Globalisation" Reith Lecture 2000; also *Biopiracy: The Plunder of Nature and Knowledge* (Boston: South End Press, 1997).

[vi] Shiva argues that informing and transforming simultaneously can ameliorate the violence. We must create continuously in our lives, she advocates, and use all our creativity in a combination of scholarship and activism. Recent disturbing events that seem uncontrollable must be tackled by academics as well as politicians (2006).

[vii] Other Caribbean writers could also be explored in this context. Earl Lovelace, for example, concerns himself in his novels with the wider vision of human history: with individual expressions of rebellion and the search for "personhood", where violence rises beyond mere political resistance to a vision of compassion, humility, and redemption (See Nasta 2000). Lovelace is also concerned with the traumatic legacy of slavery and the ongoing problem of reparation.

[viii] A relevant correlation since Malcolm Lowry refers to and quotes St John of the Cross, "What knots of self in all self-abnegation" (see introduction to *Under the Volcano*, p. xv)

[ix] And when there is *no* society or country on earth that is free from problems and suffering, how can we not talk in universal terms here?

Bibliography

Primary texts

Abouzeid, Leila. 1989. *The Year of the Elephant: A Moroccan Woman's Journey towards Independence.* Austin: University of Texas.

Achebe, Chinua. 1958. *Things Fall Apart.* London: Heinemann.

—, 1964. *The Arrow of God.* New York: Random House.

Adichie, Chimananda Ngozi. 2005. *Purple Hibiscus.* London: Harper Perennial.

Allende, Isabel. 1986. *In the House of Spirits.* London: Bantam.

—, 1996. *Paula.* London: Harper Perennial.

—, 2001. *A Portrait in Sepia.* London: Flamingo, Harper Collins.

Al-Shaykh, Hanan. 1980. *The Story of Zahra.* London: Quartet.

—, 1996. *Beirut Blues.* London: Anchor

Alvarez, Julia. 1995. *In the Time of Butterflies.* New York: Penguin.

Arnold, Edwin (tr.). 1993. *Bhagavadgita.* Toronto: Dover.

Aslam, Nadeem. 2004. *Maps for Lost Lovers.* London: Faber and Faber.

Attar, Farid ud-Din. 1974. *The Conference of the Birds: The Persian Poem Mantiq Ut-tair* (tr. C. Nott). London: Routledge, Kegan Paul.

Calasso, Roberto. 1999. *Ka.* London: Vintage.

Camus, Albert. 1965. *The Plague.* Harmondsworth: Penguin.

—, 1966. *Exile and the Kingdom.* Harmondsworth: Penguin.

Coetzee. J.M. 1974. *Dusklands.* London: Vintage.

—, 2000. *Disgrace.* London: Vintage.

Conrad, Joseph. 1995. *Heart of Darkness.* Harmondsworth: Penguin.

—, 1993. *The Secret Sharer and Other Stories.* New York: Dover.

D'Aguiar, Fred. 1995. *The Longest Memory.* London: Vintage.

—, 2004. *Bethany Bettany.* London: Vintage.

Dandicat, Edwidge. 1994. *Breath, Eyes, Memory.* New York: Vintage.

—, 2001. 'Nineteen Thirty Seven' in *The Oxford Book of Caribbean Short Stories*, in Brown, Stewart, and John Wickham (eds). New York: Oxford University.

—, 2004. *The Dew Breaker.* New York: Vintage.

DeLillo, Don. 1986. *White Noise.* New York: Penguin.

Divakaruni, Chitra Banerjee. 1997. *The Mistress of Spices.* London: Doubleday.

—, 2004. *Queen of Dreams.* New York: Anchor.

Djebar, Assia. 1980. *Women of Algiers in their Apartment.* London: Quartet.

—, 1985. *Fantasia, an Algerian Cavalcade.* London: Quartet.

—, 1987. *A Sister to Scheherazade.* London: Quartet.

—, 1999. *So Vast the Prison.* New York: Seven Stories Press.

—, 2000. *Algerian White.* New York: Seven Stories Press.

Eliot, George. 1985. *The Lifted Veil*. London: Virago.

—, 2003. *Middlemarch*. Harmondsworth: Penguin Classics.

El Saadawi, Nawal. 1983. *Woman at Point Zero* (tr. Sherif Hetata). London: Zed.

—, 1986. *Memoirs from the Women's Prison*. London: The Women's Press.

—, 1987. *The Death of an Ex-Minister*. London: Methuen.

—, 2002. *Walking though Fire: A Life of Nawal El Saadawi*. London: Zed.

Emecheta, Buchi. 1974. *Second-Class Citizen*. Oxford: Heinemann.

Garibaldi, Giuseppe. 2004. *My Life* (tr. Stephen Parkin). London: Hesperus Classics.

Green, Graham. 1966. *The Comedians*. London: Bantam.

Gurnah, Abdulrazak. 1996. *Admiring Silence*. New York: New Press.

Harris, Wilson. 1960. *The Palace of the Peacock*. London: Faber and Faber.

—, 2006. *The Ghost of Memory*. London: Faber and Faber.

Hemingway, Ernest. 1929. *A Farewell to Arms*. New York: Simon and Schuster.

Lahiri, Jhumpa. 2004. *The Namesake*. Boston and New York: Houghton Mifflin.

Langer, Jennifer (ed.). 2005 *The Silver Throat of the Moon: Writing in Exile*. Nottingham: Five Leaves.

Lowry, Malcolm. 1947, 1962. *Under the Volcano*. London: Penguin.

Mahfouz, Naguib. 1959, 1996. *Children of the Alley*. New York: Anchor.

—, 1991. *Palace Walk*. London: Black Swan.

Mann, Thomas. 1903, 1993. *Tonio Kroeger*. Paris: Gallimard.

Manto, Sadaat Hasan. 1997. *Mottled Dawn: Fifty Sketches of Partition* (tr. Khalid Hasan). New Delhi, India: Penguin.

Morrison, Toni. 1987. *Beloved*. New York: Knopf.

Naipaul, V.S. 1964. *The Mystic Masseur*. Harmondsworth: Penguin.

—, 1979. *A Bend in The River*. New York: Penguin.

—, 2004. *Magic Seeds*. London: Picador.

Ondaatje, Michael. 1982. *Running in the Family*. New York: Vintage Intl.

—, 1992. *The English Patient*. New York: Vintage Intl.

Okri, Ben. 2003. *The Famished Road*. London: Vintage Intl.

Pamuk, Orhan. 1991. *The White Castle* (tr. Victoria Holbrooke). London: Faber.

—, 2002. *My Name is Red*. London: Vintage.

Phillips, Caryl. 1994. *Crossing the River*. London: Vintage.

Rilke, Rainer Maria. 1986. Letters to a Young Poet. London: Vintage.

Robbins, Tom. 1976. *Even Cowgirls Get the Blues*. New York: Bantam.

Rushdie, Salman. 1981. *Midnight's Children*. London: Picador.

—, 1995. *East, West*. London: Vintage.

Russell, Keith A. 1999. *The Disappearance of J.D. Sinclair*. Freeport, Grand Bahama: LaVonkeish.

—, 2000. *When Doves Cry*. Freeport, Grand Bahama: LaVonkeish.

Salih, Tayeb. 1969. *Season of Migration to the North*. London: Penguin.

Sebbar, Leila. 1991. *Sherezade: Missing, Aged Seventeen, Dark Curly Hair, Green Eyes*. London: Quartet.

Soueif, Ahdaf. 1983. *Aisha*. London: Bloomsbury.

—, 1999. *The Map of Love*. London: Bloomsbury.

Vargas Llosa, Mario. 2003. *The Way to Paradise*. New York: Picador.

Wordsworth, William. 1969. *Poems of William Wordsworth* (ed. Geoffrey Parker). Saffron Walden: Parker.

Zangana, Haifa. 1991. *Through the Vast Halls of Memory* (tr. Paul Hammond and H. Zangana). Paris: Hourglass.

Zayyat, Latifa. 1994. *The Owner of the House*. London: Quartet.

Secondary texts

Abouzeid, Leila. 2005. 'Writing women's identities'. Paper presented at *Sharing Places: Searching for Common Ground in a World of Continuing Exclusion.* International conference of the European Association for Commonwealth Literature and Language Studies (Malta, 22 March).

Al-Ali, Nadje S. 1994. *Gender Writing-Writing Gender: the Representation of Women in a Selection of Modern Egyptian Literature*. Cairo: American University in Cairo.

Alexander, Charles N. and Ellen J. Langer (eds). 1989. *Higher States of Human Development: Adult Growth beyond Formal Operations*. New York: Oxford University.

Alexander, Charles N., Robert W. Cranson, Robert W. Boyer, David W. Orme-Johnson.1986. 'Transcendental Consciousness: A Fourth State of Consciousness beyond Sleep, Dream, and Waking' in Gackenbach, Jayne (ed.) *Sleep and Dream Sourcebook*. New York and London: Garland.

Alexander, Charles N. 1990. 'Growth of Higher Stages of Consciousness: Maharishi's Vedic Psychology of Human Development' in Alexander, Charles N. and Ellen J. Langer (eds.) *Higher Stages of Human Development. Perspectives of Human Growth*. New York and Oxford: Oxford University: 286-341.

Allende, Isabel. 2003. *My Invented Country: A Nostalgic Journey Through Chile.* New York: Harper Collins.

Anderson, Benedict. 1983. *Imagined Communities: Reflections on the Origin and Spread of Nationalism.* London: Verso.

Annan, Barbara. 2002. 'Subjectivity and Other: Khidr and Transformation in Liminal Encounters' in Haney, William S., and Nicholas O. Pagan (eds.) *Ethics and Subjectivity in Literary and Cultural Studies*. Bern: Peter Lang.

Antony, Michael. 2001. 'Is "Consciousness" Ambiguous?' in *Journal of Consciousness Studies* 8 (2): 19-44.

Appiah, Kwame Anthony. 1992. *In My Father's House: Africa and the Philosophy of Culture*. London: Methuen.

—, 2001. 'Liberalism, Individuality, and Identity,' *Critical Inquiry* 27 (2): 326.

—, 2006. *Cosmopolitanism: Ethics in a World of Strangers*. New York and London: W.H. Norton.

Asante-Darko, Kwaku. 2005. 'Language and Culture in African Postcolonial Literature'. On line at: http:// clcwebjournal. lib.purdue.edu/clcweb100-1/asante-darko00.html (consulted 12.12.2005).

Ashcroft, Bill. 2001. *On Post-Colonial Futures: Transformations of Colonial Culture.* London: Continuum.

—, 2002. 'Postcolonial futures'. Paper presented at USACLALS Conference. (Santa Clara University, 9-11 March 2002).

Ashcroft, Bill, Gareth Griffiths, and Helen Tiffin. 1989. *The Empire Writes Back: Theory and Practice in Post-colonial Literatures.* London: Routledge.
—, 1995. *The Postcolonial Studies Reader.* London: Routledge.
Ask, Karen and M. Tjomsland (eds). 1988. *Women and Islamization: Contemporary Dimensions of Discourse on Gender Relations.* Oxford: Berg.
Augé, Marc. 1997. *Non-Places: Introduction to an Anthropology of Supermodernity.* London: Verso.
Barber, Benjamin R. 1996. *Jihad vs. McWorld.* New York: Ballantine.
Barthes, Roland. 1977. 'From Work to Text' in Heath, Stephen (ed.) *Image-Music-Text.* London: Collins.
Baudrillard, Jean. 1983. 'The Precession of Simulacra' in Martin Jay (ed.) *Downcast Eyes: The Denigration of Vision in Twentieth Century French Thought.* Berkeley: University of California.
Bauman, Zygmunt. 1998. *Globalisation: the Human Consequences.* Cambridge: Polity.
—, 2003. *Liquid Love: On the Frailty of Human Bonds.* London: Polity.
Bennett, Robert. 1998. 'African Postcolonial Literature in English: Ben Okri (1959-)'. On line at http:// www. scholars.nus.edusg/post/Nigeria/okri/Bennett.1a.html (consulted 19.02.06).
Bhabha, Homi K. 1994. *The Location of Culture.* London: Routledge.
—, 1999. 'The Manifesto in Reinventing Britain' in *Wasafiri* 29 (Spring).
Blackmore, Susan. 1992. 'The Nature of Consciousness.' Paper presented at Cambridge University Science Society (February).
—, 2005. *Consciousness: A Very Short Introduction.* Oxford: Oxford University.
Brah, Avtar. 1996. *Cartographies of Diaspora: Contesting Identities.* London and New York: Routledge.
Bree, Germaine. 1962. *Camus: A Collection of Critical Essays.* New Jersey: Prentice Hall.
Brown, Stewart and John Wickham (eds). 2001. *The Oxford Book of Caribbean Short Stories.* New York: Oxford University.
Browning Cole, Eve and Susan Coultrap-McQuin (eds). 1992. *Explorations in Feminist Ethics.* Bloomington: Indiana University.
Bunch, Charlotte. 1992. 'A Global Perspective on Feminist Ethics and Diversity' in Browning Cole, Eve and Susan Coultrap-McQuin (eds) *Explorations in Feminist Ethics.* Bloomington: Indiana University.
—, 1993. 'Feminist Visions of Human Rights in the Twenty-First Century', in K.E. Mahoney and P. Mahoney (eds). *Human Rights in the Twenty-First Century.* Netherlands: Kluwer Academic: 967-9.
Campbell, Joseph. 1949. *The Hero with a Thousand Faces.* London: Fontana.
—, 1964. *The Masks of God: Occidental Mythology.* Harmondsworth: Penguin.
—, 1968. *The Masks of God: Creative Mythology.* Harmondsworth: Penguin.
Camus, Albert. 1953. *The Rebel.* Harmondsworth: Penguin.
—, 1995. *Summer.* Harmondsworth: Penguin.
Carter, April. 2001. *The Political Theory of Global Citizenship.* London: Routledge.
Cash, Philip, Shirley Gordon, and Gail Saunders. 1991. *Sources of Bahamian History.* London: Macmillan.
Chakrabarti, Tarapada. 1971. *Indian Aesthetics and Science of Language.* Calcutta: Sanskrit Pustak Bhandar.

Chomsky, Noam. 1982. *Towards a New Cold War: Essays on the Current Crisis and How we Got There*. New York: Pantheon.

Chrisman, Laura. 2003. *Postcolonial Contraventions: Cultural Readings of Race, Imperialism and Transnationalism*. Manchester: Manchester University.

Clements, Geoffrey. 1996. *Maharishi's Vedic Science: Awakening the Totality of Natural Law in Human Life*. Unpublished lecture notes, 1988-1996. Mentmore: Maharishi University of Natural Law.

Clements, Geoffrey and Clements, Daphne. 1985. *Tour of Universities in the People's Republic of China: Introducing the Maharishi Unified Field Based Integrated System of Education to Scientists and Educators*. Mentmore, Buckinghamshire: Maharishi University of Natural Law.

Cohen, Robin. 1997. *Global Diasporas: An Introduction*. London: UCL.

Collins, Patricia. 1990. *Black Feminist Thought: Knowledge, Consciousness and the Politics of Empowerment*. London: Routledge.

Cooke, Miriam. 2001. *Women Claim Islam: Creating Islamic Feminism through Literature*. New York and London: Routledge.

Cooper, Brenda. 1998. *Magical Realism in West African Fiction: Seeing with a Third Eye*. London: Routledge.

Coward, Harold G. 1980. *The Sphota Theory of Language: A Philosophical Analysis*. Delhi: Motilal Banarsidass.

Crick, Francis. 1994. *The Astonishing Hypothesis*. New York: Simon and Schuster.

D'Aguiar, Fred. 2007. 'The Ghost of Memory in Wilson Harris'. Paper presented at West Indian Literature conference. College of the Bahamas, Nassau, New Providence (7-9 March).

Deane, Seamus (ed.). 1990. *Nationalism, Colonialism and Literature*. Minneapolis: University of Minnesota.

Deikman, Arthur. 1996. 'I = Awareness' in *Journal of Consciousness Studies* 3 (4): 350-6.

DeLillo, Don. 2001. 'In the Ruins of the Future' in *Harpers* (December 2001).

Dennett, Daniel C. 1991. *Consciousness Explained*. Boston: Little, Brown.

—, 2006. *Breaking the Spell: Religion as a Natural Phenomenon*. New York: Viking.

Divakaruni, Chitra Banerjee. 1997a. 'The Spice of Life'. On line at: http://www.metroactive.com/papers/metro. 05.08.97/ books–9719.html (consulted 25.2.2004).

—, 1998. 'Interview with Chitra Banerjee Divakaruni.' On line at: http://www.randomhouse/com/ bold.type.Divakaruni/ essay.html (consulted 15.2.2005).

Dower, Nigel. 2003. *An Introduction to Global Citizenship*. Edinburgh: Edinburgh University.

Durkheim, Emile. 1915, 1967. *The Elementary Forms of Religious Life*. New York: Free Press.

Durix, Jean-Pierre. 1998. *Mimesis, Genres, and Postcolonial Discourse: Deconstructing Magic Realism*. London: Macmillan.

Eagleton, Terry. 2003. *After Theory*. Harmondsworth: Penguin.

Eco, Umberto. 2001. *Five Moral Pieces* (tr. Alastair McEwen). San Diego: Harvest.

Efrati, Noga. 2006. 'Negotiating rights in Iraq: Women and the Personal Status Law' in *The Middle East Journal* Summer: 577-595.

Einstein, Albert. 1972, 1995. In 'Kevin Harris : Collected Quotes from Albert Einstein'. On line at http:// rescomp. Stanford.edu/cheshire/EinsteinQuotes. html (consulted 10.10. 2006).

El-Enany, Rashid. 1998. 'The Dichotomy of Islam and Modernity in the Fiction of Naguib Mahfouz' in Hawley, John C. (ed.) *The Postcolonial Crescent: Islam's Impact on Contemporary Literature.* New York: Peter Lang.

Eliade, Mircea. 1959. *The Sacred and the Profane.* New York: Harcourt, Brace.

El-Sadaawi, Nawal. 1999. *The Nawal El-Saadawi Reader.* London: Zed.

Eno, Brian, Harold Pinter, John le Carré, Richard Dawkins et al. 2006. *Not One More Death.* London: Verso.

Fanon, Frantz. 1959. 'Reciprocal Bases of National Culture and the Fight for Freedom' in *The Wretched of the Earth.* New York: Grove.

—, 1963. *The Wretched of the Earth* (tr. Richard Philcox). New York: Grove.

—, 1963, 1994. 'On National Culture', in Williams, Patrick and Laura Chrisman (eds). *Colonial Discourse and Post-Colonial Theory: A Reader.* London: Harvester Wheatsheaf..

—, 1967, 1986. *Black Skin, White Masks.* London: Pluto.

Faqir, Fadir. 1998. *In the House of Silence: Autobiographical Essays by Arab Women Writers* (trs S. Eber and F. Faqir). Reading: Garnet.

Farrow, John T. and David Orme-Johnson (eds). 1976. *Scientific Research on the Transcendental Meditation Program: Collected Papers.* Rheinweiler, Germany: MERU.

Fletcher, M.D. (ed.). 1994. *Reading Rushdie: Perspectives on the Fiction of Salman Rushdie.* Amsterdam and New York: Rodopi.

Franklin, H. Bruce. 1978. *The Victim as Criminal and Artist: Literature from the American Prison.* Oxford and New York: Oxford University.

Forman, Robert K. C. 1998. 'Introduction: Mystical Consciousness, the Innate Capacity, and the Perennial Psychology' in *The Innate Capacity: Mysticism, Psychology, and Philosophy.* New York and Oxford: Oxford University.

Foucault, Michel. 1970. *The Order of Things: An Archaeology of the Human Sciences.* New York: Vintage.

—, 1972. *Power/Knowledge.* New York: Pantheon.

Gackenbach, Jayne. 1988. 'From Sleep Consciousness to Pure Consciousness'. Presidential Address to the Association for the Study of Dreams, London: 1988. On line at http//: www. spiritwatch.ca/from.html (consulted 6.1.2006).

Gilkes, Michael. 1975. 'An Infinite Canvas: Wilson Harris's Companions of the Day and Night' in *Caribbean Quarterly* 21 (4): 47-54.

Gilligan, Carol. 1982. *In a Different Voice: Psychological Theory and Women's Development.* Cambridge: Cambridge University.

—, 1995. 'Hearing the Difference: Theorizing Connection' in *Hypatia* 10 (2) Spring.

Gilmore, Leigh. 2005. 'Autobiography's Wounds', in Hesford, Wendy and Wendy Kozol (eds) *Just Advocacy? Women's Human Rights, Transnational Feminisms, and the Politics of Representation.* New Brunswick: Rutgers.

Gilroy, Paul. 1993, 2000. *The Black Atlantic: Modernity and Double Consciousness.* London: Verso.

Goonetilleke, D.C.R.A. 1998. *Salman Rushdie.* London: Macmillan.

Gordimer, Nadine. 1999. *Writing and Being.* Cambridge, MA: Harvard University.

Grace, Daphne. 1999. Personal interview with Ahdaf Soueif. University of Kent at Canterbury (20 November).

—, 2003. 'Women's Space 'Inside the Haveli': Incarceration or Insurrection?' in *Journal of International Women's Studies, Special Issue on Third Wave Feminism and Women's Studies*. 4 (2) April: 60-75.

—, 2004. *The Woman in the Muslin Mask: Veiling and Identity in Postcolonial Literature*. London: Pluto.

—, 2004b. Personal interview with Ghada Karmi. University of Sussex, England (14 May).

—, 2006. '21st Century Approaches to Postcolonial Studies: Incorporating Consciousness' in Meyer-Dinkgräfe, Daniel (ed.) *Consciousness, Theatre, Literature and the Arts*. Newcastle: Cambridge Scholars Press: 178-87.

—, 2006b. Personal Interview with Haifa Zangana. London (10 July).

Guevara, Ernesto Che. 1997. 'At the Afro-Asian conference in Algeria', in Deutschmann, David (ed.). *Che Guevara Reader: Writings on Guerrilla Strategy, Politics and Revolution*. Melbourne and New York: Ocean Press.

Hagelin, John. 2006. 'Achieving World Peace and National Invincibility: A Scientifically Proven Approach'. On line at http:// www.invincibility.org/foundation/html (consulted 21.12. 2006).

—, 2006b. 'Application of Quantum Wave Theory'. On line at http:// www. invincibility.org/foundation/quantum/ html. (consulted 21.12. 2006).

Hall, Stuart. 1995. 'New Ethnicities' in Ashcroft, Bill, Gareth Griffiths and Helen Tiffin (eds) *The Post-colonial Studies Reader*. London: Routledge.

—, 2004. 'Minimal Selves' in Baker, Houston, Manthia Diawara and Ruth H. Lindeborg (eds) A *Black British Cultural Studies: A Reader*. London and Chicago: University of Chicago.

Haney, William S. 1994. *Literary Theory and Sanskrit Poetics: Language, Consciousness, and Meaning*. Lewiston, New York: Edwin Mellen.

—, 2002. *Culture and Consciousness: Literature Regained*. Lewisberg: Bucknell.

—, 2006. *Postmodern Theatre and the Void of Conceptions*. Newcastle: Cambridge Scholars.

—, 2006b. 'The Phenomenology of Nonidentity and Theatrical Presence in *M. Butterfly*' in *Reconstruction* 6. (2).

Haney, W.S. and Pagan, Nicholas O. (eds). 2002. *Ethics and Subjectivity in Literary and Cultural Studies*. Bern: Peter Lang.

Harrison, James. 1992. *Salman Rushdie*. New York: Macmillan.

Hasan, Khalid. 2005. 'What is so Islamic about the Hijab?' On line at www. khalid.hasan net/fridaytimes.2005-12-02.html (consulted 15.12.2005).

Hawley, John C. 1995. 'Ben Okri's Spirit-Child: Abiku Migration and Postmodernity' in *Research in African Literatures* 26 (1): 20-29.

—, (ed.). 1998. *The Postcolonial Crescent: Islam's Impact on Contemporary Literature*. New York: Peter Lang.

Heidegger, Martin. 1997. 'The Origin of a Work of Art' in *Basic Writings*. San Francisco: Harper.

Herbert, Nick. 1985. *Quantum Reality: Beyond the New Physics*. New York: Anchor/Doubleday.

Hesford, Wendy and Wendy Kozol (eds). 2005. *Just Advocacy? Women's Human Rights, Transnational Feminisms, and the Politics of Representation*. New Brunswick: Rutgers.

Hutcheon, Linda. 1989. *The Politics of Postmodernism*. London: Routledge.

Ibn 'Arabi. 2005. *The Tree of Being: Shajarat al-kawn, An Ode to the Perfect Man* (tr. Shaykh Tosun Bayrak and al-Jerrahi al-Halveti). Cambridge: Archetype.

Innes, C. Lynn. 2000. 'Forging the Conscience of their Race: Nationalist Writers' in King, Bruce (ed.) *New National and Post-Colonial Literatures: An Introduction*. Oxford: Clarendon.

Iyer, Pundit T.V. Paremeswar. 1977. *Concept of Dhyana*. Rheinweiler, Germany: MERU.

Jaggi, Maya. 2006. 'Redemption Song'. *Guardian* December 16. On line at http//:books.guardian.co.uk/review /story (consulted 10.3.07).

James, Henry. 1884. 'The Art of Fiction' in *Longman's Magazine* 4 (September).

Jameson, Frederick. 1990. 'Modernism and Imperialism' in Deane, Seamus (ed.) *Nationalism, Colonialism and Literature*. Minneapolis: University of Minnesota: 43-66.

—, 1991. *Postmodernism, or, the Cultural Logic of Late Capitalism*. New York: Continuum.

Kanaganayakan, Chelva. 2000. 'Exiles and Expatriates' in King, Bruce (ed.) *New National and Post-colonial Literatures: An Introduction*. Oxford: Clarendon.

Khan, Izrat. 2006. 'The Spiritual Message of Hazrat Inayat Khan' on line at: http//:wahiduddin.net /inv2/x/x/_5.html (consulted 12.11.06).

King, Bruce (ed.). 2000. *New National and Post-Colonial Literatures: An Introduction*. Oxford: Clarendon.

Krishnamoorty, K. 1968. *Some Thoughts on Indian Aesthetics and Literary Criticism*. Prasaranga: University of Mysore.

Kruglinski, Susan. 2006. 'The Dalai Lama Speaks the Language of Science', in *Discover* February 27 (2).

Kureishi, Hanif. 2005. 'The Arduous Conversation will Continue' in *The Guardian* (19 July 2002).

LaCapra, Dominick. 2001. *Writing History, Writing Trauma*. Baltimore and London: Johns Hopkins University.

—, 2006. 'History, Critical Theory, Trauma: A Case Study'. Paper presented at *International Conference on Terror and Trauma,* 31st Annual Conference on Literature and Film. (Florida State University, 3-5 February 2006).

Langer, Jennifer. 2004. 'Writing Diasporas' in *Crossing the Border: Voices of Refugee and Exiled Women Writers.* On line at: http://www.swan.ac.uk/conferences/transcom/html (consulted 4. 4. 2005).

Lazarus, Neil. 2002. 'My themes of Fanon and the Burden of the Present', in *New Formations: After Fanon* 47 (Summer).

Levy-Strauss, Claude. 1969. *The Raw and the Cooked*. New York: Harper and Row.

Lodge, David. 2001. *Consciousness and the Novel*. London: Secker and Warburg.

Lye, John. 1998. 'Some issues on Postcolonial Theory'. On line at: http://www.brocku.ca/english/courses/4F70/postcol.html (consulted 12.4.2005).

Maes-Jelinek, Hena. 2004. 'Dream, Psyche, Genesis: The Works of Wilson Harris' in *The Wilson Harris Bibliography.* On line at: www.ulg.ac.bc/facphl/uer/d/german.L3/whlife.html (consulted 23.11.2006).

Maharishi Mahesh Yogi. 1969. *On the Bhagavad-Gita: A New Translation and Commentary Chapters 1-6.* Harmondsworth: Penguin.
—, 1993. *Maharishi's Absolute Theory of Government.* Vlodrop, Holland: Vedic University.
—, 1994. *Maharishi Vedic University: Introduction.* Vlodrop, Holland: Vedic University.
Malek, Amin. 2005. 'Islamic narratives: the novels of Tayeb Salih and Ahdaf Soueif'. Paper presented at the European Association for Commonwealth Literature and Language Studies conference *Sharing Places: Searching for Common Ground in a World of Continuing Exclusion* (Malta, 21-28 March 2005).
Malekin, Peter and Ralph Yarrow. 1997. *Consciousness, Literature and Theatre: Theory and Beyond.* London: Macmillan.
—, 2001. 'Imagination, Consciousness and Theatre.' *Studies in the Literary Imagination* 32 (2) Fall: 55-74.
Manto, Saadat Hasan. 1997. *Mottled Dawn: Fifty Sketches and Stories of Partition* (tr. Khalid Hasan). Delhi: Penguin.
Mascaro, Juan (tr.). 1965. *The Upanishads.* Harmondsworth: Penguin.
Massignon, Louis. 1982. *The Passion of al-Hallaj: Mystic and Martyr of Islam.* Princeton: Princeton University.
McCarthy, Cameron. 1998. 'The Palace of the Peacock: Wilson Harris and the Curriculum in Troubled Times.' Paper presented to the Curriculum and Pedagogy Institute of the University of Alberta (Summer).
McGuinness, Frank. 1992, 2002. *Someone Who'll Watch Over Me.* London: Faber.
McLeod, John. 2000. *Beginning Postcolonialism.* Manchester: Manchester University.
Mernissi, Fatima. 1977. 'Women, Saints, and Sanctuaries' in *Signs* 3 (1): 101-12.
—, 1992. *Islam and Democracy: Fear of the Modern World.* London: Virago.
Merriam-Webster 11th Collegiate Dictionary. 2004. Springfield, MA.
Meyer-Dinkgräfe, Daniel. 2001. 'Suggestion in Peter Brook's *Mahabharata*' in *Studies in the Literary Imagination* 34 (2) Fall: 115-124.
—, 2003. 'Consciousness, Theatre and Terrorism' in *Journal of Consciousness Studies* 4 (3): December.
—, 2005. *Theatre and Consciousness: Expanding Scope and Future Potential.* Bristol: Intellect.
Middleton, Peter and Tim Woods. 2001. *Literatures of Memory: History, Time and Space in Post-war Writing.* Manchester: Manchester University.
Miller, Andrew John. 2004. 'Under the Nation-State: Modernist Deterritorialization in Malcolm Lowry's *Under the Volcano*' in *Twentieth Century Literature* 50 (1).
Minsky, Marvin. 2007. 'The Discover Interview' in *Discover: Science, Technology and the Future.* January: 14-18.
Moran, Dominic. 2006. 'Interview with Mario Vargas Llosa' in *Hispanic Research Journal* 7 (3): 259-273.
Morris, Rosalind C. 2004. 'Problems of Cultural Translation and Untranslatability', in *Interventions* 6 (3).
Morton, Marcus. 1997. 'The Spice of Life: Sunnyvale novelist Chitra Divakaruni talks about *The Mistress of Spices* and the illusory power of the material world'.

On line at: http// www.metroactive.com/papers/metro/ 05.08.97/ books– 9719. html (consulted 12.5.2004).

Mudimbe, V.Y. 1988. *The Invention of Africa: Gnosis, Philosophy, and the Order of Knowledge.* Bloomington: Indiana University.

Murray, Stuart. 1997. 'Postcoloniality/Modernity: Wilson Harris and Postcolonial Theory' in *The Review of Contemporary Fiction* 17 (2) (Summer): 53-58.

Naipaul, Vidia S. 1987. *The Enigma of Arrival.* London: Penguin.

—, 1994. *A Way in the World.* New York: Vintage.

Narayan, Uma. 1995. 'Colonialism and its Others: Considerations on Rights and Care Discourses' in *Hypatia* 10 (2) (Spring).

Nanda, Meera. 2004. *Prophets Facing Backward: Postmodernism, Science and Hindu Nationalism.* New Delhi: Permanent Black.

Neshat, Shirin. 2002. *The Logic of Birds.* On line at: http://connecting flights.org (consulted 28.12.2002).

Newell, Stephanie. 2006. *West African Literatures: Ways of Reading.* Oxford: Oxford University.

Orlando, Valerie K. 1999. *Nomadic Voices: Feminine Identity in Francophone Literature of the Maghreb.* Ohio: Ohio University.

Orme-Johnson, David and John T. Farrow (eds). 1976. *Scientific Research on the Transcendental Meditation Program: Collected Papers.* Rheinweiler, Germany: MERU.

'Oxfam Issues: Conflict.' On line at http:// www.oxfam.org.uk (consulted 12.6.2005).

Phillips, Caryl. 2001. *The New World Order.* London: Secker and Warburg.

Pilger, John. 2005. 'The Other Tsunami' in *The New Statesman* (6 January 2005).

Procter, James. 2003. *Dwelling Places: Postwar Black British Writing.* Manchester: Manchester University.

Radakrishnan, S. (ed.). 1989. *The Principle Upanishads.* Delhi: Motilal Banarsidass.

Raine, Kathleen. 1997. 'Discovering Wilson Harris' in *Review of Contemporary Fiction* 17 (2) (Summer): 42-45.

Rajogopal, Arvind. 2004. 'America and its Others: Cosmopolitan Terror as Globalisation' in *Interventions* 6 (3).

Ramachandran, T.P. 1980. *The Indian Philosophy of Beauty, Part Two: Special Concepts.* Madras: University of Madras.

Richards, David. 1994. *Masks of Difference: Cultural Representations in Literature, Anthropology and Art.* Cambridge: Cambridge University.

Robbins, Bruce. 2004. 'Reflections on Culture and Cultural Rights' in *South Atlantic Quarterly* 103 (2/3) Summer: 419-434.

Rodney, Walter. 1981. *How Europe Underdeveloped Africa.* Harare: ZPH.

Royle, Nicholas. 2003. *The Uncanny.* Manchester: Manchester University.

Rushdie, Salman. 1991. *Imaginary Homelands.* London: Granta.

Said, Edward. 1979. *Orientalism.* New York: Vintage.

—, 1994. *Culture and Imperialism.* London: Vintage.

Saunders, Gail. 1990. *Bahamian Society after Emancipation.* Nassau: Beaman Porter.

Sebbar, Leila. 2005. 'The Richness of Diversity: Extracts from an Interview with James Gaasch' in *The Literary Review.* On line at: http://www. the literaryreview.org/ su98/sebbar. html (consulted 12.02.2006).

Schaub, Ute L. 1989. 'Foucault's Oriental Subtext', in *PMLA* 104 (3): 306-315.

Schweizer, Harold. 1997. *Suffering and the Remedy of Art*. New York: State University of New York.

Sen, Gita. 1988. 'Ethics in Third World Development: A Feminist Perspective.' *The Rama Mehta Lecture*, Radcliffe College, Harvard University, April 28.

Shaw, Martin. 1999. 'Global Voices: Civil society and media in global crises' in Dunne, Timothy and Nicholas Wheeler (eds) *Human Rights in Global Politics.* Cambridge: Cambridge University.

Shea, Renee H. 1996. 'The Dangerous Job of Edwidge Dandicat: An Interview' in *Callaloo* 19(2): 382-89.

Shear, Jonathan and Francesco Varela. 1999. *The View From Within: First -Person Approaches to the Study of Consciousness*. Thornverton, Exeter: Imprint Academic.

Shiva, Vandana. 1997. *Biopiracy: The Plunder of Nature and Knowledge*. Boston: South End.

—, 2000. *The Reith Lecture.* On line at: http://www.news.bbc.uk/hi/english/static/events/reith (2000)/lecture 5.stm (consulted 12.09.2005).

—, 2006. 'Icons and Iconoclasts: Vandana Shiva in Conversation with Melissa Leach'. Public Lecture at the University of Sussex, Brighton, England. 15 May.

Showalter, Elaine. 1997. *Hystories: Hysterical Epidemics and Modern Culture*. New York: Columbia University.

Singh, Jyotsna. 1996. *Colonial Narratives /Cultural Dialogues*. London: Routledge.

Smith, Ianthia. 2005. 'We need help' in *Nassau Guardian*. November 29. On line at: http://archive. Nassauguardian.net (consulted 7.05.06).

Smith, Sidonie. 1987. *A Poetics of Women's Autobiography: Marginality and the Fictions of Self-Representation*. Bloomington: Indiana University.

—, 2005. 'Belated Narrating: "Grandmothers" Telling Stories of Forced Sexual Servitude during World War 11' in Hesford, Wendy and Wendy Kozol (eds) *Just Advocacy? Women's Human Rights, Transnational Feminisms, and the Politics of Representation*. New Brunswick: Rutgers.

Sommerhof, Gerd. 2000. *Understanding Consciousness: Its Function and Brain Processes.* London: Sage.

Soueif, Ahdaf. 2004. *Mezzaterra: Fragments from the Common Ground*. London: Bloomsbury.

Soyinka, Wole. 1976. *Myth, Literature and the African World*. Cambridge: Cambridge University.

—, 2004. *The Climate of Fear: The BBC Reith Lectures*. London: Profile.

Spivak, Gayatri Chakravorti. 1988. 'Can the Subaltern Speak?'in Nelson, Cary and Lawrence Grossberg (eds) *Marxism and the Interpretation of Culture*. London: Macmillan.

—, 1999. *A Critique of Postcolonial Reason*. Boston: Harvard University.

Strachan, Ian Gregory. 2002. *Paradise and Plantation: Tourism and Culture in the Anglophone Caribbean*. Charlottesville and London: University of Virginia.

Suleri, Sara. 1992. *The Rhetoric of English India*. Chicago: Chicago University.

'Terror suspect flights defended'. BBC December 7, 2005. On line at: http:// www. BBC.UK/1/hi/uk/ 45070840 (consulted 8.08.2006).

Turner, Victor. 1998. 'Are There Universals of Performance in Myth, Ritual, and Drama?' in Brandt, George W. (ed.) *Modern Theories of Drama: A Selection of Writings on Drama and Theater, 1840-1990*. Oxford: Oxford University.

Vandervert, L.R. 1995. 'Chaos Theory and the evolution of Consciousness and Mind: A Thermodynamic Holographic resolution to the Mind-Body Problem' in *New Ideas in Psychology*. Oxford: 13 (2): 107-127.

Van de Windt, Gerda. 2005. 'Artistic Creativity: Sublime Expressions of Inner Body Wisdom' in *Consciousness, Literature and the Arts* 6 (3) December.

Vargas Llosa, Mario. 1995. 10th John Bonython Lecture, Centre for Independent Studies, Sydney, Australia, in *Reason* 26 (8): 30-35.

Vaughan-Lee, Llewellyn. 2000. *Love is a Fire: The Sufi's Mystical Journey Home*. Inverness, California: Golden Sufi Center.

—, 2002. *Working with Oneness*. Inverness, California: Golden Sufi Center.

Wa Thiong'o, Ngugi. 1987. *Decolonizing the Mind: The Politics of Language in African Literature*. Harare: ZPH.

White, Hayden. 1978. *Tropics of Discourse*. Baltimore: Johns Hopkins University.

—, 1987. *The Content and the Form: Narrative Discourse and Historical Representation*. Baltimore and London: Johns Hopkins University.

Williams, Patrick and Laura Chrisman (eds). 1993. *Colonial Discourse and Post-Colonial Theory: A Reader*. Harlow: Pearson Education.

Yogananda, Paramhansa. 2006. *How to be Happy all the Time*. Nevada City: Hansa.

Young, Dudley. 1992. *Origins of the Sacred: The Ecstasies of Love and War*. London: Little, Brown.

Young, Robert. 1990. *White Mythologies: Writing History and the West*. London: Routledge.

—, 2005. 'One Way Street: Walter Benjamin at the Border'. Paper presented at the European Association for Commonwealth Literature and Language Studies conference, *Sharing Places: Searching for Common Ground in a World of Continuing Exclusion* (Malta, 21 March).

Zangana, Haifa. 2002. 'Bombs will Deepen Iraq's Nightmare' in *The Guardian* (17 September 2002).

—, 2004. 'I too, was tortured in Abu Ghraib' in *The Guardian* (11 May 2004).

—, 2006. 'The Right to Rule Ourselves' in Eno, Brian, Harold Pinter et al. *Not One More Death*. London: Verso.

Index

170n; and consciousness 17, 34;
theory of 18, 33
Quantum mechanical world 40, 189,
220, 227-228, 231

Raine, Kathleen 219-220
Ramachandran, T.P. 89-90, 205
Rasa, theory of 204-205
Religion 22, 115, 117, 144-145, 158,
165-168
Richards, David 101
Rider Haggard, H. 140
Rilke, Rainer Maria 201
Robbins, Tom 9; *Even Cowgirls Get
the Blues* 5, 6, 12, 29, 57, 191
Rodney, Walter 175-176
Royle, Nicholas 222
Rumi 97, 108, 158
Rushdie, Salman 5, 10, 24-25, 27n,
39, 47, 69, 117, 118-124, 135n,
163, 178, 192, 214; *Imaginary
Homelands* 10, 25, 192; *Midnight's
Children* 69, 84, 119-125, 127;
"The Prophet's Hair" 22
Russell, Keith A. 174-177, 190n

Sacred, the 17, 118, 132, 138, 140,
144, 150-151, 165, 169, 170n, 202;
space 140, 142, 146, 148, 168
Said, Edward 14, 47, 60, 87, 93, 96,
98, 114n, 167, 169, 191, 230;
Culture and Imperialism 13;
Orientalism 155
Salih, Tayeb 158; *A Season of
Migration to the North* 152-161,
164, 194
Sanskrit poetics 16, 38, 49, 159
Sat-chit-ananda (eternal bliss
consciousness) 90, 220
Sebbar, Leila 76-78
Self, the 88, 100, 103-4, 138, 150,
223
Self-reflexivity 32-33, 108, 200-206,
230
Sen, Gita 80, 128
Shear, Jonathan 38, 46, 99
Shiva, Vandana 216-217, 234n
Showalter, Elaine 59-60

Slavery 21, 193, 216
Smith, Sidonie 80
Someone Who'll Watch Over Me
(McGuinness) 66
Sommerhof, Gerd 30-31
Soueif, Ahdaf 18, 73-75, 80, 231;
Aisha 76, 168; *The Map of Love*
74-76
Soyinka, Wole 18, 67, 137, 144, 158,
167
Spivak, Gayatri Chakraborti 46, 65,
78, 83, 154
Sri Lanka 98
Strachan, Ian G. 174, 190n, 192
Sufism 108, 147, 157-159, 164, 168,
169, 210, 222-224
Suleri, Sara 155

Terror, literature of 61-62, 110
Terrorism 57
Torture 65, 80-81, 112, 185, 188
Transcendental Meditation 30, 41, 42,
54, 55n, 113, 114n
Trauma 58-60, 63-64, 67, 69, 71, 87,
99, 101-102, 109-111, 178, 183
Trauma theory 60-61, 65, 81, 83
Trivedi, Harish 46
Turkey 104-106

Uncanny, the 90, 106, 131, 134, 222
Unified field theory 33, 40, 62, 189,
229-230; consciousness and 43, 51,
54, 104, 149, 189, 211n, 230
Upanishads, The 23, 33, 42, 90, 134,
148, 206, 220, 228

Vaughan-Lee, Llewellyn 158, 169,
210
Vedanta 49, 103, 224
Vedas, The 16-17, 47, 50, 160, 228;
Rig Veda 16, 26n, 49, 50
Vedic literature 45, 124, 135n, 227,
229
Vedic Science 44, 50-51, 62, 99, 117,
130, 160, 203, 220, 227, 221, 230
Vietnam 63, 85
Violence 6, 53, 58, 61-63, 83, 91, 94-
95, 109, 112, 115, 117, 127, 132,